John Pentland Mahaffy

A History of Egypt under the Ptolemaic Dynasty

John Pentland Mahaffy

A History of Egypt under the Ptolemaic Dynasty

ISBN/EAN: 9783337330514

Printed in Europe, USA, Canada, Australia, Japan

Cover: Foto ©ninafisch / pixelio.de

More available books at **www.hansebooks.com**

A HISTORY OF EGYPT

Vol. IV.

THE PTOLEMAIC DYNASTY

A
HISTORY OF EGYPT

Under the Ptolemaic Dynasty

BY

J. P. MAHAFFY

AUTHOR OF

"SOCIAL LIFE IN GREECE" "GREEK LIFE AND THOUGHT"
"THE EMPIRE OF THE PTOLEMIES" ETC. ETC.

WITH NUMEROUS ILLUSTRATIONS

CHARLES SCRIBNER'S SONS
153, 155, AND 157 FIFTH AVENUE
NEW YORK CITY
1899

H.

This History will comprise Six Volumes:

Vol. I. Dynasties I.–XVI. By W. M. F. PETRIE

Vol. II. „ XVII.–XX. By W. M. F. PETRIE

Vol. III. „ XXI. XXX. By W. M. F. PETRIE

Vol. IV. Ptolemaic Dynasty. By J. P. MAHAFFY

Vol. V. Roman Rule. By J. G. MILNE

Vol. VI. Arabic Egypt. By STANLEY LANE POOLE

PREFACE

In preparing this volume I have received generous assistance from Prof. Petrie, who has placed at my disposal many photographs of objects in his valuable collection, and of Egyptian monuments; also from the editors of the *Classical Review*, for the facsimile of the newest Ptolemaic inscription recovered (p. 138); also from Mr. M'Gregor, who has sent me a reproduction of the head-dress which corresponds to that of the child Berenike (p. 117); also from Mr. F. Ll. Griffith, for his explanation of the Ptolemaic titles (Appendix); and lastly from Dr. Botti, who has allowed me to copy his new map of Alexandria, which, although still incomplete and far from final, is yet much in advance of any map of the city hitherto attempted. It unfortunately did not appear till this book was almost ready for the press, and so could not be inserted and discussed in its proper place.

J. P. MAHAFFY

TABLE OF CONTENTS

CHAPTER I

CHAPTER II

CHAPTER III

LIST OF ILLUSTRATIONS

xi

A HISTORY OF EGYPT
UNDER THE PTOLEMAIC DYNASTY

FIG. 1. — *Obverse.* — Head of Alexander, with horns of Amon, diademed, with elephant's skin.

FIG. 2. — *Reverse.* — Pallas eagle on thunderbolt, ΑΛΕΞΑΝΔ-ΡΟΥ, and mint marks.

CHAPTER I

GENERAL AUTHORITIES.—*Ancient*—Arrian, ii. 13 *seq.*; Diodorus, xvii. 48 *seq.*; Curtius, iv. 7 *seq.*; Plutarch, *Alexander*, 26 *seq.*; Justin, xi. 11 *seq.*; Josephus, *B. J.* iv. 10. 5 *seq.*; pseudo-Callisthenes, lib. i. (ed. C. Müller). *Modern*—Grote, *Hist. of Greece*, chap. xciii.; Thirlwall, *Hist. of Greece*, chaps. xlix. sqq.; Sharpe, *Hist. of Egypt* (German ed.), i. chap. iv. *seq.*; Droysen, *Gesch. des Hellenismus*, i.; Niese, *Gesch. der Griech. und Maked. Staaten*, etc., vol. i.; Holm, *Gesch. Griech.* vol. iii.; Mahaffy, *The Empire of the Ptolemies*, chaps. i. and ii.; Pauly-Wissowa, *Realencyclopädie* (P.-W.R.), arts. "Alexander," "Alexandria," "Aigyptos," "Ammon"; Hogarth, *Philip and Alexander of Macedon*, pp. 187 *seq.*; G. Botti, *Fouilles à la Colonne Theodosienne* (Alexandria, 1897); Lumbroso, *L'Egitto dei Greci e dei Romani* (Rome, 1895).

THE condition of Egypt under the Persian dominion has been described in the previous volume. So far as we know, the Egyptian people suffered more from

IV—I

sentimental than from material grievances under that rule. We do not hear that Alexander, when he set the land in order, remitted taxes, and yet his conquest was regarded by the natives as a great boon. The main difference seems to have been in his attitude to the Egyptian gods and their priests. Instead of ignoring this great element in Egyptian life, or insulting the feelings of religious Egypt, the new conqueror sacrificed to the local gods, and probably granted some charter or security for their property to the priests. His conquest was attended with no trouble. The Satrap of Egypt, Sabakes,[1] who came with his contingent to support Darius at the battle of Issus, had fallen in the fight, and another Persian grandee, Mazakes, had succeeded to the satrapy either by the new appointment of the king, or, what is more probable, as the lieutenant of Sabakes, left in charge of the country.

The first attack upon this new governor's authority had been made by Amyntas, son of Antiochus, a deserter from the Macedonian side,[2] who had joined Darius at Issus, and who fled, with some others of his kind, with a remnant of 8000 mercenaries by way of Cyprus to Egypt. What was the policy or the intention of this person, beyond mere raiding, we cannot tell. Curtius says he was gladly received by the natives, as being opposed to the Persians, his recent patrons, and that accordingly he attacked the Persian garrison at Memphis, but was beaten off by Mazakes, and presently overpowered and slain with his accomplices by the natives, who soon found that plunder was his object. The story is not clear. What position can he have assumed against the Persians and also against the Macedonians, unless he pretended that he was fighting for the natives—an excuse which could only last a few weeks? And surely such a person could never hope to set up for himself an independent

---

[1] This man, to judge from his name, was a grandee of Ethiopian extraction. Shabak occurs as a king's name in the XXVth dynasty.—PETRIE.

[2] *Prætor hic Alexandri fuerat, tunc transfuga.*—Curt. iii. 11, 18.

monarchy. Yet this is the view of Q. Curtius, who alone among our authorities gives us any details.[1]

There was, no doubt, great uncertainty, and a great collapse was impending throughout all the Persian provinces. Had Alexander perchance died shortly after Issus, the whole Eastern world would have indeed been the prize of the boldest adventurers. But Curtius by himself is a poor authority. At all events, Mazakes, who was loyal and strong enough to repel and crush this wholly unauthorised raid upon his province, was not strong enough to offer any resistance to Alexander. The whole population was excited with the news of Issus, and ready to fall into the arms of the new deliverer. So Alexander, appearing at Pelusium (probably September 332 B.C.), entered Egypt without resistance, and ascended the river to Memphis. His march was a triumphal progress, for the inhabitants felt that he would free them not only from the hated Persian yoke,[2] but from the more pressing danger of other raids like that of Amyntas, and from the piracy which must have been rampant during the great crisis of the last year's campaign. Not only was Memphis surrendered by Mazakes, but with it 800 talents of treasure, a most welcome addition to the military chest of the victor, for the expenses of the campaign must have been great, and the profits (excepting the plunder of Tyre) not yet very large.

[1] *Quum in illo statu rerum id quemque, quod occupasset, habiturum arbitraretur, velut certo jure possessum, Ægyptum petere decrevit.* He exhorts his soldiers, shows the weakness and unpopularity of the Persians in Egypt, and how the natives would regard any new power as an ally against their hated masters. He gets admission to Pelusium under the pretence of being the new satrap of Darius, and then calls the natives to join him in crushing the Persian garrison. At first successful, and proceeding to the siege of Memphis, he takes to raiding the neighbourhood, and is defeated and slain in a sortie of the besieged Persians. —Curt. iv. 1, 27 *seq.*

[2] Oxyrynchus Papyri, I, xii. col. iv.: Ολυμπιαδι εκατοστη δωδεκατη . . . ταυτης κατα το πρωτον ετος Αλεξανδρος ο Φιλιππου Τυρον ειλεν· και Αιγυπτον παρελαβε εκουσιως αυτον προσδεξαμενων των ενχωριων δια το προς Περσας εχθρον.

We are told by all our authorities that he forthwith offered sacrifices to the local gods, especially to Apis, and celebrated gymnastic and musical contests with the help of Hellenic artists, who were on the spot at the required moment. Some historians regard this coincidence as a proof that Alexander had foreseen his movements and their success, and had ordered these distinguished people to meet him at Memphis. I think it more likely that, like camp-followers, they watched campaigns, and found themselves in the vicinity of conquests, knowing that under no other circumstances would their profits be so great as when celebrating the glories of victorious armies. It was worth while sailing to Egypt, and having a little acting season at Naukratis, among their Greek friends, upon the chance of being summoned by the recklessly extravagant Macedonian youth to adorn his successes. The festival must have been chiefly intended for his soldiers, and for the various speculators, petitioners, and other adventurers who came from Greek lands. For it is not very likely that the natives would understand or appreciate Greek gymnastics, still less Greek music.

But from the outset, the policy which Alexander

FIG. 3.—Cartouches of Alexander the Great.[1]

marked out for himself was to protect and promote Eastern nationalities, without abating aught from the primacy of the Greeks in culture. Hence his musical and gymnastic celebrations were a counterfoil to his sacrifices to Apis and to Ptah. The latter god is not indeed mentioned by our Greek authorities, but as his temple was the greatest feature of ancient Memphis, and his priests were the greatest corporation there, it was most probably in this metropolis of Greek religion that Alexander was formally crowned king of Egypt.[2]

[1] For explanations of these and other cartouches cf. Mr. Griffith's Appendix to this volume.
[2] On this question M. Gaston Maspero has recently published a most instructive essay (*École des hautes études*, annuaire for 1897),

It is to be noted that when Alexandria had become the recognised capital of Egypt, the earlier Ptolemies

FIG. 4.—King Ramses II. worshipping the Ram-headed Amon.

did not trouble themselves with the sacred ceremony at Memphis. With Ptolemy V. the solemn national

which examines the nature of Alexander's deification. He has not, however, cited the only direct Greek authority for the ceremony, which he establishes upon *à priori* grounds. The pseudo-Callisthenes, who gives a very important, though much distorted, account of Alexander's visit to Egypt, says expressly (i. 34): καὶ ἐλθόντος αὐτοῦ εἰς Μέμφιν τὴν πόλιν ἐνεθρόνισαν οἱ Αἰγύπτιοι αὐτὸν εἰς τὸν τοῦ Ἡφαίστου (*sc.* Ptah) θρονιστήριον ὡς Αἰγυπτίων βασιλέα. This is not the only important fact preserved to us in the *Romance*, as will appear in the sequel.

enthronement was resumed, as the Rosetta stone tells us with the emphasis of reiteration.

FIG. 5.—View of the Western Bank of the Nile over against Thebes.

There was also another great Egyptian god, served by a separate, and probably rival corporation of priests, who was better known to the Greeks, and whom Alexander desired to honour. This was Amon,[1] whose shrine and city Thebes, in the upper country, had for centuries been the real metropolis of the whole land. Alexander must have thought it an important part of his policy to conciliate this great spiritual authority. But it does seem strange, at first sight, that he should not have ascended the river to Thebes, a very charming and instructive journey, showing him the greater part of his new possessions, at the goal of which he would see the wonders which attract travellers from all the world even to the present day. In the palmiest days of Memphis, its religious appointments were not equal to those of Thebes. Why then did Alexander select the long and difficult route to the oasis of Jupiter Ammon, to perform a ceremony which could have been more splendidly performed at Thebes?

There are several adequate reasons to explain this apparent waste of time in a very busy man, full of ambitious plans for the conquest of the East. In the first place, something may be due to the jealousy of the priests of Ptah at Memphis, whose old rivals were those of Amon at Thebes, and who might dread the effect which the splendour of Thebes would have upon Alexander, while the shrine of the god in the far oasis was in outward appearance and appointments insignificant. Secondly, while the splendours of Thebes were unknown to the Greeks, the reputation of the oracle in the desert was old and well established. From Pindar's day onward, mention of it crops up occasionally in Greek history, showing that it was well known and honoured in the Hellenic world.[2] Very probably it was through the comparative proximity of

---

[1] On the various forms of the name, Ammon, Hammon, Amoun, etc., cf. the art. "Ammon," in Pauly-Wissowa's *Realencyclopädie*. He is represented frequently as ram-headed, and so associated with that form in the legends of the pseudo-Callisthenes. The Greeks identified him with Zeus, and hence Thebes was called by them Diospolis.

[2] Cf. the catalogue of consultations by Greeks in early days in P.-W.R., "Ammoneion," p. 1858.

Cyrene, and the trade of this city with the desert, that it became thus known in the Levant.

But there were other than religious interests working in the minds of the Greeks of Egypt. Alexander had come into the land by its eastern gate, and if he left again by the same route, he might never see the western Delta, and so never become personally acquainted with the only purely Greek city in the land, the old mart of Naukratis. This consideration escaped the notice of historians,[1] because they did not know the site of Naukratis, discovered by Mr. Petrie a very few years ago. As soon as Alexander spoke of founding a capital, the first alarm of the Greeks must have been that he should choose Memphis, or some site near it, at the head of the Delta. It was highly necessary to lure him away from too great an Egyptian centre. They may have hoped that he would select Naukratis itself, which he must have visited on his way to the Canopic mouth ; but in any case they obtained this, that Alexandria was founded near it, and far from any great native city. The conqueror chose the strip of ground between Lake Mareotis and the sea, with the island Pharos over against it, so that this natural break-water might afford means of making a good anchorage for ships.

Our best authorities agree that he planned this new and momentous foundation on his way to the oasis[2] (which, by the way, he could more easily have reached across the desert), and perhaps immediately after he had been solicited by the Greeks of Naukratis to remember Hellenic interests in Egypt. I have already argued that there is no need for attributing special insight or prophetic genius to Alexander's selection of the site.[3] Any site along the coast, or near it, on

---

[1] Cf. now *Empire of the Ptolemies*, p. 10.

[2] To judge from the foundation feast afterwards kept on the 25th of Tybi, at Alexandria, the formal act appears to have taken place on or about January 20, 331 B.C. Cf. the authorities quoted by Holm, *Griech. Geschichte*, iii. 383, note 5.

[3] Mr. Hogarth (*Philip and Alexander*, p. 189) contests this, and thinks the site behind Pharos the only suitable spot for a harbour

one of the larger arms of the Nile, must have proved successful, if we give it the conditions supplied by the great conquests in the East, and then the wise and practical rule of the first Ptolemy and his successors. Wherever the mart was established for the meeting of the merchandise of the Mediterranean and the Nile, a vast concourse of people must inevitably take place.

We hear many accounts, more or less detailed, of the founding of this great city, but of these the most fabulous (that in the *Romance*) is apparently the most instructive, for the writer was personally intimate with the city, and records the traditions of the inhabitants.[1] But they all presuppose the city to be so well known that they omit details which to our comprehension of it are vital. The only earlier attempt to fix the plan by excavations was made for Napoleon III. by Mahmoud Bey (1866). Dr. Botti's map in this volume gives the results of his researches up to 1897. On one point we must lay peculiar stress, because most authors produce a false impression, that Alexandria was a city in which Jews and Greeks counted for everything, the natives for nothing. There is good evidence that the majority of the poorer classes was from the first Egyptian, and that to the end the city remained very different from

along the whole Delta coast. Of course if this were so, it would detract greatly from Alexander's credit, as his choice was controlled by necessity. But it is not so. Ancient ships did not require the deep water that ours do, and the precautions taken at the Sebennytic and Pelusiac mouths prove that landing at these points was easy even for ships of war. Even Nelson's ships could fight in the bay of Aboukir.

[1] I quote from the Didot edition of Arrian, etc., edited by C. Müller. The importance of pseudo-Callisthenes, especially according to our oldest text, and the Armenian translation, was first shown by G. Lumbroso, whose varied and curious learning has not marred his natural acuteness. Both in the case of this book and in that of the pseudo-Aristeas, he has shown that what the learned world up to his day had rejected as purely fabulous, contained valuable historical indications. Cf. his *l'Egitto*, etc., cap. xvi. ; and also Zacher's *Pseudo-Callisthenes* (Halle, 1867), p. 96.

other Hellenistic foundations.[1] The native element, though at first thrust out from power and influence, gradually asserted itself, and the city that opposed Cæsar was probably far more Egyptian than that which opposed Antiochus Epiphanes. This is not an extra-ordinary or exceptional course of events. The city of Dublin, for example, has been settled with Danes and English for many centuries, during which the whole control and government of the city lay in these foreign hands. Yet, though they imposed their laws, their language, and to some extent their religion, upon the native population, the English never made it an English city. The masses of the poor, long subjected to harsh control, nevertheless so influenced the settlers, that to this day Dublin has remained and will continue an Irish city, with the national characteristics strongly and clearly marked. Such was the case with Alexandria.

It is therefore not out of place in this book, which deals with the people of Egypt and their condition under the Macedonian dynasty, to enter into some details regarding the origin of this great foreign mart in the north-west corner of the land. For this capital in its day became, like Paris in France, the normal con-troller of the fortunes of the whole country.

The first point which deserves special notice is the statement of Strabo (xvii. 1, 6), corroborated by the *Romance*, that the site, when Alexander found it, was not an open coast, only occupied by a fishing village. "The former kings of Egypt, content with home produce and not desirous of imports, and thus opposed to foreigners, especially to Greeks (for these were pillagers and covetous of foreign land, because of the scantiness of their own), established a military post at this spot, to keep off intruders, and gave to the soldiers as their habitation what was called Rakotis, which is now that part of Alexandria which lies above the dockyards, but was then a village. The country lying round

---

[1] The expression of Justin (xi. 11), *coloniam Macedonum caput esse Ægypti jubet*, is, I believe, accurate. The Macedonians, so called, were always a small and privileged part of the population.

about this spot they entrusted to herdsmen, who themselves also should be able to keep off strangers."

Strabo's statement commends itself to common sense. If Pharos, and the coast it protected from the heavy sea, were not occupied, it could hardly fail to become the favourite haunt of Greek pirates, as it was the nearest point of Egypt both to Cyrene and to Crete. The island was well known to the Athenians in Thucydides' time. The *Romance* adds that the population round Rakotis was divided into separate villages, in all twelve, and that each had a separate watercourse coming from the fresh-water canal skirting Lake Mareotis, and crossing the tongue of land into the sea. This also seems very probable. If the land was given up to careful agriculture as well as grazing, a systematic water supply at intervals along the coast was absolutely necessary. Each group would depend upon its own canal, and so form a separate village. We are further told that in the plan of the city the streets were built over these parallel canals, and formed the thoroughfares from north to south, which intersected at right angles the great Canopic street running along the whole tongue of land which separates Lake Mareotis and the sea. The old names of these villages are given in the text of pseudo-Callisthenes, but in such corrupt forms that Lumbroso has only been able to identify three of them [1] by later allusions; enough, however, to show the historical character of the tradition. The large sheet of water called Lake Marea or Mareotis, at that time in touch (by several channels) with the Nile, and therefore affected by the summer rising of the river, afforded to the city a fresh-water harbour (λιμὴν ὁ λιμναῖος), which in Strabo's day was more crowded with vessels and merchandise (coming down to it from the upper country) than were the harbours on the sea.

The native portion of the city was undoubtedly the western, where the great pillar (so-called that of Pompey) marks the site of the old temple of Serapis, which

[1] Rakotis, Aspendia, Argeon. Cf. his *Egitto* (1895), pp. 166 *seq.*

existed, we are told, before Alexander's foundation.[1]
To the west of this was the Egyptian necropolis, with
a suburb devoted, says Strabo, to all the preparations
for embalming bodies, another very clear proof of the
Egyptian character of this part of the city.   Here also
have been found at various times statues, etc., in
granite, which point to a certain adornment of the
old Rakotis and its temples.   The necropolis on the
east side was, so far as we know, rather Greek in
character.   There were also from the commencement
many Jews attracted,[2] as they ever have been, by the
mercantile advantages of the new emporium, and they
became a very important section
of the population.   It does not
appear that Alexander gave
these foreigners any privileges
apart from other immigrants;
but that he gave special consideration to Egyptian feeling
appears from his either founding,
or more probably embellishing,
a temple of Isis, which always
remained an important building
in the city, and with its Egyptian
façade forms a very curious feat-

FIG. 6.—Coin of Alexandria,
showing Temple of Isis.

ure in the coins of Alexandria under the Roman Empire.
   It does not seem necessary to enter here more
minutely upon the topography of the new city.[3]   It
was laid out on the principles which the architect
Hippodamus had made fashionable in Greece, and
which, unfortunately, have again become fashionable
in Southern Europe.   The intersection of two great
thoroughfares at right angles marked the approximate
centre of the city, and the lesser streets were cut

   [1] Dr. Botti has found many relics of the older occupation of this
site, even so far back as Ramses II.   Cf. his *Fouilles* (Alexandria,
1897).
   [2] This statement, denied by many German anti-Semite authorities, will be supported by evidence in the sequel.
   [3] The most recent discussion of it is by Puchstein in P.-W.R.
art. "Alexandria."   Cf. the map at the end of this book.

parallel to these. The main thoroughfares, which ran from gate to gate, were a plethron (101 English feet) wide, and adorned with colonnades on both sides for the shelter of pedestrians. But it is added by our authorities that even the lesser streets were passable for horses and wheel traffic, a convenience not usual, apparently, in Greek towns. The narrowness of the site from north to south (across the main lie of the city) was remedied by building a causeway, the Hepta-stadion,[1] to the island Pharos, which not only conveyed water to the island, but divided the bay into two main harbours, which were entered round the east and west ends of the island respectively. Thus this great natural breakwater was converted into a suburb or part of the town,[2] and fortified accordingly. The royal or eastern harbour had inner docks and special quays for the navy, and round it were situated the royal palace and other notable buildings. The western harbour was for the merchant shipping; but this too contained special recesses, and there was a way here from the sea into Lake Mareotis. This harbour, which is spoken of as open, in contrast to the other, was afterwards known as Eunostus, in memory, possibly, of a king of Cyprus, who was a friend and connection of the first Ptolemy. But this seems an unsatisfactory account of the title. There were two passages kept open in the causeway to allow vessels to be transferred from the eastern to the western harbour.

How far the original plan of Alexander corresponded to the results in after days we shall never know. For we are told that after the foundation had attracted

---

[1] This causeway is now so broad as to hold a large population; indeed, the whole Turkish town was contained by it 200 years ago. The accretion and consequent shallowing of the harbour is attested as growing since the first century, and is quite inconsistent with the theory that the sea has encroached largely upon ancient Alexandria.

[2] The population, however, apart from that of the forts, always remained native, poor, and addicted to plundering wrecked ships, an ancient privilege, according to Cæsar, *De Bell. Civ.* iii. 112. Compare Heliodorus, *Aeth.* i.

many settlers, besides the neighbouring natives, whose former possessions were made into a privileged (and possibly untaxed) territory, the city grew rapidly, and then history is silent about it for many years. The splendour of Alexander's conquests dazzled the historians, so that they were blind to all lesser or more gradual changes in the world. The conqueror spent but little time superintending his new plan. The stories about the prosperous omens noted at the moment are hardly worth repeating now. What is called the accident or sudden expedient of marking out the circuit with meal or flour appears to have been a Macedonian habit founded upon some old superstition. The real marvel would have been if this meal had not been picked up by the numerous birds that people the country. So that it required the talents and the veracity of courtiers to make a portentous phenomenon out of this perfectly unavoidable occurrence. Probably there were more birds to do it in Egypt than there were upon such occasions in Macedonia.

We may, therefore, hurry on with Alexander to the oasis of Ammon, and consider the bearings of this adventure upon the history of the country. He probably followed the usual, though not the shortest, route. Greeks coming to visit the oasis from Cyrene or elsewhere would probably go as near as possible by sea, and disembark due north of the oasis. To this point Alexander could sail or march, with the aid of a provisioning fleet. The rest was a caravan march across the desert. We are told by some of our Greek authorities that at Parætonium, the roadstead from which the march started, he was met by an embassy offering submission and valuable presents from the Cyrenæans.[1] It is far more likely that they offered him

---

[1] Diod. xvii. 49: "Midway an embassy from the Cyrenæans met him, bearing a crown and magnificent gifts, among which were three hundred war-horses, and five four-in-hands of the highest quality." To this a new chronological fragment adds some details (Oxyrynchus Papyri, xii. col. 5): ανεβη εις Αμμωνος και εν τη αναβασει Παραιτονιον κτιζει πολιν; so also the *Alexander*

guides. For this was not the Egyptian road to the
oasis, and it is quite possible that even the Greeks of
Naukratis were not familiar with it. For they would
probably take the road through the Nitrian desert, when
making the journey. But this is only a conjecture. The
marvels related concerning Alexander's journey are such
as could be easily constructed from an exaggeration of
natural phenomena. That two ravens, when flushed
from some carrion in the desert, should fly towards
the oasis was almost certain, and was a well-established
index used by every straying traveller. That the party
suffered from drought, and were relieved by a sudden
downpour of rain, was an unusual, but not unpre-
cedented occurrence then, as now. It is more interesting to note that none of our authorities makes any
mention of the use of camels in this journey, thus indi-
cating that they were not yet domesticated in Egypt,
or at least in the west of Egypt. The name *Camel's
Fort* near Pelusium occurs in the next generation.

On the whole, the accounts we have from our various
sources are very consistent as regards the visit and
its probable objects. There is a description of the
temple and its appointments in Diodorus (xvii. 50. 2)
which is said to correspond with what still remains of
ancient ruins on the spot. Still more closely does it
correspond, according to M. Maspero,[1] with the very
analogous ruins in the Great Oasis. It seems that in
the days of Darius, temples of Amon had been built
or restored in both these outlying sites. They were
constructed, with less expense and grandeur, upon the
same principles as the other shrines of the god, and
the ceremonies attending the accession of a new king
were depicted, as upon the walls of the temple of
Karnak and that of Erment. If Alexander had been
a legitimate Pharaoh, he must visit the god in his
temple, he must enter alone into the inner shrine,

Romance, i. 31: κτίσας οὖν ἐκεῖ πόλιν μικρὰν καὶ καλέσας ἐκ τῶν ἐγχωρίων
τινὰς λαμπροὺς ἄνδρας, κατῴκισαν αὐτοὺς ἐκεῖσε, καλέσας αὐτὴν Παραιτόνιον.

[1] *École prat. des hautes études,* annuaire for 1897 : "*Comment
Alexandre devint dieu en Egypte.*"

where the statue of the god in his sacred boat was
kept, and after due homage, Amon answered with a
declaration that the new king was his beloved son, on
whom he would bestow the immortality of Ra, and
the royalty of Horus, victory over all his enemies, and
the domination of the world, etc. etc. These wildly
exaggerated formulae, which had none but a liturgical
meaning for a poor king of decaying Egypt, were
translated into a prophecy of some import when
addressed to Alexander. The god, in this case, not
only received him in his shrine, but answered him in
words, instead of mere motions of his head. The
priests had all these things well arranged. But the
important point in the affair is that the declaration of
the king's divinity, and of his actual descent from Amon
as his father, was the only formula known by which
the priests could declare him *de jure* king of Egypt, as
he already was *de facto*.

As every king for centuries back had been declared
the son of Amon, it was natural and necessary that
Alexander should be so also. But most of these earlier
native kings had been of the royal stock, where any new
interference of Amon was unnecessary. In the case,
however, of illegitimacy, when a conqueror became king
of Egypt (and that had been no unfrequent occurrence),
the first precaution had been to marry him to one of
the royal princesses, whose right of succession was as
recognised as that of their brothers. Thus the next
generation, at all events, showed partial royal descent.
But, as M. Maspero has shown, even this was not
enough; by a fiction of the priests, represented in several
instances upon the hieroglyphic decorations of temples,[1]
the god was declared to have taken the place of the
non-royal husband, and to have become the actual
father of the new prince. It seems even likely that
among the strict prescriptions for all the solemn acts
of the king it was directed that he should assume the
insignia of the god, his ram's horns, fleece, etc., when
visiting the queen. We find from the *Romance* of

[1] Cf. the instances cited by Maspero, *op. cit.* pp. 15-19.

Alexander's life, afterwards so popular in Alexandria, that the invented paternity of the hero by means of Nektanebo and his magic arts conforms exactly to all this ritual. As last legitimate king of Egypt, Nektanebo had fled to Macedonia, seduced Olympias by magic visions, and then appeared to her under the form either of a serpent, the Agathodæmon, or of the ram-headed god Amon.

Here is another argument to be added to those of Lumbroso in his rehabilitation of the traditional literature of this period. The theological details have now been shown by M. Maspero to correspond so accurately with the doctrine of the priests of Amon in pre-Ptolemaic days, that I hesitate to date the composition of the *Romance* after that dynasty was extinct. I do not think that the decayed priesthood under the Roman Empire could have found any interest in reviving these solemn fictions. I had argued long ago that the remarkable absence of all importance of the Ptolemies throughout the whole book pointed further in the same direction. Either the legend arose before they did, or after they had passed out of public memory. The latter seems to me impossible, so that I contend that at least the earlier portions of the *Romance*, and those regarding Alexander's acts in Egypt, must have taken shape almost at once, and the story of his birth must have become current before it became necessary to make similar inventions for the Ptolemies.

As regards Alexander's acceptance of his own divinisation, there is no reason to think that he received it with reluctance or with scepticism, or that either Greeks or Orientals were shocked at it, and unwilling to accord him this honour. The insurgent Macedonians indeed twitted him concerning his father Amon, and one or two sceptical philosophers may have expressed their scorn; but the Attic public that lavished divinity a few years later on Demetrius the Descender, or the natives of the Cyclades who conferred it with enthusiasm upon the first Ptolemy, can hardly have thought the notion strange or shocking a few years earlier. Strack even maintains the general conclusion (*Dyn. der Ptolemäer*, p. 112) that the deification of the Ptolemies and other Hellenistic sovereigns was a distinctively Greek invention, not a piece of Orientalism.

To the completion of Alexander's divinity, and his foundation of the new capital, our historians well-nigh confine their account of his Egyptian doings. We are even uncertain whether he ever saw Alexandria after his first laying out of the place on his way to the oasis. For though some of our inferior authorities actually place the foundation on his return journey, it seems more likely that he returned across the desert straight to Memphis, and hastened to descend the eastern channel to Pelusium and to Syria. He had received some Greek deputations from cities of Asia Minor, and had ordered some political prisoners to be put in ward at Elephantine, which seems to have been regarded in some way as a penal settlement. But with the natives he had no further intercourse.

FIG. 7.—A King (in this case the Emperor Tiberius) worshipping Amon.

It remains for us to consider, so far as our materials

permit us, the general effect of the conquest upon these natives and their condition. For this is properly the history of Egypt. The founding of the new city was doubtless accompanied by some hardships. Probably to the natives the closing of the mart at the Canopic mouth was the least, for the whole literature of the papyri of the succeeding generations does not afford us any evidence that native Egyptians engaged in foreign trade. That must have been altogether in the hands of Greeks or Syrians. But the unsettling of all the villages round Rakotis, and the sweeping in of the country population into a new city—this must have caused much annoyance and trouble, notwithstanding the many privileges with which Alexander sought to soften it. The Egyptians are, however, a patient people, and provided their priests were satisfied, and recommended the new dynast, we may imagine the poorer people soothed with the reflection that a change of masters would not do any harm, and might possibly bring some relief. We hear, indeed, that he demanded from them the same amount of taxes as they had paid to the Persians. But the odiousness of the Persian rule had not been so much extortion, as a reckless and cruel disregard of Egyptian sentiment. In our day we have heard grievances made light of because they were *sentimental*, as if such were not the worst, nay, perhaps the only real grievances. . The violation of sentiment is a far worse form of tyranny than the violation of material rights. Outrages, for example, on property are not resented with the same fierceness as outrages on religion. But these latter had often been committed by the Persians. It was on this point that there was now every probability of a great change.

As regards the political settlement of the country there is a curious chapter in Arrian (iii. 5) giving us the names and offices of those to whom Alexander entrusted the country. Upon his return to Memphis he had received various embassies from Greece, and also (what was more welcome) about 1000 mercenaries sent him by Antipater by way of reinforcement. He then celebrated

a great musical and gymnastic feast to "Zeus the
king," apparently in Hellenic fashion, and perhaps in
contrast to the various Egyptian ceremonies to which
he and his army had submitted.   Then he ordered the
country as follows:—"He made two Egyptians nomarchs
of (all) Egypt, viz. Doloaspis and Peteesis,[1] and divided
the country between them; but when Peteesis presently
resigned, Doloaspis undertook the whole charge.   As
commanders of the garrisons he appointed from among
his companions Pantaleon of Pydna at Memphis, and
Polemo of Pella at Pelusium ; as general of the mercenaries,[2] Lycidas the Ætolian ; as secretary over the mercenaries, Eugnostos, one of his companions; as overseers
over them, Æschylus and Ephippus of Chalcis.   Governor
of the adjacent Libya he made Apollonios, of Arabia
about Heroopolis Cleomenes of Naukratis, and him he
directed to permit the nomarchs to control their nomes
according to established and ancient custom ; but to
obtain from them their taxes, which they were ordered
to pay him.   He made Peukestas and Balakros (two
of his noblest Macedonians) generals of the [whole]
army he left in Egypt, and admiral Polemo. . . .   He
is said to have divided the government of Egypt into
many hands, because he was surprised at the nature
and (military) strength of the country, so that he did
not consider it safe to let one man undertake the sole
charge of it."   So far Arrian.

[1] The Greek text gives Petisis, but the true form is found frequently in papyri, and means *gift of Isis*, in fact, the Greek
Isidorus.   Doloaspis is not known to me as an Egyptian name,
and is probably Persian.—P.

[2] I see that Droysen (*Hell.* i. 1. 324) understands Ξένοι in the
sentence to mean immigrant Greeks, who were thus set under
special magistrates.   This he did, I presume, because Μισθοφόροι
occur a few lines earlier in describing the succours sent from
Macedonia.   I think he is wrong, and that both terms apply to
mercenaries, but the earlier to Alexander's "foreign legion,"
permanently enlisted (probably from Greek exiles), the latter to
those who were engaged for a short and definite time.   That each
body of mercenaries had a secretary appears from such texts as
that of Thera : Γραμματεις των κατα Κρητην, κ.~.λ., στρατιωτων και
μαχιμων, etc.

But his meagre statement of facts leaves room for many conjectures. Alexander's military arrangements do not specially concern Egypt. It is more than probable that the general, secretary, and *episcopi* were a regular feature in the hazardous control of every great mercenary force; separate military governors of Memphis and Pelusium, with trusty Macedonian garrisons—all these forces under command of two of his highest officers, leave no room for surprise except in the last item. Here was shown the young king's suspicion. For either Peukestas or Balakros might well have sufficed as the commander-in-chief. Apollonios was made *Libyarch*, a term known from early papyri; but to the corresponding *Arabarch*, Cleomenes, a man of Naucratis, was given another most important function. He was made Chancellor of the Exchequer (afterwards known as διοικητής[1]), and was responsible to Alexander for the whole tribute of Egypt. Yet he was not entrusted with the collection of it. This was left in the hands of two native general nomarchs, who must have had under them a host of local nomarchs. I suppose the division of the country between them was into Upper and Lower Egypt. Perhaps the resignation of Peteesis, taken with the evil reports we hear of Cleomenes' extortions, show that the office became unpopular, and that the gain from the Macedonian rule was not so great as people had anticipated. It is plain that the man of Naucratis had most influence with Alexander; the native nomarchs sank into insignificance; the garrison was gradually withdrawn into the East, and so the Greek, as usual, monopolised all the power and profit. It is remarkable, that though Alexander must have been in much want of troops, no hint is given us that he even thought

---

[1] ὁ ἐπὶ τῶν προσόδων which Droysen suggests, is a title I have never found in early Ptolemaic papyri, so that it possibly dates only from Roman times (*e.g.* the Cleopatra stele from Thebes, C.I.G. 4717). It is likely that Cleomenes' control of the finances was at first connected with raising the money for the building of Alexandria from the taxes of the country.

of enrolling the military caste of Egypt, as he afterwards enrolled Persians in his service. He was no
doubt quite young and inexperienced, and proposed to
himself to conquer the world with Macedonians and
Greeks only. It should be added that the separation
of administrative from military functions was a principle
carried out elsewhere by Alexander, probably on the
Persian model. In his Eastern conquests his habit
was to set a satrap over each province, but beside him,
and independently, a commander of the forces, and an
official in charge of the revenue.

It would be a matter of no small interest to determine with certainty whether Ptolemy accompanied
Alexander to Egypt, and to the oracle of Amon. He
was at that time still an officer of no prominence in the
Macedonian service, whose promotion was yet to come.
Yet it is hard to avoid the conclusion that it was now
that the wealth and isolation of Egypt struck the far-
seeing man, and made him in after years claim this as
his province without hesitation. But if we merely
regarded his account of Alexander's adventure, we find
him so well inclined to the marvellous as to dispose us
to believe that he wrote from hearsay. Arrian reports
(iii. 3. § 5) that "Ptolemy son of Lagus says that
two serpents (δράκοντας) went before the army (in
the desert march to the oasis) *uttering a voice* ; and that
Alexander commanded his guides to follow them as
inspired ; that these led the way to the oracle *and back
from it again.* But Aristobulus and the majority say
that two ravens flew in advance of the force," etc.
Either, therefore, Ptolemy, writing his history of the
campaigns in long after years, copied down one of the
legends that clustered about the conqueror, without
any criticism, or, having himself accompanied the
expedition, he deliberately chose to propagate the most
miraculous version. Subsequent acts, to which we
shall come in due time, incline us to believe that the
latter was the case.

Alexander never revisited Egypt, but his corpse was
conveyed with solemn pomp to Memphis, and ultimately

laid at rest in the centre of his new capital, as its hero-founder (œkist).   He seems even to have neglected the proper care of the land in the midst of his enormous engagements.   He was informed that Cleomenes had proved an unjust and tyrannous steward ; he promised to pardon him for all his crimes, provided his instructions regarding the worship of his friend Hephæstion were duly carried out at Alexandria. Arrian (vii. 23) quotes the very words of Alexander's letter without suspicion,[1] and thinks they are justified by the promptness with which Cleomenes procured an oracle from Amon ordering Hephæstion's deification (Diod. xvii. 115), and the importance of his loyalty to Alexander when other financial officers were proving dishonest and mutinous.   The fact remains that the administration of Egypt during Alexander's short reign was in bad hands, and that though the king knew it, he either could not or would not interfere.   Probably

[1] " The sacred embassy returned from the temple of Amon, whom the king had sent there to inquire to what extent it was lawful for him to give honours to Hephæstion, and said that Amon permitted him to have sacrifices as a hero. . . . And to Cleomenes, a worthless person who had done much injustice in Egypt, he wrote a letter which I do not criticise so far as it concerns his loving memory of Hephæstion, but in many other respects I do.   For the letter directed that a *heroon* should be erected to Hephæstion in Alexandria—one in the city and another in the island of Pharos, where the tower is in that island, most famous for its size and beauty—and that it should become the habit to call it after Hephæstion, and that on the mutual contracts of the merchants the name of Hephæstion should be inscribed." So far well, though it shows an undue attention to trifles.   But here is the objectionable part.   " If I find," continues the letter, "the temples in Egypt and the *heroon* of Hephæstion well appointed, I shall condone your former transgressions, and whatever wrong you may do hereafter, you shall suffer nothing disagreeable at my hands."   I cannot understand how modern historians (Niese, i. 185, Grote, xii. 341 (who mistranslates the passage), Droysen, i. 2. 336) can accept this letter as genuine. The details about the Pharos lighthouse contain the grossest possible anachronism, for it was not built till at least forty years later.   But I presume that the forger of the letter knew the still-existing shrines of Hephæstion, one of which was near the subsequent lighthouse.

the tribute of Egypt was at all events promptly paid. The charges against Cleomenes in Demosthenes' speech *against Dionysodorus* are only to be taken for what they are worth in an Athenian law-court. The defendants are one and all conspirators with Cleomenes, "who has the control in Egypt (τοῦ ἐν Αἰγύπτωι ἄρξαντος), who, from the time that he received this government, did no small harm to your city (Athens), nay, rather to all the Greeks, retailing upon retail (παλιγκαπηλεύων) and raising the prices of corn with his associates." Possibly this sharp practice only damaged the Greek traders, and did no harm to the natives. On this point we have no information. But the promptness with which Ptolemy put him to death when he took over Egypt, may be a proof that he was a power among the natives, not merely that he was detested by the merchants.

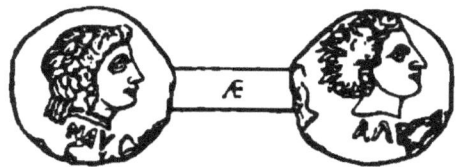

FIG. 8.—Coin found by Mr. Petrie at Naukratis. Two female (?) heads (Aphrodite? Naukratis?) with NAT on obverse and ΛΛΕ on reverse, showing that the city had a right of coinage under Alexander, and indeed the head on the reverse seems to me that of the youthful Alexander.

CHAPTER II

GENERAL AUTHORITIES.—*Ancient*—The sequel in the historians quoted above, chap. i.; Josephus, *Antiq. Jud.* xii.; Plutarch, *Demetrius*; Pausanias, i. 6. *Modern*—Droysen, Niese, and Mahaffy as above; Strack, *die Dynastie der Ptolemäer* (1896).

WE are not here concerned with the various quarrels among Alexander's generals for the possession of his empire. Happily there was not from the first any doubt concerning the satrapy of Egypt. Ptolemy, a favourite and familiar companion, who had fought his way up from an obscure military position to one of the highest and most trusted in the army, demanded and obtained Egypt for his share. This was in 323 B.C., immediately after the death of Alexander.

FIG. 9.—Head of Ptol. Soter in Egyptian dress, from an Onyx seal (Petrie collection).

I do not know that we have a single scrap of evidence concerning the condition of the country since the Macedonian conquest, beyond what has been quoted already from Demosthenes, and corroborating anecdotes in Aristotle's *Œconomics*. In the second book of that pseudonym work, which gives a number of instances from various sources of sharp practice in public economy, the conduct of "Cleomenes the Alexandrian, satrap of Egypt," receives special consideration. "Cleomenes the Alexandrian, satrap of Egypt, when a severe famine occurred in the neighbouring countries, but in Egypt to only a small extent, forbade the exportation of corn. But when the nomarchs complained that they

were unable to pay their tribute, owing to this
regulation, he allowed the export, but put so high a
tax upon it, that for a small quantity exported he
obtained a large sum of money, besides getting rid
of the excuse made by the nomarchs. And as he
was going by water through the nome where the
crocodile is a god, one of his slaves was carried off
by them, so calling the priests together, he said he
must have revenge for this wanton attack, and
ordered them to hunt the crocodiles. Thereupon the
priests, in order that their god might not be insulted,
collected and gave him a great quantity of gold, and
so appeased him. When Alexander directed him to
found a city at Pharos (Alexandria) and to move the
trade-mart of Canobus thither, he went to Canobus
and told all the priests and wealthy people that he had
come for the purpose of moving them out. They
therefore collected a large sum of money which they
gave him, in order to keep their mart. He departed
with this, but after a while, when his new foundation
was in order, he came again and asked them for an
enormous sum, declaring that he estimated the difference of the mart being there or at Alexandria at this
figure. And when they said they could not pay it,
he transferred them all to the new city. [The next
example has no local colour.] And when corn was
selling at 10 drachmæ (for the medimnus) he called
together the peasants (τοὺς ἐργαζομένους) and asked them
on what terms they would work for him; they said
they would do so at a cheaper rate than that at which
they sold to the merchants. Then he told them to
sell to him at the same price as to the rest, but fixed
the price of corn at 32 drachmæ, and sold at this
rate. [This seems to mean that he got rid of the
middlemen, and so made all the profit himself for the
Crown.] And having called together the priests, he
told them that the expenses of religion in the country
were extravagant, and that a certain number of
temples and priests must be abolished. Then the
priests offered him both privately and from their

temple-funds money, as they thought he was really going to reduce them, and each wanted to preserve his own temple and his own priesthood." [If this argument meant, either you must sacrifice some of your endowments or give a large contribution to the Crown, then anyone who knows the enormous wealth of the old Egyptian priesthood will hardly quarrel with Cleomenes.]

It does not seem to me that any of these instances show an oppression of the poor, but rather of the financiers and priests. From what we know of them and their doings, we shall be slow to condemn Cleomenes upon their complaints. The anecdotes seem to be genuine, and the famine in the Levant by which he profited was doubtless that known to us by inscriptions as having affected Athens in 329 B.C. At all events, we can say nothing more now, than that Cleomenes was the authorised satrap of Egypt, and in no fear of dismissal, while its future master was winning fame and influence in Alexander's campaigns.

When the great king's death supervened (June, 323 B.C.), and a division of the empire under Macedonian chiefs, the nominal lieutenants of the royal heir, took place, we are told by Pausanias, a bad authority, that Ptolemy was the main advocate for making these chiefs independent of the central power, and that it was with this object clearly before him that he asked for and obtained Egypt as his portion. It is stated in the compendium of Arrian's history of the sequel to Alexander's reign (Phot. *cod.* 92) that Cleomenes, now acknowledged satrap of the country, was formally named as his colleague, though not his equal.[1]

It is plain, therefore, that Cleomenes had not made himself disliked by the generals, and probably Perdikkas, who seems from the first to have suspected and feared Ptolemy, thought it safe to have a powerful friend, well acquainted with the country, to help him to counteract any schemes of the new satrap. "Ptolemy," says Diodorus (xviii. 14), "took over Egypt without

[1] ὕπαρχος is the word.

disturbance, and treated the natives with kindness; found there a treasure of 8000 talents, collected a mercenary force, and organised his power; moreover, there ran together to him a crowd of friends, on account of his personal popularity." To protect himself against the coming hostility of Perdikkas, who desired to keep the whole empire together, and act as regent, with the chance of succeeding, he made alliance with Antipater, master of Macedonia, and what was perhaps more urgent, he put to death Cleomenes, upon what pretext we do not know (Paus. i. 6. 3).

His first care was to put the country into a state of defence against the expected attack of the regent. When this was successfully beaten off,[1] and the regent slain, Ptolemy could have taken his place, being highly popular, for the army and the princes, who had lost their director and protector, were ready to adopt any prompt solution of their difficulties. But his prudence and moderate ambition did not permit him to make such a mistake. He conferred the doubtful and dangerous honour on two of his supporters, and remained as he was, the confirmed and now very powerful satrap of Egypt.

One of the most open causes of quarrel with Perdikkas had been the securing of the body of Alexander, which had set out from Babylon, upon a splendid funeral car, and which had reached Palestine, when Ptolemy met it with a large escort, and conveyed it to Egypt. The regent himself seems not to have seen the danger at the outset; for the original plan he sanctioned was the burial of Alexander in the temple of his father Amon in the oasis. When the procession had started, he saw that this would give Ptolemy control of a great sentimental advantage, and directed that it should go to Ægæ, the resting-place of the old Macedonian kings. But Ptolemy, partly by force and partly by persuasion, had brought the remains to Egypt.

This is a matter which does affect our history,

[1] Cf. the details, *Emp. Ptol.* pp. 30 *seq*

and is worth closer consideration, especially as our authorities vary concerning it, some
(Pausahias) asserting that the
body of the king was laid in
Memphis, and not brought to
Alexandria till the following
reign, others, and the majority,
that it was conveyed straight
to Alexandria.   The *Romance*
even asserts that the people of
Memphis refused to receive it,
as being a source of danger to
any city where it lay.[1]

[1] After the oracle of the Babylonian
Zeus had answered that the king
should be buried at Memphis, the
Romance proceeds : "Then no one
objected any further, but allowed
Ptolemy to depart and take with him
the embalmed body in a leaden coffin,
which he placed upon a cart and
brought to Egypt. When the people
of Memphis heard of it, they went out
to meet the body of Alexander and
brought it into Memphis.   But the
high priest of the temple of Memphis
said, 'Do not settle him here, but in
the city which he has built at Racotis,
for wherever this body may lie, the
city will be uneasy, disturbed with
wars and battles'" (iii. 34). I will
here add, to save the reader from
misapprehension, that the only recognised route from Syria to Alexandria
lay through Memphis.   To sail from
Palestine to Alexandria was most
difficult, owing to the prevalence of
violent north-west winds and the
shoaly coast.   To cross the Delta by
road was impossible. It is therefore
quite certain, that whatever Ptolemy's
intention was as to the final resting-
place, the body must have been first
brought to Memphis.   There may

FIG. 10.—Hunting Scene from the great Sarcophagus of Sidon (wrongly supposed to be the Tomb of Alexander).

But the *Romance* seems to know nothing of the
gold coffin in which the great Alexander lay during
Ptolemaic times, nor of the glass one with which it
was ultimately replaced near the end of that period.
It is even still possible that the legend arose before
the second Ptolemy had formally laid the body in the
Sema at Alexandria; for the golden coffin may only
date from that time (nearly forty years subsequent); it
is also possible, but very unlikely, that the fable was
not composed till the memory of these details had been
totally forgotten.

The quarrels concerning the division of the empire,
concerning the entombment of Alexander, and the ultimate
expedition of Perdikkas against Egypt, and his death,
seem to have occupied fully two years. For Perdikkas
had not ventured to attack Egypt without first sub-
jugating some of the recalcitrant satraps of Asia Minor,
still more the "kings" of Cyprus, whom Ptolemy had
brought over to his side, and who supplied him with
a fleet. Perdikkas' attack upon the new allies of Egypt
had been kept in check by obtaining from Antipater
the help of ships commanded by Antigonus, afterwards
the most dangerous neighbour of Ptolemy in Syria.
And during the breathing time afforded him by
Perdikkas' campaign in Asia Minor, the Egyptian satrap
had managed to secure the adherence of Cyrene.

That famous Greek settlement, famous since the
days of Pindar, and so isolated that it could be really
independent, had exchanged its voluntary submission
to Alexander for the sweets of autonomy, which in
those days usually meant an internecine struggle
between the rich who had most property and the poor
who had most votes. As soon as one party had force
enough to exile its opponents, these opponents appealed to any foreign nation to avenge them of their
enemies. In this case, the banished aristocrats—they
had been sent into exile by a Macedonian soldier of

---

even then have been some hesitation whether to bring it to the
oasis or to settle it in the tomb of the Founder (οἰκιστής), in the
centre of Alexandria.

fortune, Thibron, who had seized the remaining
treasures of Harpalus, a defaulting fiscal agent of
Alexander—tried every other ally, even Libyans and
Carthaginians, while Ptolemy's troops, under his
general, Ophelas, were waiting for the full-ripe fruit
to fall into their grasp; and so it happened. And
for some years Cyrene became a province of Egypt,
governed by a soldier, Ophelas, who was one of the
"men of Alexander," and therefore a personage to be
respected in that generation.

This addition of Cyrene to Egypt was merely the
tacking on of a Hellenic settlement, which added
nothing to the real life of the Egyptian people, unless
it be that it furnished many distinguished literary men
to the Museum, and added largely to the number of
foreign settlers who obtained farms and other privileges in Egypt. The papyri show that both in the
Fayyum and in Upper Egypt a large number of
veterans, or soldiers in reserve, were Cyrenæans.
By and by Cyrene also became a sort of outlying
province, held by a crown prince as heir-presumptive
of Egypt. The right of Ptolemy to hold it was
formally acknowledged in the second settlement of the
empire at Triparadeisus (321 B.C.), after the defeat
and death of Perdikkas, wherein Ptolemy again was
awarded Egypt, and whatever lands he might conquer
to the West.[1] In 320 B.C. he formally occupied Cyprus
with his fleet, and so added to his kingdom the second
outlying province, which was held by his dynasty permanently as a part of its empire.[2] The condition of
Cyprus seems to have been peculiar, and very different
from that of Cyrene. I need only mention the fact
that among the many foreign settlers in Egypt the
papyri hardly ever mention a Cypriote.

Having occupied and secured Cyprus, Ptolemy next
proceeded to seize the satrapy of Syria, held by Lao-

[1] Arrian in Photius, § 34; Diod. xviii. 39.
[2] I must remind the reader that Ptolemy was still in theory satrap
under Philip Arridæus, who had been nominated regent to the
whole empire, pending the accession of the child Alexander (IV.).

medon (320 B.C.).   In this he succeeded with hardly an
effort, and became master of a new and important
province.   But if his success was permanent in the
previous two extensions, it was not so in this.   For
about five years, while Antigonus was occupied with
wars in Asia, he maintained his possession ; but afterwards, when attacked, and notwithstanding his great
victory over Demetrius, who commanded for his father
Antigonus, at Gaza (312), he felt no confidence in his
power to carry on foreign wars ; and though he again
seized Syria at opportune moments, he never showed
any determination in risking another great battle for
its permanent possession.   But these several inter-
mittent occupations of Syria in part, and therefore of

FIG. 11.—Granite Shrine of Philip Arridæus (Luxor).

all Palestine, were accompanied (according to Josephus,
Antiq. xii. 1) with great hardships to the Jews, inas-
much as he carried away not only spoil, but thousands
of people to add to the strength of Egypt.

Alexander the Great was said to have induced many
Jews to come to Alexandria, and even to have settled
them in the upper country.   This is hardly probable ;
but it need not be doubted that, during the reign of
the first Ptolemy, very many Jews came as captives or
as settlers to Egypt.   Even this has been denied by
recent historians,[1] who very naturally suspect Josephus

[1] Lastly by Willrich, *Juden und Griechen*, an able pamphlet which
seems to me to import modern anti-Semitism into ancient history.

of exaggeration when he seeks to enlarge the early national importance of his race. But there is growing evidence of the early residence of Jews in Ptolemaic Egypt. The Petrie Papyri disclosed to us the existence of a village or town called Samaria in the Fayyum in the middle of the third century B.C., certainly founded before the conquests of the third Ptolemy, and therefore most likely due to the policy of the first. It also appears that the discussions on the legend of the translation of the LXX tend more and more to establish the general truth of that story, and the fact that it was the second Ptolemy who favoured the formation of a Greek version of the Hebrew Scriptures. If this be so, it is a proof of the number and importance of the Jewish population in Egypt at a very early point in this epoch. Josephus says that the first Ptolemy was a hard and oppressive master in Palestine; but his evidence is not quite consistent, and probably the deportations of which he complains were not so violent as he pretends. At all events, I believe that with the first Ptolemy, and at this moment, there began that growing intercourse of the Jews with Egypt, which led to large transfers of population, and to a great influence of the Jews in Egypt all through Ptolemaic history.

Another point of no small interest is mentioned by Diodorus (xix. 80) in his account of the battle of Gaza (312 B.C.). He says that Ptolemy employed a great number of natives in the army, not only in the transport service and as attendants, but among his armed forces. We may presume that they were only light-armed troops, if such were indeed to be had among the tall and stalwart Egyptians; for it is not till the very similar battle of Raphia, just a century later, that the natives formed the body of the phalanx and practically won that great battle. There is mention of the μαχιμοι or soldier-caste, if there were still castes in Egypt, in the Rosetta inscription (Ptolemy V.); but there is also a text found at Thera (1895), which speaks of a certain Eirenæus as secretary of the soldiers and the

μαχιμοι quartered in Crete, Thera, and Arsinoe in the
Peloponnesus, and this very possibly dates, as we shall
see, from the second or third Ptolemy.   These facts
lead one to abandon the received opinion, that the
soldier class of natives had become so insignificant as
to be of no account in Ptolemaic days.   It seems
rather to have been part of the prudent policy of the
satrap to strengthen his army, and perhaps his navy,
by recruiting from his native subjects.   But texts from
his time are so scanty and few that we cannot as yet
pretend such a conclusion to be more than probable.

Concerning the satrap's home policy towards the
natives,—his arrangements regarding revenue, internal
security, and commerce,—we know absolutely nothing.
But concerning his domestic affairs some very important events are recorded which belong to this
period of his life.

Ptolemy had the reputation of being much addicted
to women.   At the great "marriage of Asia and
Europe" in Babylon, Alexander had given him a
Persian grandee, Artakama, to wife ; but this lady
disappears from history without another trace.   Then
we are told a very improbable story by Athenæus
(576 d), that after Alexander's death (as if the lady
had been Alexander's mistress!) he consorted with
the Greek courtezan Thais,[1] and had by her at least
two children—a son called Leontiskos or Lagus (so I
read the text), and a daughter Eirene, afterwards
married to the "king" of the Cyprian Soli.   But
these unions do not affect our history.   During the
crisis of Perdikkas' attack on Egypt and the new
settlement at Triparadeisus (321 B.C.) Ptolemy contracted his distinctly political marriage with Eurydike,
daughter of Antipater, the senior and then the most

[1] This story is so improbable that I believe our authorities, who
knew the story of the notorious Thais having excited Alexander,
in a drunken revel, to set on fire the royal palace at Persepolis,
confused with her a mistress of the same name, whom Ptolemy
brought with him in the campaign.   The clause "after the death
of Alexander" is therefore to be expunged, as based on this misapprehension.

important of the satraps, who held Macedonia. This lady brought him several children, of whom the eldest was called Ptolemy, and so perhaps designated for the succession in Egypt. But within four years we find that he married a lady who seems to have come in the retinue of Eurydike to Egypt, a widow with children (the eldest, Magas, perhaps eleven years old), and who exercised no small influence upon his life. This was Berenike (I.), grandniece of Antipater, according to some the daughter of Lagus, and therefore his stepsister; her children, who afterwards made royal marriages, he seems to have adopted. The point of interest to us is that he did not divorce his first wife, so far as we know, but openly adopted the practice of polygamy, recognised both at the Macedonian and the Egyptian courts. In the latter case I do not know whether more than one was ever recognised at the same time as the *great wife*, whom the king visited in the garb of Amon; but Egyptian kings certainly did marry foreign princesses for political purposes, who could hardly have been considered mere inmates of his harem. In Macedonia we know what troubles Philip, the father of Alexander the Great, brought upon his house by his polygamy; and such may also have been the practice of Macedonian nobles. But it was distinctly opposed to Hellenic sentiment and custom, and must therefore be put into the scale with the arguments against the new theory[1] that the sovereignty founded by Ptolemy was upon Greek principles and according to Greek ideas. Both polygamy and incest were odious to the Greeks; they were not so to the Macedonians and Egyptians. But Ptolemy was as yet only a satrap in name, and his public acts pretended to be done according to the orders of Philip Arridæus, and when the latter was murdered (in 317 B.C.), according to the orders of the boy Alexander (IV.). Still we must attribute to Ptolemy's internal policy that he restored the outer shrine of the great temple of Luxor (Thebes) in the name of Philip Arridæus, and therefore at the open-

[1] M. L. Strack, *die Dynastie der Ptolemäer*

ing of his satrapy.   This proves plainly enough that
from the commencement he sought to conciliate the
priesthood, and through them the national feeling.

 ˙ The restoration of the inner shrine was continued in
the name of the young Alexander, probably at this
very time,[1] for in the succeeding years Ptolemy's
attention became riveted on Hellenic affairs and in the
great struggle for supremacy between Antigonus and
his son on one side and the rival but inferior satraps
on the other.   Seleukos had been driven out of Babylon
by Antigonus, and arrived a fugitive at the Egyptian
court in 316 B.C.   Of course he urged Ptolemy to make
war in time, before Antigonus became all-powerful.
But in any case, at this moment Ptolemy held Syria
and Cyprus, which were beyond his original share of
the empire, and upon this ground Antigonus attacked
him.   We are fortunately not concerned with the
intricate details of these wars, which affected Egypt
very indirectly.

At the beginning of the new struggle (314 B.C.)
Ptolemy for a short time lost control of both Cyrene
and Cyprus, the former by a revolution, the latter by
the attack of Antigonus.   The revolt in Cyrene was
(we may be sure) occasioned by the proclamation of
Polyperchon, the nominal regent after Antipater's death
(319 B.C.), giving autonomy to all Greek cities, and
commanding them to receive back all their political
exiles.   The other satraps—Antigonus and his son and
Ptolemy — were obliged to follow suit, and so far
humour the Greeks.   But with Ptolemy it was only a
device to leave him a free hand regarding his fleet in
Greek waters, nor did he have recourse to it as yet.
He regained both provinces, and in the case of Cyprus,
with the high-handed proceedings of a downright conqueror.   As regards Syria and Palestine, after a series
of chequered campaigns, including one great victory at

[1] It is from this inner shrine that we have (in the Museum at
Cairo) the statue of the young Alexander (IV.), which is very
remarkable as a hybrid production, containing both Greek and
Egyptian artistic features.   Cf. Fig. 12.

FIG. 12.—Græco-Egyptian Colossal Statue of Alexander IV. (Karnak).

Gaza (312) over Demetrius, and several lesser defeats, such as the loss of Tyre and the capture of his general, Killes, with a division, Ptolemy was content to make peace with his formidable foe in 311 B.C., without recovering this valuable province.[1] It is during its course that he is supposed to have carried off so many Jews to Egypt.

Throughout this war we find the policy of Egypt rather cautious than brilliant; nor did Ptolemy ever again, after his victory at Gaza, entrust his fortunes to the risk of a great pitched battle, the loss of which meant the loss of all the mercenaries in his army, who as a rule went over to the conqueror. With the exception of one great naval defeat suffered at Rhodes, Ptolemy never engaged in any more heroic conflicts. He had probably seen enough of fighting under Alexander to appreciate the changes and chances of campaigns. From henceforth his policy on land is purely defensive; on sea more political than naval. But now at last we arrive at a historical text which gives us some insight into his activity at home.

"In the year 7 (i.e. 312–311 B.C. of the boy king Alexander IV., whose formal reign began at the death of Philip Arridaeus), at the beginning of the inundation, under the sanctity of Horus, the youthful, rich in strength, the lord of diadems, loving the gods who gave him the dignity of his father, the Horus of gold, lord in the whole world, the king of Upper and Lower Egypt, the lord of both lands, the delight of the heart of Amon, chosen by the Sun, of Alexander the ever-living, the friend of the gods of the cities PE and TEP. He being as king in the world of strangers, his Holiness was in the interior of Asia, so that there was a great victory in Egypt, Ptolemy was his name.

---

[1] It is to be specially noted regarding these campaigns that, according to Diodorus (xix. 80), the forces at the battle of Gaza included, in addition to 22,000 Macedonians and mercenaries, a crowd of Egyptians, partly to supply transport service, partly armed, and to be used in battle.

"A person of youthful vigour was he, strong in his
two arms, a king in spirit, mighty among the people,
of stout courage, of firm foot, resisting the furious, not
turning his back, striking his adversaries in the face in
the midst of the battle. When he had seized the bow,
it was not (for) one shot at the assailant, it was a (mere)
play with the sword ; in the midst of the battle not a
question of staying beside him, of mighty hand there
was no parrying his hand, no return of that which
goeth out of his mouth, there is not his like in the
world of foreigners. He had brought back the images
of the gods found in Asia ; all the furniture of the books
of all the temples of north and south Egypt, he had
restored them to their place. He had made his residence the fortress of the king's loving Amon's name the
chosen of the sun, the son of the Sun, Alexandria it is
called on the shore of the great sea of the Ionians,
Rakotis was its former name. He had assembled
Ionians many, and their cavalry and their ships many
with their crews, when he went with his people to the
land of the Syrians, who were at war with him. He
penetrated into their land, his courage was mighty as
that of the hawk among little birds. He taking them
at once carried their princes, their cavalry, their ships,
their works of art all to Egypt. After this, when he
had set out for the territory of Marmarica (Cyrene), he
laying hold of them at one time, led captive their men,
women, horses, in requital for what they had done to
Egypt. When he returned to Egypt, his heart being
glad at what he had done, he celebrated a good day,
and this great viceroy was seeking the best (thing to
do) for the gods of Upper and Lower Egypt. There
spoke to him he that was at his side, and the elders of
the land of Lower Egypt, that the sea-land, the land of
Buto is its name, had been granted by the king, the
image of Tanen, chosen by Ptah, the son of the Sun,
Chabbas living for ever, to the gods of PE and TEP,
after his Holiness (Chabbas) was gone to PE TEP to
examine all the sea-land in their territory, to go into
the interior of the marshes, to examine every arm of

the Nile which goes into the great sea, to keep off the
fleet of Asia from Egypt.

" Then spoke his Holiness (Ptolemy) to him who was
at his side.   This sea-land let me get to know it.
They spoke before his Holiness.   This sea-land it is
called the land of Buto, is the property of the gods of
PE TEP from earlier time.

" The enemy Xerxes reversed it, nor had he given
anything of his to the gods of PE TEP.   His Holiness
spake that there should be brought before him the
priests and magistrates of PE TEP.   They brought
them to him in haste.   There spoke his Holiness :
Let me learn to know the souls of the gods of PE TEP,
as to what they did to the miscreant on account of the
wicked action which he had done, what ?   They answered : The miscreant Xerxes had done evil to PE TEP,
he had taken away its property.

" They spake before his Holiness : The king our Lord
Horus, son of Isis, son of Osiris, the ruler of rulers,
the king of the kings of Upper Egypt, the king of the
kings of Lower Egypt, the avenger of his father, the
lord of Pe, being the beginning of the gods hereafter,
not a king after him, cast out the miscreant Xerxes
with his eldest son, making himself known in the town
of Neith, Sais, on this day beside the holy mother.
There spoke his Holiness : This powerful god among
the gods there is not a king after him, that it may be
given (me to know him) in the way of his Holiness.
I swear by it.   Then spake the priests and the magistrates of PE TEP, that your Holiness may command,
that there may be granted the sea-land, the land of
Buto it is called, to the gods of PE TEP, with bread,
drink, oxen, birds, all good things, that there may be
repeated his renewal in your name on account of his
loan to the gods of PE TEP as requital for the excellence of your actions.   This great viceroy spake :
Let a decree be drawn up in writing at the seal of the
writing of the king's scribe of finance, thus—I Ptolemy,
the Satrap, in the land of Buto I give to Horus, the
avenger of his father, the lord of Pe, and to Buto, the

lady of PE TEP, from this day forth for ever, with all its villages, all its towns, all its inhabitants, all its fields, all its waters, all its oxen, all its birds, all its herds, and all things produced in it aforetime, together with what is added since, together with the gift, made by the king, the lord of both lands, Chabbas, the ever-living. Its south (limit) the territory of the town of Buto, and Hermopolis of the north towards the mouths of the Nile. Its north: the downs on the shore of the great sea. Its west: the mouths of the plier of the oar—towards the downs. In the east the home of Sebennys, so that its calves may be (a supply) for the great hawks, its bulls for the countenance of Nebtanit, its oxen for the living hawks, its milk for the august child, its fowls for him in Sa, to whom is life-all things produced on its soil on the table of Horus himself, the lord of Pe and Buto the head of Ra-Harmachis for ever. This land in extension had been given by the king, the lord of both lands, the image of Taven, chosen by Ptah, the son of the Sun, Chabbas living for ever, renewed these gifts has this great viceroy of Egypt, Ptolemy, to the gods of PE TEP for ever. As a reward for this that he has done, may there be given him victory and strength to his heart's content, so that fear of him may continue even as it is among strange nations. Whosoever shall propose the land of Buto, so that he shall touch it to take ought from it, may he be under the ban of those that are in Pe, under the curse of those that are in Tep, so that he may be in the fiery breath of the goddess Aptari in the day of her terrors, not his son, not his daughter, may they give him water."—*Greek Life and Thought*, pp. 180-192.

Though it is the plan of this book to regard only the history of Egypt during the long and complicated external wars of Ptolemy's life, it is necessary to say a word more concerning the peace or rather truce of 311 B.C., which was made among the satraps after five years' fruitless struggle. The young Alexander, now unfortunately interned with Casander in Macedonia, was growing up, and his titular sovereignty over the empire was undisputed. On the other hand, not only had Antigonus made himself a great ruler in Asia, but Seleukos in Babylon, Ptolemy in Egypt, Casander in Macedonia, had become practically sovereigns. The truce of 311 B.C. proclaimed the *status quo*, without daring to question the young Alexander's rights. But with it all Greek cities were declared to be free and autonomous. This was the immediate bone of contention. Was it to apply to Cyrene, held in subjection by Ptolemy, to Cyprus, ruled by him through local kings, to the cities of Cilicia, dominated by Antigonus, or those of Greece which Casander claimed as under his dominion? It was the obvious policy of each of the rival satraps to accuse the other of not fulfilling this clause of the peace; it was the insight of Ptolemy which made him the first to understand that in this contest of pseudo-liberality the satrap with the dominant fleet would exercise practical sway over all the coasts and islands of the Ægean. So while the youthful heir to the empire and his mother were being secretly hidden away and murdered by Casander, not without the connivance of the other satraps,[1] Ptolemy fitted out an ample fleet and proceeded along Cilicia and Caria to the Levant, "freeing" all the Greek cities under the sway of Antigonus, and proclaiming to the islands of the Ægean their autonomy. This led to a general league of the islanders, under the "presidency" of the ruler of Egypt, which lasted so long as the Egyptian held the supremacy of the sea. It was presently interrupted by the rival and victorious fleet of Demetrius (the Besieger), who retook even Cyprus, and held the Levant for nearly ten years, again for a moment by his son Antigonus Gonatas after his naval victory at Kos. But these were only passing alterations. The control of the Cyclades and adjoining coasts, as well as of Palestine and Cœle-Syria, were secured by the tenacious policy of Ptolemy to Egypt for a century.

---

[1] This seems to me almost certain from the silence of the rest, and the utter absence of any protest or complaint against the conduct of Casander.

What effects had this naval supremacy upon the land? It is beyond doubt that a large number of natives must have been employed in the management of the necessary ships, and we know from one inscription (of Thera) that the military caste did duty in the islands with the Hellenistic troops. So far then this foreign service must have tended to teach many natives some knowledge of Greek, and some wider view of business affairs than the narrow traditions of the valley of the Nile. There were also material advantages. Not only did this influence bring much additional traffic to Alexandria and fill the port with visitors from the islands, but in days of distress, when the failure of the inundation threatened Egypt with famine, the control of the sea and the pressure of guardships could divert the corn traffic of the Black Sea from going west and send it south. Moreover, the ports of Greece could be made to receive Egyptian merchandise on terms of "the most favoured nation." This it was which made it possible for the third Ptolemy, as the Canopus stone tells us, to import corn to Egypt and save his people from starvation. An inscription, recently discovered, tells us of the gratitude of the islanders, and how they displayed it.[1] Here is the passage which concerns us now:[2] "Since the king and saviour Ptolemy was the cause of many great benefits to the islanders and the rest of the Greeks, having liberated the cities and restored their laws, and established for all their hereditary constitution, and lightened the burden of their taxes . . . it is therefore befitting that all the islanders who

---

[1] Cf. M. J. Delamarre's publication of this text from Nikourgia, close by Amorgos, in the *Revue de Philologie*, xx. (April 1896). I beg the reader to remember, however, that this is an official expression of gratitude, in which fact and flattery are usually compounded so inextricably that the plain truth can hardly be extricated by us now.

[2] Επειδη ο | βασιλευς και σωτηρ Πτολεμαιος πολλων | και μεγαλων αγαθων αι | τιος εγενετο τοις | τε νησιωταις και τοις αλλοις ελλησιν τας τε πο | λεις ελευθερωσας και τους νομους αποδους | και την πατριομ πολιτειαμ πασιγ καταστησας | και των εισφορων κουφισας και νυν ο βασιλευς | Πτολεμαιος διαδεξαμενος την βασιλειαν, etc.

were the first to honour Ptolemy the Saviour with
equi-divine honours on account of his public benefits
and his personal help . . . should join heartily in celebrating the feast now being established in his honour
at Alexandria," etc.   The question of these divine
honours is one of special interest to the history of
Egypt. The most recent author upon Ptolemaic history [1]
holds that the deification of these and other Hellenistic
sovereigns at this epoch was a Greek fashion, and not,
as we all had supposed, due to Egyptian and Syrian
influences.   Here there seems to arise a direct corroboration of this theory.   The islanders boast that
they were the first to accord to him divine honours.
Our historians tell us that it was the Rhodians after
the first siege of 306 B.C. who called him *Soter*, and
set apart for him a shrine and sacrifices.   The evidence
that the Greeks of that age were quite ready to deify
any great benefactor or any one of whom they were
greatly afraid is beyond dispute, but I cannot accept
this as a complete account of the deification and cult
which the Ptolemies enjoyed in Egypt.

   With the death of the young Alexander a complete
change took place, at least officially, in Ptolemy's
position.   Up to that moment he was set down in all
formal protocols as the satrap holding the country
under Alexander's sovereignty.   In the year 310–9 (we
cannot tell the more precise date) he must of necessity
have adopted a new title.   From the fact that in 308
he sends his stepson Magas as regent to the again
subdued Cyrene, it seems hard to avoid the conclusion
that he was proclaimed king in Egypt on the death of
Alexander becoming known.   Or shall we give credit
to the theory that this death was (officially) ignored or
kept secret, and that he still ruled by the grace and in
the name of the young Macedonian? [2]

[1] Max. L. Strack, *die Dynastie der Ptolemäer*, p. 112.
[2] Strack, *op. cit.* p. 191, quotes from Revillout three demotic
papyri, dated in the year 13 Athyr of the king Alexander, son of
Alexander, which means the beginning of 304 B.C.   I quote these
demotic documents and readings with all reserve.   As Revillout

This is the view adopted by Strack, who holds fast to the canon, which makes the royalty of the dynasty not begin till the opening of 304 B.C., and who even brings down the birth of his successor to this or the subsequent year.[1] This he has done because he accepts the theory that the rule of the dynasty only permitted sons born in the purple to succeed. To my mind there is little doubt that this was the case, and it was most probably the excuse or plea urged by Ptolemy to his court for preferring his youngest to his eldest son. But there is great difficulty in altering the date of the prince's birth from the year 308-7, during which Ptolemy was still completing his triumphal progress through the Ægean. After the siege of Rhodes in 306 B.C., when the Rhodians repeated what the other islanders had already done, and deified Ptolemy, his adversary Demetrius was still undoubted master of the sea. We know from good authority[2] that the young prince was born at Kos. Is it likely, is it possible in these troublous times, that Ptolemy would have risked leaving his favourite wife at this crisis of her life in an island now beyond his control? I think this is impossible, and that therefore he must have been acknowledged king in Egypt upon the death of Alexander, and his son born while he was undoubted master of the Ægean, that is to say, before Antigonus and his son Demetrius built a rival fleet and ousted him from his new acquisition. There may be added a lesser difficulty. If Ptolemy nominated his stepson Magas as regent of Cyrene in 308 B.C., this regent must have

never gives us facsimiles of his texts (except in one disastrous case), no scholar can verify his alleged readings.

[1] There is another far clearer and more explicit argument urged by Strack, which is the indication given by the funeral stele of Anemho, who was born in the sixteenth year of a Ptolemy, lived 72 years, and died in the fifth year of Ptolemy Philopator. This, allowing for the received periods of the intermediate kings (38 and 25 years), leads to the inference that the first king reigned only 20 years officially (Strack, *op. cit.* p. 160). This is an Egyptian recognition of the canon.

[2] Theocritus, xvii. 58 *seq.*

been at least twenty years old (one would think) to
undertake such a responsibility. For Cyrene was not
only an isolated province, at a long distance from
Egypt, but a very turbulent one, which had frequently
revolted. If then Berenice had a child in 328 B.C., it
is not very likely (though possible) she should have had
one in 304. Such are the arguments which make us
hesitate to accept the statement of the canon, and even

M. Revillout's demotic
papyri, as regards
Ptolemy's Egyptian
sovereignty. He cer-
tainly exercised its
functions practically,
and his sending Magas
as regent may even im-
ply that he was himself
king, if the term regent
does not come from a
later period of Magas'
life.

The appointment of
Magas came about on
this wise. It appears
that the first viceroy
appointed by Ptolemy—
the Macedonian Ophelas
—became disloyal about
312 B.C., and sought to
set up an independent
kingdom in Cyrene. He
was so experienced a
soldier, having served

FIG. 13.—Part of Wooden Coffin of
Pete-har-Si-Ese in the form of
Hathor, 3rd century B.C. (Berlin
Museum).

with distinction in Alexander's campaigns, and his
position was so strong and isolated, that Ptolemy
seems to have long hesitated to attack him, and ultimately vanquished him by diplomacy rather than
by arms. Having probably raised discontent against
Ophelas among the democrats of Cyrene by his ostenta-
tious proclamation of Hellenic liberties,—a declaration

which he was as ready to forswear as the rest of the Diadochi,—he seems to have purchased the aid of the Sicilian Agathocles, who had made an expedition into Africa against Carthage, and at the time seemed the coming sovereign of the far West. Agathocles, by brilliant offers of African provinces to be added to Cyrene when the Carthaginians were conquered, persuaded Ophelas to wander with his troops across the desert of the Syrtes, and murdered him on his arrival. It is likely that the bribe offered by Ptolemy was the hand of his stepdaughter Theoxena, which helped to give the upstart Agathocles a position among the Hellenistic rulers of the world.

But these Cyrenæan affairs, now settled by the appointment of Magas (308 B.C.), are only Egyptian history so far as they disturbed Egypt. The birth of Ptolemy's youngest son at Kos (probably 308-7 B.C.) was a matter of greater moment. The favourite wife, Berenike, the mother of Magas during her former marriage, had hitherto borne him only daughters (Arsinoe, perhaps Philotera), and though daughters, according to Egyptian notions, if their mother was declared queen, had strong claims upon the throne, a son was of course the more obvious heir. We may hesitate concerning the exact date of Ptolemy's proclamation as king; there can be little doubt that it was Berenike, not Eurydike, who was proclaimed queen.

The years 306-5 were years of the greatest anxiety for Ptolemy. His whole kingdom, and probably his life, were at stake. These dangers began by the signal victory of Demetrius the Besieger over his fleet at Cyprus, by which Ptolemy lost not only the command of the sea for many years, but also his province of Cyprus and its revenues. The campaign in or about Cyprus, of which Ptolemy's brother Menelaos was military governor, is described rhetorically by Diodorus (xx. 47 *seq.*) and by Plutarch in his life of Demetrius; the details seem rather intended for effect than derived from a record of the actual facts. But there is one notice of interest to our history. When Menelaos had fought his first battle against Demetrius near Salamis, and lost it, the victor, as was usual in these days of mercenary armies, proceeded to enrol his prisoners under his own banner. But he found that they were deserting to their Egyptian master, because all their goods lay in Egypt, so he sent them off to his father Antigonus to Syria. This assumes that the Ptolemaic army in Cyprus consisted purely of mercenaries, whose families and chattels Ptolemy retained as pledges of fidelity in Egypt ; I think it worth considering whether he had not already enrolled many natives as soldiers and sailors in this army, as he had in the army that fought at Gaza in 312. These natives would naturally cling to the Ptolemaic side abroad even in defeat, for the chance of regaining their homes.

The pretended cause of this war was the occupation of Greek cities such as Corinth and Sikyon by Ptolemaic garrisons, in distinct contravention to the fashionable pretence of "liberating the Greeks." But the real issue was whether Ptolemy should retain his hold on Egypt with its influence over the Ægean, or whether his rival Antigonus should succeed in reconquering the whole dominions of Alexander. For with his possession of all Asia Minor and Syria, and his now assured supremacy of the sea and the islands through the activity and the genius of his son Demetrius, such an issue seemed at this moment, when he and his son formally assumed the title of *king*, not at all improbable.

To attack Ptolemy in his lair was well known to be a matter of no small risk. Perdikkas had essayed it, and had lost his army and his life in the attempt. Since that day, now seventeen years ago, Ptolemy had obviously spared no pains in fortifying all the in-ways to Egypt — Pelusium, at the eastern outlet of the Nile ; the marshes and lakes leading to the lesser mouths — all the coast had been amply garrisoned. Very probably his largesses to the priests of Pe and Tep now began to bear him high interest. The superior fleet of Demetrius could only be defeated by the difficulties of landing, the want of anchorage on the coasts of Egypt, the impossibility of lying off that coast without encountering N.W. gales.

In all these matters Antigonus took unusual precautions.[1] The whole campaign was planned at Antigoneia, the new capital on the Orontes, and from thence the troops and ships were sent to assemble at Gaza, which was the proper starting-point for the march against Egypt. Ancient historians are utterly untrustworthy as regards figures; I therefore only repeat the alleged numbers of Antigonus' attacking force to show what kind of armament Egypt was supposed able to resist. Antigonus advanced, we are told, with more than 80,000 infantry, 8000 cavalry, 83 elephants, 150 ships of war, 100 transport ships. He had obtained from the nomad Arabs a great convoy of camels which he loaded with 130,000 medimni of corn and green fodder for the beasts. His siege-train, now an important arm of attack, was on the transport ships.

Two obvious dangers threatened the invasion. In the first place, the army was of unwieldy size, and unable to undertake quick or stealthy operations. Secondly, the season was wrongly chosen, or rather, I suppose, the expedition was accidentally delayed till the setting of the Pleiades, early in November (B.C. 306). For not only were storms now to be expected along the harbourless and shoaly coast, as the seamen expressly warned Antigonus; but at this time the Nile is still high, and the passage of any of its mouths accordingly difficult, especially in the face of a watchful enemy. Antigonus must have had the strongest counter-inducements to advance in spite of these well-known obstacles. We can only conjecture that it was thought all-important to attack Ptolemy so rapidly after his great defeat at Cyprus as to find his troops still dispirited and his fleet disorganised. He had lost about 140 ships at Cyprus. In a few months of dockyard activity these might be replaced, and the supremacy at sea become again doubtful. An attack by land along the narrow coast-

[1] Diod. xx. 73 *seq.*

line without a superior fleet to protect its flank, and
secure its communications with Syria, was held to be
more risky than to brave the weather.

But the elements did their work for Ptolemy.
Demetrius, who commanded the fleet, found his task
almost hopeless by reason of the strong north-west
winds which set in, as was predicted by the seamen.[1]
He first met a storm which drove several of his heaviest
ships on shore at Raphia, so that but for the arrival of
the land army to succour them, and make his landing
secure from the enemy, the expedition might then and
there have been given up. When the combined forces
arrived at Pelusium, they found it amply defended ; the
entrance of the river blocked with boats, and the river
above covered with small-armed cruisers to resist any
attempt at crossing, ready, moreover, to circulate
among the invaders promises of large bribes and good
service if they would desert and join Ptolemy. As
these bribes amounted to two minae for the private, a
talent for the officer, it was with difficulty, and by
punishing such deserters as he could stop with death
by torture, that Antigonus escaped an end similar to
that of Perdikkas. Demetrius, finding any entrance at
Pelusium impracticable, attempted to land farther west,
first at a so-called ψευδόστομος, or sham outlet, probably
from the present Lake Menzaleh, and then at the
Damietta mouth (Phatnitic). In both places he was

---

[1] The wind, which blows so persistently from the sea and up
the valley of the Nile into far Nubia, is commonly called north,
but is really north-west, as I can certify from two seasons' careful
observation. Hence it blew right on shore along the coast from
Gaza to Pelusium. The rarely visited site of Pelusium was
described by Mr. Greville Chester in the *Palestine Exploration
Fund, Statement for* 1880, p. 149. There are two Tells or mounds,
called by the natives the Mound of Gold and the Mound of Silver,
from the number of coins found in them. These now stand in a
salt marsh which no camel can traverse, and which Mr. Chester
waded across with difficulty, sinking at times to his knees in mud.
The sea must therefore have advanced here too, as at Alexandria,
and turned the lower level of the city into a swamp. But it must
always have been easy to defend it with canals and dykes as well
as with walls.

beaten off, and was then overtaken by another storm, which wrecked three more of his largest ships ; and with difficulty did he make his way back to his father's camp east of the Pelusiac entrance.

We can imagine the feelings with which Antigonus called a council of war to weigh the situation. The fate of Perdikkas stared them in the face. Mercenary armies will not tolerate ill-success and increasing want in the face of a courteous, well-supplied enemy ready to welcome deserters. Another couple of storms would certainly destroy any fleet, however well-handled, on this inhospitable and harbourless coast. The nomad tribes friendly to a successful invader would be certain to fall upon a dispirited, retreating army. It was determined, we may say of necessity rather than of wisdom, to retreat while retreat was a military evolution, and not an irreparable disaster.[1]

Diodoros tells us (xx. 53) that Ptolemy's soldiers hailed him with the title βασιλεύς as soon as Antigonus and Demetrius had assumed it just after the defeat of the Egyptian fleet at Cyprus. They answered, he thinks, the presumption of these satraps with a counter presumption. But if after a defeat, then certainly after his victorious defence of the land against Antigonus, must he have been so hailed. The title was, however, at this moment not of much consequence. It did not of itself imply any distinct sovereignty.[2] Antigonus' son, for example, assumed it with his father. I have already spoken of the beginning of Ptolemy's formal sovereignty. It is to this moment that we may ascribe the beginning of the independent Egyptian coinage of money. Most

[1] Modern critics have found fault with Antigonus for not fortifying and holding a station opposite Pelusium, with Demetrius for not attacking Alexandria forthwith, and thus separating Ptolemy's troops. Such censure should only be based upon very ample knowledge, and upon some claim to understand the situation better than Antigonus and Demetrius did—two men of great ability and experience in practical war. I assume that they knew what was possible far better than any modern professor of history can know in his study.

[2] Cf. Strack, *Dyn. der Ptolemäer*, pp. 5-7.

strange to relate, there appears in the native dynasties
up to this period a complete absence of coined money,
and Persian or Greek satraps had actually had no right
to utter anything but the coins of their suzerains.   But
now there begins the whole series which has been
expounded in the admirable numismatic volume of Mr.
Poole (British Museum).   It is also well worthy of note,
though I have in vain sought an explanation of it from
the specialists, that the scarabs produced in quantities
during the many native dynasties now suddenly cease.
No such thing as a Ptolemaic scarab has, I believe,
ever been found.   It seems, therefore, possible to
suppose that these scarabs may have, in some way,
filled the place of coins, and their sudden disappearance seems to point to legislation on the question.

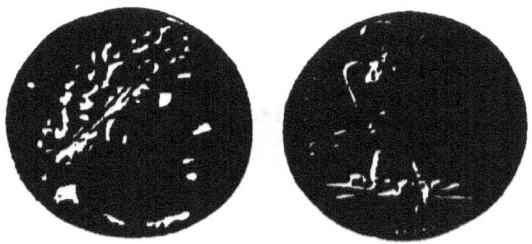

FIG. 14.—Coin of Ptolemy Soter.

This Ptolemy is the only one of the series whose
cartouche seems uncertain.   There are, however, at
Teranneh instances of double cartouches, the former
identical with the prænomen of Alexander or Arridæus,
the latter simply Ptolemy, which seem to belong to him.

The divine honours, which had already been conferred
upon him by the islanders of the Cyclades, were repeated
by the Rhodians, who were next attacked by Demetrius
(306–5 B.C.) as being allies of Egypt, and whose conquest
might have made Antigonus so strong at sea, that a
naval attack upon Alexandria could be attempted.   But
Ptolemy, though unable to meet Demetrius on the sea
in open battle, managed to throw in such constant succour to the beleaguered city, which was never really

invested, that Demetrius, after enormous efforts which lasted nearly a year, made peace and withdrew his forces. The Rhodians only gained the single advantage of maintaining their neutrality if Antigonus attacked Egypt. The main fact shown by these transactions was the mutual importance of Rhodes and Alexandria in working the mercantile traffic of the Hellenistic world. Rhodes was, indeed, not only the mart but the bank of all the princes and cities round the Levant, and so all manner of common friends offered mediation between Demetrius and the Rhodians. But to these friends the friendship of Egypt must have been the most vital. Yet on this all-important question for the history of Egypt we have no clue beyond our inferences from this Rhodian policy. Concerning the internal affairs of Egypt there is absolute silence.

The following years (up to 302 B.C.) were spent by the Hellenistic sovereigns in preparing a coalition against Antigonus and Demetrius, which ended in the great battle of Ipsus (in Phrygia) wherein Seleukos and his son Antiochus with their Indian elephants, Lysimachus with his Thracian power, and Casander the Macedonian, met the new monarchs of Syria and hither Asia. Antigonus was defeated and killed in the battle (301 B.C.), but his son escaped and remained the scourge and terror of the Greek world for some years to come. Ptolemy had indeed joined the coalition, but behaved in a half-hearted and pusillanimous way. He advanced, by way of diversion, into Cœle-Syria, and occupied the coast cities, but retired precipitately upon the false news that Antigonus was victorious, and would presently reappear in Syria. From the great deciding battle he was absent. But the kings who partitioned the empire of Antigonus without regarding Ptolemy found that he had again occupied Lower Syria and Phœnicia, which he claimed as his share in the alliance. Seleukos, the man principally concerned, though objecting to this arrangement, did not think fit to contest it with arms. Perhaps the danger of throwing Ptolemy into alliance with Demetrius, and so losing all hope of recovering the islands and coasts dominated from the sea, was the restraining motive.

At all events, from this time onward, for about a century, the sway of Egypt over Palestine, Lower Syria, and Phœnicia was established, and so one of Ptolemy's great ambitions was satisfied. The support of Sidon, with the forests of Lebanon, for his fleet was of the highest importance, and we hear of at least one king of Sidon, Philokles, acting as his principal admiral and controller of his power over the Ægean islands. In 295 B.C. Ptolemy recovered Cyprus, as the naval power of Demetrius waned with that adventurer's wild enterprises. It had for ten years been the residence of Antigonid princesses, so secure was he of his maritime supremacy. But now that supremacy passed back again into the hands of Ptolemy, thus completing for him the Empire of the Ptolemies, in its largest real sense. It included, as Polybius tells us, not only Egypt and the coast of the Red Sea down to far Berenike and the elephant coast,—in this direction as yet ill defined,—but Cyrene, under the viceroyalty of Magas ; Palestine and Phœnicia, up to and including Mount Lebanon ; Cyprus, where the remaining local dynasts were controlled by an Egyptian garrison ; Rhodes, not subject, but in close alliance, and treating Egypt as the most favoured country in its commercial policy ; the "free" cities of the coast of Asia Minor, under the influence of Rhodes in their policy, and in any case overawed by the Egyptian fleet, and the islands of the Ægean, combined under a league (κοινόν) which formally recognised Ptolemy as its president. How far this Egyptian influence would reach in the Levant, whether it might not include the coasts of Greece— Ptolemy had long kept garrisons in Sikyon and in Corinth — and even those of the Propontis and the Euxine, was still uncertain,[1] and varied with the strength of the Macedonian and Thracian kingdoms.

[1] We know, for example, from inscriptions (C.I.G. 2254, 2905), that Samos belonged to the dominion of Lysimachus, we may presume up to the battle of Korupedion, where he lost his empire

But Ptolemy had sought to weaken the former by supporting the young king Pyrrhus of Epirus, to whom he gave a daughter in marriage, and whose military genius was sure to be a thorn in the side of Macedon. He married two daughters into the royal house of Thrace, one, the famous Arsinoe, to the old king himself, the other, Lysandra, to his heir Agathokles. It is even possible, though I think the evidence insufficient, that he married another Lysandra — these people thought it quite sane to call two sisters by the same name—into the royal house of Macedon.[1] Thus Ptolemy seemed to have secured his dominion by military defences, by his fleet, by his commercial and diplomatic relations, by his alliances with royal neighbours, so far as it was possible in those days to secure anything.

At all events, the last fifteen years of the old king's life were spent in peace at home and in great prosperity. The occupation of Cœle-Syria by his troops and Cyprus by his fleet were not accompanied with great campaigns, or determined by bloody battles. He had ample security and leisure to turn to the development of his home affairs. Here, therefore, the proper history of Ptolemaic Egypt, so long obscured by foreign complications, ought to begin. But, alas! the materials are almost totally lost. We would fain believe that the whole policy of the dynasty had its broad lines laid down by the great founder. Though his early life was spent in wars, and in them he had made his mark, his later life shows that his genius was not military, but diplomatic. His great superiority in wealth points to a careful economy of his internal resources; the total absence of any national reaction among the priests against the new Hellenism to his prudence in dealing with religious privileges and endowments. But of these things no evidence in detail remains save (1) his

and his life. Nor is it likely that this was the only island held by the Thracian king.

[1] Cf. the note in Strack, *op. cit.* p. 190, who is in favour of accepting the evidence for two Lysandras.

introduction of the god of Sinope as Sarapis, and his building of a temple for him at Alexandria ; (2) his foundation of two cities ; (3) his foundation of the Museum and Library at Alexandria.

The story of the founding or re-founding of the famous Serapeum at Alexandria is told us by Plutarch (*de Iside*, etc., 28) and Tacitus (*Hist.* iv. 84), with some additional notices from Athenodorus of Tarsus, quoted by Clemens Alex. (F.H.G. iii. 487). This last tells us the true meaning of the name, a mixture of Osiris and Apis (Hapi), the Apis bull passing into Osiris after death.[1] There was, in fact, an old Serapeum at Memphis where the Apis bulls were buried, and the earliest Greek document which gives us the name, the well-known imprecation of Artemisia, which palæographers

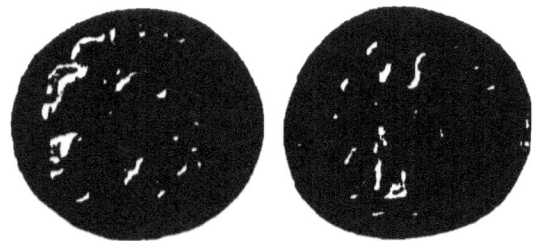

FIG. 15.—Coin of Ptol. Soter, with Head of Serapis.

place about 300 B.C., or even earlier, gives us the form Osirapis. Hence, if a statue was brought from Sinope to Egypt by Ptolemy, it was no new god, but merely a fusion of a Greek Hades, or god of death, with an old Egyptian god. The accounts of the transference are not quite consistent in their details, and Lumbroso, who has turned his acute intellect to the sifting of them (*Egitto*, second edition, pp. 143 *seq.*) declares himself in favour of Plutarch's version. The main facts reported are, however, that the king saw in a dream

[1] οὗ καὶ τοὔνομα αἰνίττεται τὴν κοινωνίαν τῆς κηδείας καὶ τὴν ἐκ τῆς ταφῆς δημιουργίαν σύνθετον ἀπό τε Ὀσίριδος καὶ Ἄπιος γενόμενον Ὀσίραπις.

a vision of the god, who ordered that his image should be sought and brought to Alexandria. With the aid not only of Egyptian priests—probably of Manetho—but of Greek theologians, the statue of Zeus-Hades at Sinope was found to correspond with the king's vision, and was either stolen or coaxed by bribes from its place, the people of Sinope ultimately consenting to the transference.

In this legend, which we have from the Greeks, the king plays the leading part, and with him the Greek theologian Timotheus whose professional advice he sought. But the site chosen was the old site of a Serapeum at Rakotis, and if we have indeed redis-covered that site,[1] there is clear evidence that Ptolemy made no new foundation, but merely increased the stateli-ness, and so the celebrity, of an ancient fane. Lumbroso well points out that the story of the translation has a suspicious family likeness to the importing of the Mother of Pessinus and the Æsculapius of Epidaurus to Rome, and he recalls Letronne's forgotten suggestion that the existence of a hill called Sinopium near the Serapeum of Memphis may have given rise either to the actual performance of Ptolemy or to the legend of his doings.[2] But I think the story of the finding of the image too explicit to be a mere invention, and therefore one requiring some political explanation. It can hardly have been necessary to attract Greeks to Egypt by such means. The habit of consulting oracles in Egypt was very old. Not only at the oasis of Amon, but at the temple of Osiris at Abydos in Upper Egypt, Greeks seem to have consulted oracles from early times.[3] Why then all this fuss to enhance an old and well-

[1] Cf. Dr. Botti's *Fouilles* (Report to the Arch. Society of Alexandria), 1897.

[2] Cf. *op. cit.* p. 145: " Les Grecs, fidèles à leur méthode de tout rapporter à eux, se sont imaginés que Serapis nommé *Sinopites* du mont Sinopion près de Memphis était une divinité venue de Sinope en Paphlagonie."

[3] Cf. Mr. Sayce's account of the graffiti he found on the temple, some of which he dates as far back as the sixth century B.C. (*Soc. Bibl. Arch.* for 1888, p. 377).

established Egyptian cult?[1]   The worship of Isis
spread from Alexandria very rapidly over all Hellenistic
lands, without any such elaborate publication.   In
whose interest, and for what special purpose, was all
this ecclesiastical pomp and circumstance brought into
play?

I have in vain sought any more special solution than
the desire of the prudent king to fuse as far as possible
the Greeks and natives in Alexandria.   Possibly the
native quarter, with its old shrine of Osirapis, was not
visited or frequented by the new population, and there
may have been a danger of such severance of interests
between Racotis and newer Alexandria as to make
them two distinct cities.   By this religious act Greek
worshippers would be attracted to the native west end,
and so counteract its threatening isolation.   It might
also have been done to allay fears among the settlers
that the king was drifting too far into an Egyptian
policy.   This I think most improbable.   The first
Ptolemy, a Macedonian prince and a companion of
Alexander, is never mentioned as one of the few who,
like Peukestas, adopted the Oriental style of life.
Further speculation seems idle, till we learn some more
facts concerning this most obscure period.

We come now to his foundation of new cities.   In
this we know that he was very sparing.   He had
evidently no taste for those pseudo-Hellenic politics,
with their senates and public assemblies, which excite
the admiration of so many modern historians.

The negative evidence against any Hellenic constitution at Alexandria is too strong to be resisted.   Some
decrees of the senate and assembly must inevitably
have been found, if not at Alexandria, at least at
some one of the many shrines (Delphi, Delos, Teos,
etc.), where such decrees were set up in duplicate.
Even the miserable archæological remains of Ptolemais
in Upper Egypt furnish us with such.   There were,
however, privileges accorded, beyond the dominant
"Macedonians," to the Greeks, the Jews, and the

[1] Cf. Wellmann in *Hermes*, xxxi. on fusion of cults.

natives respectively. But what these privileges were, is yet obscure. There seem to have been *demes* at Alexandria called after national Greek heroes, as Wilcken was the first to perceive. It is more than likely that the population outside these demes, such as new immigrants, were in an inferior position.[1] The Macedonian guards about the palace seem to be the historical forerunners of the prætorian guard at Rome, probably with greater constitutional authority. It may have required their acclamation, after the old Macedonian fashion, to make a coronation legitimate. But the management of the city was by semi-military authority, under a governor with his subordinates. It seems that the Jews were dealt with through a responsible head of their own, and this was interpreted by later writers to mean that they had the same privileges as the Greeks. The weight of evidence is against it, at least in early days. So far as the natives were concerned, certain immunities from taxation, and certain securities of food supply, were probably their only privileges over the country population. The territory of Alexandria was specially excluded from the nomes, and specially supplied (cf. Revenue Pap. col. 60, *sqq.*).

Until the remains of Ptolemais (at the site of the modern Menshieh) are further examined, we can add but little concerning this, the principal foundation of the first Ptolemy. We know that a cult of him as Soter God,[2] was established there, doubtless as Founder, in the same way that there was an eponymous priest of Alexander the Great at Alexandria. There was a council and assembly, after the Hellenic fashion ; there was also sufficient Greek life and language pervading it to give scope and profits to a permanent

---

[1] We have the actual phrase " An Alexandrian of those not yet enrolled " in a deme (Petrie Papyri, and elsewhere).

[2] Other Ptolemies afterwards associated themselves, and several queens, but not in pairs, as was the case in Alexandria and Philæ. Hence Berenike I. (so far as I know) was not set up with her husband here.

corporation of Dionysiac artists, who have left us two
or three honorary decrees. The importance of Ptolemais
is further to be inferred from the fact recently ascertained
that in Ptolemaic finance all Upper Egypt (above
Kynopolis) was put under one division, the Thebaid,
and had no separate nomes with their capitals. Hence
there were no rival towns to compete with Ptolemais,
like those of the Delta, which exceeded Naucratis and
Menelaos in importance. The latter two were not in
any sense metropolitan. Menelaos, which Mr. Ll.
Griffith seems to have identified by cartouches of the
founder-king at Kum abn Billuh (or Terenuthis), was
merely the key or stepping-stone to the Nitriote country.
Its name points to the Menelaos whom we have already
met in the Cypriote wars. But it is very odd that a
separate Menelaite nome should have been marked out
on the other side (N.E.) of Alexandria. Naukratis was
an old Hellenic city favoured by the second and later
Ptolemies, but not specially by the first king, so far
as we know. We are not told that he made any
establishments for colonists or soldiers either in
Greece,[1] Cyprus, or Palestine. Thus then, in contrast
to the activity of his rivals, — Antigonus, Seleukos,
Lysimachus, — Ptolemy Soter was no founder of
cities.

The most brilliant and permanent of his new creations
was undoubtedly what may be called the University of
Alexandria—the famous Museum and Library. The
very authorship of this great scheme has been denied
him owing to the flatteries lavished on his successor,
and the heedless acceptance of them by modern scholars.
When Ptolemy was in the Greek waters (308-7 B.C.)
and in possession of Corinth, Sikyon, and Megara, he

---

[1] The inscriptions of the mercenaries at Thera, recently discovered by Hiller von Gärtringen, contains one with 279 names
of subscribers to a gymnasium, among whom there appears but
one Ptolemy. I guessed at once that this list must date from
Soter, otherwise the name Ptolemy would be far more frequent
(as we know from later inscriptions). Mr. Smyly's (unpublished)
researches seem to show that its double date (L18, Audnaios 15,
Epeiph 15) fits exactly into this reign, and nowhere else.

endeavoured, we are told (Diog. L. ii. c. 11), to induce
the famous Stilpo to leave Megara, and come with
him to Egypt. He made similar efforts to attract
Theophrastus and Menander. He had no difficulty in
persuading Demetrius the Phalerean, when overthrown
and driven out of Athens by his namesake, to migrate
to Egypt. These facts are the hints from which we
infer that the king was then planning a great institution
upon the model of the schools at Athens, already
famous as the homes of philosophy and centres of
education for Hellenic and Hellenistic youth. But of
course he did not contemplate the establishment of free
and democratic corporations at Alexandria, which
would have been as incomprehensible to him as our
free universities, electing their own governors and
professors, are to the Germans or the French, where
the Government interferes in all academic appointments.
The Museum, though an old title for such a foundation
in the Greek world, was now to be a State institution,
regulated and controlled by the Crown. The original
scheme does not seem to have been educational, in the
stricter sense, certainly not in any way educational
for the natives. To them it was and remained the most
foreign thing in Alexandria. Seneca, when speaking of
the alleged conflagration of the Library, says this part
of the establishment was merely intended as a display of
royal luxury, such, for example, as the Queen's Library
is at Windsor, or the Sunderland Library once at Blen-
heim Palace. The Museum with its learned men was
certainly used as an amusement by later Ptolemies.
We are not told anything whatever of the relations of
the founder to his work.

There is indeed no topic in Hellenistic history
so disappointing as the history of the Alexandrian
Museum. While new discoveries are certainly throwing light on many obscure points of Ptolemaic history,
so that we may hope ere the end of our generation
to obtain some intelligible account of their acts and
policy, there seems to be no progress whatever in our
knowledge of the Museum. The summary of all the

special studies in Susemihl's *Alexandrian Literature*, or
in the articles in Pauly-Wissowa, tell us nothing more
than we knew twenty years ago.   Perhaps they tell
us even less, because they have freed us of many un-
founded assumptions.   We know that there was a
nominal head of the Museum who was a priest and a
Greek ; we know that when the library was founded,
it soon required a librarian, whose office grew in
importance with the size and fame of his charge, and
that is all.   No excavations have discovered any
remains of these buildings, the very site of them is as
yet uncertain.   The list of the famous librarians seems
not to commence till the second king, and recently an
inscription has recovered for us the name of one we
never heard of before.[1]

Mr. Poole's researches into the very complicated
numismatics of the dynasty show that the first Ptolemy
established a silver coinage on the basis of the Attic
drachme as the ordinary silver unit.   Owing to the
vast treasures of precious metal let loose by Alexander
the Great from the Persian treasures into the Hellenistic
world, silver may have been at the moment very cheap.
Hence, when years elapsed, it seems to have been
necessary to reduce the standard drachme first to the
Rhodian, and lastly to the Phœnician standard (67.5 and
47.5 grains respectively).   This silver seems to have
been coined in relation to an older Egyptian copper
currency in the ratio of 1 : 120 of respective values.
Of course the lightening of the drachme would raise
the ratio from 120 to 140 and even 150 to one.   But
the nominal ratio was maintained, and later kings
preferred to debase the silver, rather than to change
the weight of the coin.   At all events, in Soter's day
both silver and copper were in daily use, and there
appears to have been so little preference for either at
the established ratio, that the Crown allowed many

---

[1] An inscription recently found at Cyprus (J.H.S. ix. 240),
tells us of a certain Onesander, son of Nausikrates, town-clerk of
Paphos, who was "appointed over the great library in Alexandria" apparently by Ptolemy Soter II.   This is indeed news !

taxes to be paid in copper, in which case we find a small charge made for the conveyance of the money.

Instead of letting us know anything concerning the internal policy of Egypt, the means taken to attract settlers, to satisfy national sentiment, to develop the material resources of the country, our historians only give us a few hints of the external policy of the king, of his matrimonial alliances with his neighbours and rivals, of his recovery of Cyprus from Demetrius, and his resumption of naval supremacy in the Ægean. He had a daughter married to Pyrrhus of Epirus, to Lysimachus of Thrace, and to his son the crown prince Agathocles ; probably to the young king of Macedon, Casander's son ; to the rival claimant of Macedon, and actual king, Demetrius ; even to the distant Agathocles of Syracuse, and to one of the petty kings of Cyprus. He was said to be the richest of all the Hellenistic sovereigns, and princesses with large fortunes were probably as much sought after then as they are now. Regarding his sons, it is only the eldest and the youngest that are of any importance in Egyptian history. The eldest, called Ptolemy (afterwards the fixed name of the heir-apparent), and nicknamed Keraunos or the Thunderbolt, possibly because this emblem may have appeared on the coinage at the time of his birth, was son of Eurydike, the daughter of Antipater of Macedon, and hence of the noblest Macedonian blood. His natural claim to the throne was backed by Demetrius the Phalerean, Antipater's friend, and by a party at court. But his temper was said to be sullen and gloomy, and his mother Eurydike had not the influence of the king's favourite wife Berenike.

Ancient authorities give us no further reason for the postponement of the elder son for the sake of the youngest, the boy born of Berenike about 308 B.C. But since I have called attention to the Ptolemaic habit of requiring *porphyrogenitism* in the heir, critics are disposed to think that it was on this principle that the old king acted, and this it was which he explained when abdicating, and declaring his successor.[1] I have above stated the difficulties in accepting this view, but in substance I believe it to be right. How complete the abdication was is also a matter of doubt ; the Attic inscription,[2] which speaks of him as the elder Ptolemy along with his son, points to some such arrangement as was afterwards usual when the crown prince was associated with his father. But in the present case the majority of critics are satisfied with the statement that Ptolemy Soter, abdicating in 285 B.C., lived a private man at his son's court for two years, and died at the age of eighty-four, leaving his mark upon the world, and affording us a striking example of great and permanent success attained by the exercise of moderate abilities, good temper, good sense, and reasonable ambition.

[1] Justin xvi. 2: *Is contra jus gentium minimo natu ex filiis ante infirmitatem regnum tradiderat, ejusque rei populo rationem tradiderat.*

[2] C.I.A. ii. 331 ; Strack, No. 12: πρεσβευσας δε προς τον βασιλεα τον πρεσβιτερον Πτολεμαιον is the expression, which seems as if the elder man was still regarded as a king after his abdication.

FIG. 16.—Stone Sarcophagus (Ptolemaic work).

CHAPTER III

FIG. 17. Cartouches of Ptolemy II.

AUTHORITIES.—*Ancient*—The Greek historians fail us on this reign. But we have some contemporary documents, viz. the Revenue Papyrus (Oxford, 1895), the Petrie Papyri (cf. next chapter), of which many date from this reign; the inscriptions collected in Strack's *Ptolemäer*, Nos. 13–37; the poets Aratus, Callimachus, Theocritus, and Herondas, and the Greek scholia upon them. *Modern*—Pauly-Wissowa's *Realencyclopädie*, articles "Alexandria," "Arsinoe"; Susemihl's *Literatur der Alexander-Zeit*; Revillout's *Revue Egyptologique*, vols. i.–vi.

THE accession of the second Ptolemy comes at a moment of Hellenistic history upon which we are very badly informed. The better authorities of earlier years, notably Diodorus, whose remains only reach to 301 B.C., desert us, and as yet we have a great scarcity of those Egyptian documents which throw much light on subsequent reigns. We know in general the complications which threatened Egypt from without, and which might have even overturned the dynasty under easily conceivable conditions.[1] Demetrius the Besieger was still alive, and making great plans with his sea-power. Lysimachus of Thrace and Seleukos of Syria were indeed old, and ought to have been tired of wars, but

[1] Cf. my *Empire of the Ptolemies*, cap. iv.

if either of them attacked Egypt, what might be the consequences? For Ptolemy had enemies within his own family. His eldest half-brother, Ptolemy the Thunderbolt, though now an exile at the court of Thrace, must have had a party in Egypt, and, at all events, must have known every vulnerable spot in the kingdom If this personage could have persuaded either of the old kings to attack Egypt, he might count upon the support of Ptolemy's other stepbrother, Magas, now regent of Cyrene, who showed in the sequel plainly enough that he was not minded to submit to a younger member of the family. He might also have enlisted on his side Pyrrhus, now king of Epirus, the rising soldier of the generation, who was presently removed, by a public subscription among the other kings, to make war in Italy, instead of troubling the Hellenistic lands of the East. There were indeed Egyptian princesses, queens, or crown princesses at almost all the Hellenistic courts, but these ladies and their retinues seem rather to have promoted or detected hostile intrigues than to have cemented alliances. Ptolemy II. had married, immediately upon his accession, a crown princess of Thrace, Arsinoe, who promptly bore him three children ; but his own sister, of the same name, first married to his father-in-law, the king of Thrace ; then, upon his murder, to his murderer, Ptolemy the Thunderbolt ; then, after the murder of her Thracian children by this ruffian, exiled from Macedonia, and a fugitive at Samothrace, ultimately found her old home and a third throne by marrying her brother Ptolemy, and ousting her namesake the Thracian princess.

These astonishing adventures are only connected with the history of Egypt as showing reasons for the cautious and diplomatic conduct of the young king during the early years of his reign. He very probably promoted the quarrels by which his rivals were led into internecine struggles. He put to death at once such of his brothers as he could reach, and the terrible outburst of the Gauls upon the northern frontiers of

Hellenism rid him of Keraunos, his most dangerous
brother, for it turned all the force which might have
invaded Egypt to struggle with the heathen of the
north. Magas of Cyrene delayed his insurrection,
probably for want of support from Macedonia, and so
our Ptolemy steered his way safely through the rocks
and shoals of this dangerous quinquennium in peace
and rising prosperity, while the rival kingdoms were
being shaken to their very foundations.

Such is the general aspect of the foreign relations of
Egypt at this moment, which only concern us here as
helping to explain the internal condition of the country.
The empire of Egypt, founded by the first king, still
included Palestine and Cœle-Syria, as well as the outlying and not very secure province of Cyrene.   There
is even evidence that in Syria, at one time in this reign,
there were Egyptian garrisons as far as the Euphrates.[1]
As soon as Demetrius disappeared, and the great
empires of Thrace and Syria lost their established
sovereigns, Ptolemy resumed control of the Ægean Sea,
with its coast cities and islands.   How far this naval
supremacy reached, and what cities it did not include,
we cannot as yet tell with certainty.   At all events, the
confederacy of the Cyclades, some cities on the
Thracian coast, perhaps even on the Euxine, recognised the sway of Egypt, administered apparently by
the king's high admiral, Philokles, himself king of
Sidon.   It must also be remembered that such influence
implied tribute from all the controlled cities, and hence
a large increase to the resources of Egypt.   The
stations from which all this naval empire was controlled were Thera, and probably Cyprus, now managed
by petty kings, ruling sham Greek politics under the
strict suzerainty of Ptolemy, who kept a large garrison
in the island.

With these external advantages, and the absence of
dangerous wars, there would have been little excuse for
Ptolemy if he had not developed the resources and the
splendour of his kingdom, and so we turn with interest

[1] Cf. Epping u. Strassmeier, *Z. für Assyr.* vii. 200.

to question the vague or fragmentary notices concerning his internal administration. Above all, the question which should interest us is this: Did he pursue a national policy, raising and improving the condition of the natives, or did he merely seek to make himself a brilliant Hellenistic sovereign, ruling his native subjects not ἡγεμονικῶς as Alexander the Great would have done, but δεσποτικῶς as Aristotle recommended his pupil to do? The evidence on this point is conflicting, and consequently a decision not easy to attain.

We have no account of his coronation at Alexandria, for the great pageant to which we shall presently refer is now shown to be the foundation of a Five-years' Feast in honour of his deified father, Ptolemy Soter. Yet the coronation must also have been something splendid. Direct information upon it we have none. So also his marriage with the first Arsinoe, the Thracian princess, which must have been in close proximity of time to his coronation, is passed over in silence. She bore him three children before she was exiled (or possibly divorced, if such a practice existed) by the plots of her supplanter, the second Arsinoe. This exile must surely have happened shortly after, if not before, the second marriage, and this took place, as we shall see, very early in the 70's of that century (279 B.C.).

We have already decided that the Museum was the foundation of the first king, but it is more than likely that in the early years of Philadelphus, and perhaps before the old king was dead, the appointments of that great College and its Library received special care. It is said that Demetrius the Phalerean, the expert consulted upon the requirements of the Museum, was against the succession of the youngest son, as contrary to monarchical precedent, and was therefore banished by the new king. But his work remained, and if there was any institution in Egypt which owed him its great promotion, it was surely this. We know further, from the inscriptions recovered at Menshieh, the ancient Ptolemais in Upper Egypt, that the corporation of Dionysiac actors there enjoyed the special favour of the

young king. The city was from the outset a Hellenistic, not an Egyptian, city, and very possibly it may
have been necessary to provide for these far-off Greeks
such national amusement as would make them content
in their distant and isolated home. The principal text
indeed (Strack 35) speaks of the *Gods Adelphi*,[1] and
therefore dates after the formal deification of the king
and his second wife ; but his favours were evidently
neither isolated nor were they all subsequent to the
date of the decree.

The greatest of all the scenes of his early reign
shows these very artists holding a capital place in the
splendours of Alexandria. It is the monster procession
described by Callixenus, whose account Athenæus has
preserved for us. The details are so voluminous, and
have so often been given elsewhere,[2] that it will not
here be necessary to do more than appreciate the
general character of the display. In the first place, the
discovery of the inscription of Nikourgia has shown
that we have an account not of the king's coronation,
but of a Five-years' Feast ($\pi\epsilon\nu\tau\epsilon\tau\eta\rho\iota\varsigma$) founded in honour
of the deified Soter. Many indications point to an
early date in the reign, probably 280 B.C. For the
frequent use of the term $\beta\alpha\sigma\iota\lambda\epsilon\upsilon\varsigma$—in fact the plural is
regularly used in referring to the sovereigns—shows that
the king was already married, possibly to his second
wife, who may even have been the special instigatrix
of the great Five-years' Feast in honour of Soter and
Berenike I. The whole feast has a distinctly Bacchic
tone. It reminds us strongly of the poetical story of
Alexander's triumphal return through Karamania to
Babylon after he had escaped the horrors of the
Gedrosian desert.[3] Indeed, the prominence given to

---

[1] Arsinoe Philadelphus was early associated with the cult of
Soter, and had her canephorus at Ptolemais. Her husband was
not so till the time of Philometer, when the whole series of kings
was added.

[2] Athen. iv. 196 ; *Greek Life and Thought*, pp. 216 *seq.*; *Empire of
the Ptolemies*, § 74.

[3] Arrian discredits it (vi. 28); it is told by Plutarch (*Alex.* 67),
Diodorus (xvii. 106), and Curtius (ix. 42).

Persian and Indian captives and curiosities among the spoils of the god Dionysus, when brought together with the assertion of the Pithom stele, that before his sixth year the young king had gone to Persia and brought home the captive images of the Egyptian gods, leads me to conjecture that there was some campaign as far as the Euphrates made by the king at the moment that the death of Seleukos had freed him from anxiety—nay even had given him hopes of extending the Syrian province of his empire. In general the whole pomp has a non-Egyptian air, discounting the small detail that some of the gilded pillars of the banqueting-room had floral capitals, and even this might be in accordance with Dionysiac ornament. If we except the curious products of Nubia and Ethiopia in ivory, giraffes, antelopes, hippopotami, etc., there is nothing Egyptian in the whole affair. We seem to see a Hellenistic king spending millions upon a Hellenistic feast.

In consonance with this is the information obtained for us by Mr. Petrie, that this king took pains to repair and adorn the Hellenion at Naukratis, the ancient common shrine of all the Ionian trading cities which had marts at this once famous place. The specimen deposits which Mr. Petrie found under the four corners of the pylon or gateway, with the king's cartouches, make the fact of this restoration certain ; though neither in histories nor in inscriptions does a single hint of it remain,—an instructive instance of that silence in history, from which some modern scholars are wont to draw dogmatic conclusions.

This considerable series of Hellenistic works undertaken or promoted by the second Ptolemy led me formerly to set him down as a king who took but little interest in his Egyptian subjects and their land beyond the revenues of the fields and the curiosities in fauna with which he could adorn his zoological gardens. We know that his wealth exceeded that of any contemporary sovereign ; we know, not only from the procession of beasts at the great show just mentioned, but from Diodorus (iii. 36), that he had a

peculiar interest in bringing up the huge animals and
serpents of the Soudan, and exhibiting them to his
visitors in his gardens at Alexandria.   But in none
of these things does he show us that he was a king
of Egypt rather than one of any other domain.   It
does not appear that even
among his many mistresses he
favoured a single native.   The
famous Belestichis, in spite of
her odd (but Greek) name, was
probably a woman from Argos.

The great settlement in the
Fayyum, of which I shall speak
at length in due time, was, as
we now know certainly, a settlement essentially Hellenistic.
The new settlers were all mercenaries from his Greek phalanx
or cavalry.   Not a single native
appears as a privileged landholder among the many whose
papers—wills, contracts, etc.—
have been recovered.

But now I proceed to discuss
a series of acts of a different
kind, which, had they alone
been preserved, would have indicated to us with equal probability that the king was devoted
to native interests, and sought
to emulate in every reasonable
way national sentiment.   But
though these pompous texts
are very explicit, they probably
prove no more than that

Fig. 18.—Ptolemy II. (red
granite, Vatican).

Ptolemy had come to a compromise with the Egyptian
priesthood, and succeeded through them in persuading
the populace and the old nobility of the land to
acquiesce in his rule.

The text of the Pithom stele, as given in revised

translation (from Brugsch) by Erman in the *Z. für Æ.*
for 1895, I have already reproduced in a previous work.[1]
I now give an abstract of the second great Egyptian
document[2] with the important recent addition on the
death of Arsinoe II.

The famous Mendes stele, now at Gizeh, relates to
the offerings and endowments granted to the god by
Ptolemy II. and his queen Arsinoe II. The following
extracts from this very voluminous praise of the god
will give the drift of the matter. Under the uraeus is
a headline divided in the middle, which declares : " The
holy Ram-god, the great god, the life of Ra, the
engendering ram, the prince of young women, the
friend of the royal daughter and sister, queen and
lady of the land Arsinoe, living for ever," *and*: " The
lord of the land, the lord of power Meri-amon user-ka-ra,
the son of Ra begotten of his body, who loves him, the
lord of diadems Ptolemy, the ever-living."

Then there is a row of figures of gods and goddesses,
with the king and queen, the latter entitled " the
daughter, sister, and great wife of a king, who loves
him, the divine Arsinoe Philadelphos."

The text of the main inscription begins again with
all the titles of Ptolemy, and his intention to support
and enrich the temple of Mendes, which god had really
begotten him " to be lord and king, the son of a king,
born of a queen, to whom was granted the royal dignity
over the land, while he was yet in his mother's womb."
Then follow fulsome praises of Ptolemy in peace and
war. He determined that a new ram should be enthroned at Mendes according to all the traditional
practices, and so went down in state by the canal Aken
to the Mendesian nome. He then visited the buildings
of the holy ram. When he found the temple which
was being built according to his orders—foreign workmen were excluded—was still unfinished, his majesty
ordered it to be completed as quick as possible [with
many details of his order]. When this was done

---

[1] *Empire of the Ptolemies*, pp. 138 seq.
[2] First published by Brugsch in *Z. für Æ.* for 1875.

(line 30) the king returned to his capital, and was rejoiced at what he had done. Then his majesty [desired to honour?] and combine the first of his wives *Netef-auch* with the goddess Ba-abot. And he granted the following titles : the charming princess, the most attractive, lovely and beautiful, the crowned one, who has received the double diadem, whose splendour fills the palace, the friend of the sacred ram and his priestess Uta-ba, the king's sister and wife who loves him, the queen Arsinoe.

"In the year 15, the month Pachon [the day is lost]. *This great lady went to heaven*," etc. [This is the new fragment.] Then follow all the honours bestowed upon her as a deified queen, and the consequent feasts and sacrifices. Furthermore the king remits the tax on shipping, and the tax on bread, paid by all Egypt, to this nome, and fixes its liability for offerings, which must be supplied for the temple at 70,000 coins [the exact coin is lost in a gap]. "In the year 21, they came to his Majesty to tell him : the temple of your father, the holy ram, the lord of Mendes is complete in every respect. It is far more beautiful than ever it was. According to your orders, the inscriptions have been carried upon it in the name of thee, thy father, and of the divine lady, Arsinoe Philadelphos." The rest of the text describes the feast and enthronement of the new Mendes ram in his restored temple. It may be noticed how the last mention of the queen speaks of her quite simply, without titles, as a mere goddess, just as the Revenue Papyrus does. This is additional evidence that she was really dead, and that the plain statement of her demise contains no mere allegorical meaning.

These documents bring us back to the question of Ptolemy's royal wives, of whom the second had very great influence upon his life ; and as he was left a widower finally about the age of forty, an estimate of these ladies belongs rather to the earlier part of his reign.

Among the scholia on the Encomium of the second

Ptolemy which Theocritus has left us,[1] we are told
that after the first Arsinoe had borne three children, she
was discovered plotting against the king, whatever
that may mean, and that therefore she was banished to
Koptos in Upper Egypt. We have found traces of her
here, as well as of her son Lysimachus. To the latter
we have recovered a dedication in hieroglyphics (cf.
Krall, *Studien*, ii. 40): "Goddess of Ascher, give life
to Lysimachus, brother of the sovereigns, the Strategos,
year vii." (viz. of the next king). If he was therefore
Strategos of Koptos, it is likely that he was sent there
into nominal authority, but real exile, with his mother.
She is also commemorated (as I first pointed out) in a
stele found at Koptos in 1894 by Mr. Petrie.[2] It is the
memorial of Sennukhrud, an Egyptian, who in an
account of his life says he was her steward, and for her
rebuilt and beautified a shrine. The late Mr. Wilbour
examined this stele for me, and reported that though
the lady is called "the king's wife, the grand, filling
the palace with her beauties, giving repose to the
heart of King Ptolemy," she is not qualified as *loving
her brother*, and, what is perhaps more significant, her
name is not enclosed in a royal cartouche as a queen's
name should be. This then seems to be a record of
the first Arsinoe during her exile, and the only mention
of her in any inscription.[3] Concerning her character
and fortunes we know absolutely nothing else. But
we may infer, with the strongest probability, that she

[1] Idyll. xviii. The recent editors of the poet seem to take care
to conceal these valuable Greek notes, wherefore that on v. 128
is here quoted—

Πτολεμαίῳ δὲ τῷ Φιλαδέλφῳ συνώκει πρότερον Ἀρσινόη ἡ Λυσι-
μάχου, ἀφ' ἧς καὶ τοὺς παῖδας ἐγέννησε Πτολεμαῖον καὶ Λυσί-
μαχον καὶ Βερενίκην. ἐπιβουλεύουσαν δ' αὐτὴν εὑρὼν
ἐξέπεμψεν εἰς Κοπτὸν τῆς Οηβαίδος καὶ τὴν οἰκείαν ἀδελφὴν
Ἀρσινόην ἔγημε. καὶ εἰσεποιήσατο αὐτῇ τοὺς ἐκ τῆς προτέρας
Ἀρσινόης γεννηθέντας παῖδας· αὐτὴ γὰρ ἡ Ἀρσινόη ἄτεκνος
ἀπέθανεν.

[2] Cf. also Maspero, *Recueil*, xvii. 128, now No. 1357 in the Gizeh
Museum.

[3] An inscription from Samos (Strack, 18) may be, as Strack
says, an exception. But it merely mentions her name.

was deposed through the intrigues of her former stepmother at the court of Thrace, the Egyptian princess
who was wife of Lysimachus, then of her half-brother
Ptolemy Keraunos ; then, when her children by Lysimachus were murdered by Keraunos and herself

FIG. 19.—Arsinoe II. Philadelphos (Vatican).

repudiated, an exile, first at
Samothrace, lastly at her own
brother's court in Egypt. She
must have been born not later
than 316 B.C., for she became the
wife of Lysimachus in 301–300,
and had at least three children,
so that some have even supposed
that Arsinoe I., whom she replaced in Egypt, was her own
daughter. Though sufficient time
had elapsed to make this possible,
I do not believe it, nor is there
any hint in the extant gossip of
the time of so remarkable a circumstance as a mother sup-
planting her own daughter. But
when she came to Egypt, probably
in the end of 280 B.C., she was
about thirty-six years old, and
though she may have hoped for
more children, who would certainly have supplanted those of
her predecessor, as her husband
had supplanted Keraunos, when
her hopes were baulked, she
advised or acquiesced in the
adoption of her stepchildren, of
whom the eldest was therefore
the declared crown prince.

Here we come upon the most Egyptian feature in
this king's reign. Polygamy was common among all
the successors of Alexander, as indeed it had been at
the Macedonian court in older days. But to marry a
uterine sister was a thing abhorrent to Greek senti-

ment, as transpires from contemporary allusions. The poet Sotades, like John the Baptist, spoke out his mind upon the scandal, and lost his life in consequence. It is only in the researches of our own day that the Egyptian dogmas and sentiment on this matter have been duly examined, and it is now clear that, far from being a licence or an outrage, the marriage of full brother and sister was in the royal family of Egypt the purest and most excellent of all marriages, the highest security that the sacred blood of kings was not polluted by inferior strains. This is what M. Maspero has recently explained in his remarkable essay.[1]

This glorification of what we brand as incest had great importance in all questions of royal succession. A king's son born of a concubine took rank below a daughter born of the king's sister, and she succeeded before him. When the father was not of the old royal race, but some adventurer who had won the throne and married the rightful heiress, the priests imagined a direct intervention of Amon to maintain this so-called purity of blood. We have, accordingly, one strong political reason for Ptolemy's second marriage. The priests, despite their ingenuity, which had explained the legitimacy of Alexander in a fashion, must have been put to great straits to give a theological justification to the succession of the first Ptolemy and his Macedonian wife to the throne. There was apparently no princess of the native dynasty surviving. But having once sanctified Soter and his queen, it was a great concession to their traditions for Ptolemy II. to make a marriage conflicting so violently with the

---

[1] *Annuaire de l'école des hautes études* for 1896, p. 19: "The nobility of each member of a Pharaonic house and his claim upon the crown corresponded with the amount of the divine blood (of Amonra) which he could show ; he that derived it both from father and mother had a higher claim than he who had it from one parent only. Here the Egyptian social laws permitted what would be impossible in any modern civilisation. The marriage of brother and sister was the marriage *par excellence*, and it contracted an unspeakable sanctity when this brother and sister were born of parents who stood in the same relation."

customs of the invaders. The lady had already indicated her freedom from such prejudices by marrying
her half-brother, Keraunos.

At all events, though she bore no more children and
was obliged to adopt the son of her disgraced rival, she
became a great figure, not only in the Egyptian, but in
the Hellenistic world. Of no other queen do we find
so many memorials in various parts of the Greek
world. She was honoured with statues at Athens
and Olympia; her policy is specially commended in
an Attic inscription. The honours done to her in
Samothrace and in Bœotia, where a town Arsinoe is
named, may have been during her early life, when she
was queen of Thrace. But besides these, we have
votive inscriptions in her honour from Delos, Amorgos,
Thera, Lesbos, Cyrene, Cyprus, Oropus, and doubtless
more will yet be found. The dedications to her in
Egypt are numerous, and are only the formal part of
the many exceptional honours heaped upon her by her
husband. There seems to have been a statue of her,
seated upon an ostrich, at Thespiæ in Greece.

Though not a co-regent in the sense that some later
queens were (as we shall see in due time), she was
associated in every titular honour with the king. It
is noted by Wilcken (P.-W.I. p. 1283), from Naville's
transcription of the Pithom stele, that the Egyptian
priests had even assigned her a *throne-name* in addition
to her ordinary cartouche, an honour quite exceptional
for a queen. We have many coins issued with her
effigy only, as well as those with the king her brother,
as Gods Adelphi. She was deified together with him,
and gradually declared co-templar (σύνναος) with the
gods of the great shrines throughout Egypt. She
accompanied the king on his state progresses through
the country to Pithom, Mendes, etc. She had such influence upon the life of the king, that we used to assume
a long joint reign. The wording of the Revenue Laws,
drawn up in his year 23, first made me suspect that this
was not so, and the late Mr. Wilbour pointed out to me
that on the newly found fragment of the Mendes stele

above quoted we have express mention of her death
in year 15, month 9, day [lost], in other words, in the
year 270 B.C., when she had been at most 10 years queen
of Egypt.[1] The disconsolate king kept adding to her
honours throughout the remaining 22 years of his
reign. As early as his year 16 (immediately after her
death), they were deified together as θεοι αδελφοι;

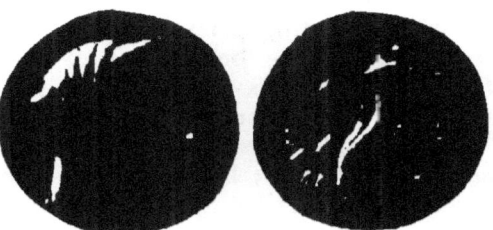

FIG. 20.—Coin of Arsinoe Philadelphos.

about the same time a yearly priestess (kanephoros)[2]
was appointed for her as the goddess Arsinoe Philadelphos, a title given long after to her husband also.
It is indeed maintained by Strack (D.P. p. 117) that

[1] This discovery runs counter to so many ingenious hypotheses
concerning the queen's life, that it will not find ready acceptance.
But there is no doubt whatever as to the meaning of the text. A
well-known Attic inscription (C.I.A 332), which is apparently from
the time of the Chremonidean war (about 262 B.C.), is considered
by some to be inconsistent with it, because it speaks of the king's
policy ακολουθως τει των προγονων και τει της αδελφης προαιρεσει. But
surely this text distinctly implies that she was already dead. Had
she been alive we should have had some of her titles, even as the
Mendes stele is profuse in them, till it comes to mention her as a
goddess, when she is "the great lady Arsinoe," and nothing more.
Secondly, she is expressly classed with his ancestors, as among
those who were no longer with him. It seems to me, therefore,
that the inference hitherto drawn from the inscription was exactly
the reverse of the right one.

[2] I believe the earliest evidence for this kanephoros is a demotic
document of the year 19. But we had no evidence of the θεοι
αδελφοι before year 21 till the Petric Papyri were published. It is
to be noticed that there is another Egyptian title extant attached
to her name, of which I can give no further account, viz.
"Secretary of Ptah and Arsinoe Philadelphos" (Krall. Studien,
ii. 48). It points to her association in some temple with Ptah.

Philadelphos was the original proper name of this
prince, which he exchanged for Ptolemy when promoted
to the crown.   But I think this hypothesis unlikely, as
we should probably have had ere this some direct evidence of it.   So far as we know from the new evidence
produced by Mr. Grenfell (Grenfell Papyri, i. p. 31),
that title was first applied to distinguish the king when
his priesthood was added (with other members of the
series) to the pre-existing priesthoods of the Ptolemies
at Ptolemais, and this between the 21st and 28th
years of Philometor (160–153 B.C.).   It is obvious
why this should have been so.   In the priesthoods of
Ptolemais the kings were consecrated separately from
the queens (and of these but a few), so that in a list
of kings some distinctive appellation for the second
Ptolemy must be found.   At Alexandria, on the contrary, the Ptolemies were consecrated in pairs (θεοι
αδελφοι, etc.), so that there was no need of the distinction ; and indeed this Ptolemy seems to have made
it a principle to associate his favourite wife with himself in all public acts and ceremonies.   Where he did
not appear as one of the Gods Adelphi, the specification
" Ptolemy, son of Ptolemy Soter " was sufficient, or
even " Ptolemy, son of Ptolemy," as this latter was
the first.   On the whole, therefore, I incline to the
belief that the title Philadelphos was not applied to the
king till some time after his death.

A pompous shrine, the Arsinoeion, was built for the
queen apparently within the precincts of the Serapeum
at Alexandria, and there the king set up the greatest
obelisk of Aswan granite hewn in Egypt, which he had
found partly prepared in the upper country by some
old Pharaoh, but still lying *in situ*.   This obelisk, 85
cubits high, was the wonder of men in Roman days.
I have sought to explain its unaccountable disappearance by the hypothesis that the extant pillar known as
Pompey's pillar was constructed out of it.   Other
Arsinoeia were consecrated to her in the Fayyum and
elsewhere in Egypt ; several towns were named after
her, and ultimately she was declared the guardian

goddess of the whole rich nome round the Lake Mœris, which was named the Arsinoite nome. She was identified with Aphrodite Zephyritis in a temple on the promontory east of the bay of Alexandria.

This list of honours is by no means exhaustive, but will suffice to show her vast influence over the king. He never raised any woman to the rank of queen after her death. He is said to have been planning a new temple and new devices to have her image floating in its midst at the time of his death. But we could not have suspected how much her deification was employed in domestic and practical legislation, till the Petrie Papyri, notably the Revenue Papyrus, gave us new and strange information.

We now know that, not only was her deification at the various local shrines completed after her decease, but that in the year 23 of the reign, after it was complete, a great financial revolution and an invasion of the temple estates and priestly corporations were made in her name. The landed property and the orchards and vineyards of all Egypt (with certain exceptions) paid a duty to the gods of the nearest temple amounting to one-sixth of the yearly crop. This great revenue was transferred by a single act into a duty to Arsinoe Philadelphos the new goddess, who sat as an equal in the temple of each god in Egypt. It was simply a disendowment of the State religion for the benefit of the Crown. And yet this act of spoliation seems to have been carried out without any open resistance on the part of the priests. How so curious a result was attained we can only guess. In both the Pithom and the Mendes stelæ great gifts of money and other honours to the gods are commemorated on the part of the priests. The king there posed as the greatest benefactor of the gods of the country. What proportion these occasional largesses bore to the yearly income now taken from the temples we have no means of determining. But we may not only surmise that the king made a good bargain, we may see clearly that by substituting benevolences or yearly subventions

IV—6

(συνταξις) for a revenue from land, the king brought the
priesthood of Egypt under his immediate control, for
they now depended more and more directly upon his
royal bounty.   How far the taxpayers were affected is
also uncertain, but it is more than likely that the Crown
officials were stricter collectors than the Church, and
not so likely to allow arrears from compassion or neigh-
bourly feeling as the local priests.   Moreover, debts
to the Crown were recovered by a process far more

FIG. 21.—Philæ.   South Approach to the Great Pylon.

summary than those due to other creditors.   Unfortunately, the Revenue Papyrus gives us no evidence, even
approximate, of the amount derived from this ἀπόμοιρα,
so that we cannot venture upon an estimate.

But in addition to the large gifts of money mentioned
in the Pithom and Mendes stelæ, we know that this king
began the great series of Ptolemaic temples which are
still the wonder of the modern traveller.   His great
Arsinoeion at Alexandria has vanished, and so no doubt

have many other of his buildings throughout the upper
country. We still possess the finest chamber of the
temples of Philæ, which he built and adorned, though
the formal dedication fell to his son.[1]   So strictly was
he regarded as the founder of the new splendours of
Philæ, that in the list of Ptolemies as co-templar gods,
which we find in inscriptions, etc., at Philæ, the Gods
Adelphi stand first, in the position that Soter occupies
at Ptolemais.[2]   The sacred island, which seems to have
begun to supplant the older sanctum of Biggeh (a
neighbouring island) as early as Amasis' reign,[3] was
specially consecrated to Isis, the patroness of Ptolemy
II., and to her he also reared a great temple of Aswan
granite 600 miles away in the Delta, where its ruins
now mark the Roman *Iseum*, the temple of Hebt.   The
building of this temple, whose site has not yet been
properly explored, was of the most costly nature.   To
carry down and carve granite blocks for single statues
or shrines was common enough in both Pharaonic and
Ptolemaic times.   To construct a whole temple of red
granite is, if I mistake not, unique even in the archi-
tectural extravagances of Egypt.

What, it will be asked, is the political and religious
significance of these temples built by nearly every
Ptolemy to Egyptian gods quite foreign to any Hellenistic creed?   That it signified any religious conviction,
or any dread of vengeance from the unseen ruling
spirits of the country, we may set aside as implying
an anachronism.   But as these great structures were
built out of the royal purse, what it did mean was
that a large sum of the royal income, levied in taxes,
was refunded to the people in the shape of wages for
architects, stonecutters, carriers, masons, designers.
Moreover, the completion of such a temple implied a

[1] This was discovered by Captain Lyons in 1896.
[2] This was first made clear by U. Wilcken in his article on the
stele of Euergetes II. at Philæ, *Hermes*, vol. xxii.
[3] This I owe to the late Mr. Wilbour, who found Amasis'
cartouches there.   The common belief is that Nectanebo II. was
the first builder at Philæ.

permanent establishment of a staff of priests and
servitors for its maintenance. We have no hint in

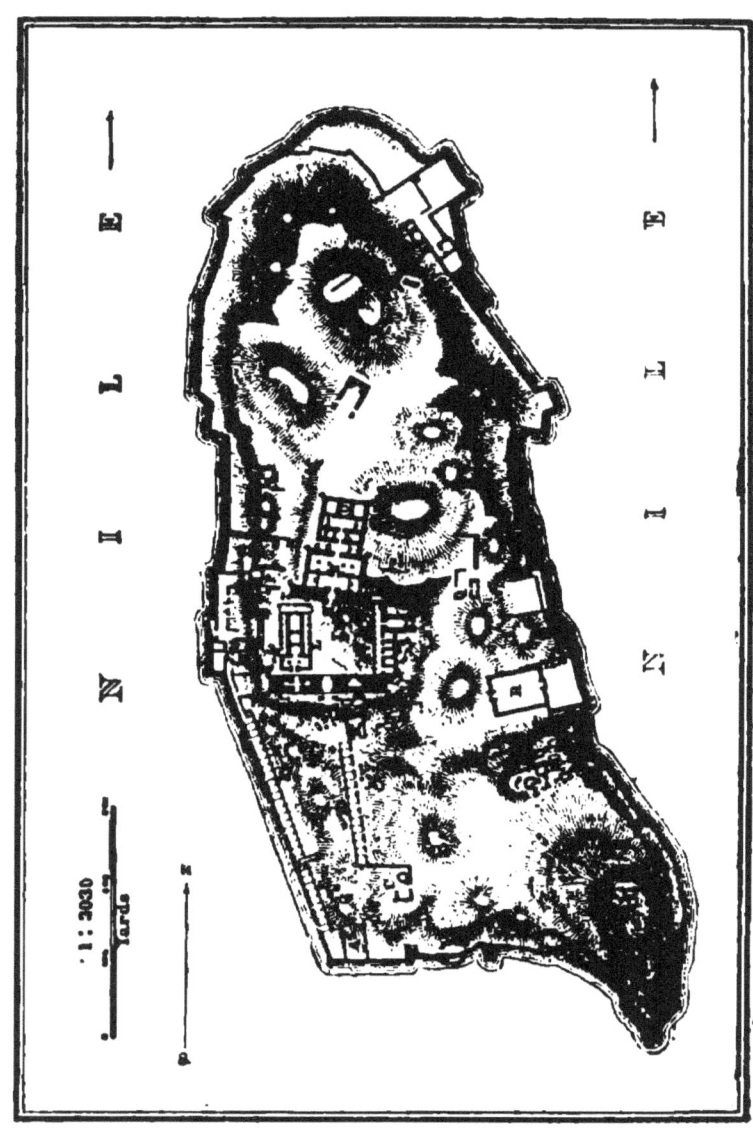

FIG. 22.—Plan of Philæ (the chambers round the adyton O are the work of Philadelphos).

any papyrus known to me that the building of these temples was done by *corvée*, like that of the pyramids in the IVth dynasty, of the dykes, or of the treasure cities which tormented the Israelites. On the contrary, it appears that some exalted native official was entrusted with this work, of which he would boast on his tomb as his most distinguished public service.

While these internal measures tended to make the king popular among the natives, Alexandria became, owing to its Museum and Library, more and more a great centre for Hellenistic literature and learning. Callimachus, Apollonius, Theocritus — these were the men who gave the tone to the literature of that age, and from them we still can judge its character when we supplement it with other work, such as that of Aratus or Herondas, who, though not Alexandrian in their birthplace, were truly Alexandrian in their spirit. For to us Alexandria sums up the Hellenism of the third century B.C. Perhaps the solitary Egyptian feature in this literary splendour was the taste shown by Philadelphos (if we may so call him for convenience sake) in having the old records of Egypt translated by the high priest Manetho. But the figure of Manetho is so hazy, our authorities concerning him are so late and poor, the silence concerning his Egyptian history in early Ptolemaic days is so complete, that it was very clearly no leading feature in the king's policy to have the national history in the dry form of Greek annals. The work of Manetho was undoubtedly of serious value. Josephus, Julius Africanus, Eusebius, in discussing his chronology, show us that he had honestly examined such hieroglyphic and hieratic records as the famous Turin Papyrus, and that his surviving dicta about the old dynasties are to be examined with care.

But this was not the kind of Egyptian history that the court of Philadelphos valued. There had been a history or sketch of the country and its wonders already composed by Hecatæus of Abdera, who visited Thebes in the days of Ptolemy Soter; we know the general character of it clearly enough from the first

book of Diodorus, who cites Hecatæus as his chief
authority.   This account of Egypt runs upon the
general lines of Herodotus' account, in its spirit, and
its efforts to amalgamate Hellenic and Egyptian mytho-
logy ; and one of the few things we know of Manetho
is that he specially controverted Herodotus and exposed
the ignorance of that traveller.   But if we estimate
aright the spirit of the Alexandria of that day, we shall
shall not hesitate to say that Manetho's dry enumera-
tion of early dynasties of gods and kings stood no
chance in popularity against Hecatæus' agreeable
romancing.   Possibly the high priest, who is cited as
one of the first Ptolemy's religious advisers, made an
honest attempt to counteract the uncritical rubbish
which was talked at the Museum concerning the earlier
history of his country.   In its day his work was a failure,
though centuries later Jews and Christians in their
controversies raked it out of oblivion, and cited enough
to show us how serious a loss we have sustained in its
disappearance.

    It is this apparent carelessness of the king about an
honest and thorough inquiry into ancient Egypt and
its traditions which throws strong suspicion upon the
story of the pseudo-Aristeas that the king promoted
and superintended the translation of the Law of Moses
into Greek.   That this version, known from the legend
in Aristeas as the LXX, was begun under the early
Ptolemies, and perhaps under this king, seems to me
probable, in spite of the scepticism of most modern
critics.   But it is also more than probable that it took
place quietly and gradually to meet the practical wants
of the Jews of Alexandria, who were forgetting
Hebrew, and their Hellenistic proselytes.   It is quite
in keeping with the temper and policy of these
Jews, that this great work, when found complete and
of capital importance for the propagation of their
doctrine, should have a formal and pompous birthday
assigned to it.

    None of these traditions, therefore, is sufficient to
prove that the king took any serious interest in fusing

Greeks and Egyptians, in giving the natives their due share of power, in making his kingdom more than the city of Alexandria, with a rich territory to supply it with every luxury. The course of recent discovery has made us acquainted with more and more of his internal administration, while our knowledge, or rather ignorance, regarding his foreign policy remains unchanged. His foreign wars are quite vague and undefined. We know that he resisted the attack of Magas from Cyrene with the aid of Celtic mercenaries, whom he was obliged to massacre because they saw that Egypt was too rich and pleasant a place to abandon when their engagement was over. We hear that he had wars with the king of Syria, but without any decisive battle being named. We hear that he sustained one great naval defeat at Kos from Antigonus, king of Macedon, and so lost control of the Ægean till another battle off Andros restored his prestige. The dates of these two battles are set down conjecturally at 262 and 247 B.C. In the other wars we have no definite dates at all.

Equally vague is our information regarding his city foundations in the Hellenistic world. As regards Egypt it is not so. We can affirm positively that he founded no new Greek polity in the country, though we know that he stood in friendly relations with the Greek artists of Ptolemais, his father's creation, and with the people of Naukratis, whose Hellenion he restored. His many foundations along the Red Sea, from the Isthmus down to the Straits of Aden, and perhaps even farther, were made to protect the trade from India and Arabia, and to obtain safe ports for the catching of elephants and other tropical curiosities in Abyssinia. But in this southern country the work of this king is hard to separate from that of his son, who may indeed have been there, acting in his father's name, before he went to Cyrene.[1] But why did this king found cities called

---

[1] There were apparently three towns called Arsinoe on the Red Sea, three in Cyprus, and many elsewhere. We also find the king's sister Philotera in town-names, and wonder that he did

Arsinoe, Philotera, etc., in Syria and in Asia Minor?[1]
We can understand his founding many towns in
Cyprus, his possession, in Syria, upon his military
frontier towards Antioch, but why in Lykia and Pamphylia, why in Ætolia? I adhere to my old view that
in the case of Lykia and Ætolia it was for the purpose
of having a voice in the politics of the leagues existing
in these countries. According to an extant inscription,
an Arsinoite occurs as chief magistrate of the Ætolian
League (Droysen, iii. 2. 327, note), and thus the
Egyptian king could have a legitimate voice in the
important politics of that influential confederacy.
Similar reasons would apply in Lykia. But both in
these lands and in Crete the foundation of an Arsinoe
or a Philadelphia may also be connected with the
question of mercenaries—either as a depôt for hiring
them, or as a place of pension when they had done
their service. The most far-reaching and lasting act
of his foreign diplomacy was, however, the offer of
friendship which he sent to the Romans (273 B.C.), to
which they replied by a most dignified embassy,[2] and
by cementing a friendship which lasted all through the
dynasty. It was thus that Puteoli became a great and
favoured harbour for Alexandrian merchant ships.

This digression upon the king's foreign policy is
perhaps no more than just, as offering some reason for
a less assiduous attention to his home affairs. But
even here, in addition to the evidences of building now
recovered, we can point to one great foundation which
may very well counterbalance the absence of all new
city foundations in Egypt during this reign. In older
authorities it is consistently stated that he founded a

not marry her after Arsinoe II. had departed. The third statue
in the Vatican, which stands with those of the Gods Adelphi,
seems to me to be probably that of Philotera. Cf. below, Fig. 26.

[1] The Arsinoe in Bœotia, though called after the same queen,
might have been a foundation of Lysimachus, while she was his
wife, as Mr. Woodhouse has pointed out; but Strabo says expressly (x. 2. § 22) that it was as Ptolemy's wife that she founded
it.

[2] Livy, Epit. xiv. ; cf. also *Empire of the Ptolemies*, p. 296.

Greek city Arsinoe in the Fayyum as the capital of that nome. This is not true. The chief town of the nome was not called Arsinoe till long afterwards; it was Crocodilopolis, and was not a "Greek city," though it was the chief town of the Arsinoite nome, which he renamed and settled with a new population about the 28th–30th years of his reign.[1]

We now know that Arsinoe herself, being more than ten years dead, could have had nothing to say personally to this foundation. In the documents of

FIG. 23.—Philæ from the N.E.

the 23rd and 27th years of the reign, long after her decease, it is still called *the Lake* (Λιμνη). But the fact that one village there was named the Mound of Arsinoe (Αρσινοης χωμα) points to the queen having paid some attention to the banking out of the great lake, which covers a huge area of so gradual a downward

---

[1] The dates in P.P. II. viii., which are L (year) 11 (or 14) and 16, make it uncertain whether the foundation may not have begun much earlier. In future I shall denote *year* in these dates by the symbol L

slope, that a dyke might reclaim thousands of acres.
Diodorus tells us that the fish of the lake, which are
exceedingly numerous, were of old the perquisite of
the queen of Egypt.   Arsinoe may therefore have fore-
gone part of her perquisites for the benefit of the
province, and this may have suggested her being made
the special goddess of the nome.   At all events, a large
number of veterans [1] were granted lands, possibly the
lands obtained by the embankment of Arsinoe, and of
these the largest lots seem to have been 100 arouræ [2]
(acres of about 55 yards square, or 3000 square yards).
Cavalry soldiers were evidently more favoured than
infantry, but they were bound to keep a horse for their
service, which was under the inspection of a govern-
ment officer ($\iota\pi\pi\sigma\sigma\kappa\acute{o}\pi\sigma\varsigma$). [3]   That they were not the only
cleruchs in the country appears from the general mention
of the class in the Revenue Papyrus (col. 36, 12), at which
time there were possibly none yet settled round the
Lake.   They were divided into two grades, cleruchs of
100 acres or less, and men of the Epigone, of which
I take the former to mean settlers who had come as
soldiers, and brought with them their wives, from
the Greek world, being foreigners by birth, as distinguished from the latter, who were born of a soldier
and a native woman, a race still so privileged that

[1] My German critics persistently object to my calling them
veterans, because they were still liable to be called out for active
service.   As they seem disinclined to inform themselves on this
matter, I must point out that in the English language *veterans* do
not mean *pensioners*, and that any soldier or general who has
served many years is a veteran, whether still in active service or
not.   But I am quite sure that the settlers in the Fayyum were
reserve men, not performing ordinary camp duties.

[2] Herod. ii. 168 says this was the allowance of land, tax-free,
given to each of the old warrior caste and his family.   Hence the
Ptolemies probably borrowed the figure, which seems very large
for the land of Egypt, if some parts of it were not $\mathring{\alpha}\beta\rho\sigma\chi\sigma\nu$ or
$\mathring{\alpha}\phi\sigma\rho\sigma\nu$, as appears in P.P. II. p. 103.   For it amounts to about 166
acres.   E. Revillout (*Mélanges*, p. 250) thinks that the whole of the
land of the military caste had been *common* land, and was divided
into separate freeholds by the Ptolemies, and distributed to both
Greeks and natives of the old caste.   This I do not believe.

[3] Cf. P.P. II. [116].

the title became hereditary, but not equal to the former.[1]

What the relation of these people was to the native population around them does not appear from any of the numerous documents in the Petrie collection. That the latter, as yet, stood apart from the Greek-speaking people seems pretty clear ; that the mutual relations were friendly appears from the absence of any trace of disturbances or riots, and the very few complaints of mere ordinary assaults. In a few of these a native may have been insolently treated by a Greek.[2] Perhaps indirect evidence of some value can be gathered from the correspondence of Kleon the *Architect*, a chief commissioner of works in the nome, from whose correspondence many fragments dating from L 27-32 of the reign are among the P.P. (II. p. 83 *sqq.*). It seems likely that his great and various activity in the construction of dykes, quarrying in the desert, etc., is connected with the organisation of the settlement of soldiers in the nome. We find on the whole that this great piece of land legislation appears to have been carried out without outrage or war of races, and the prosperity of the nome was not impaired but increased. The phrase which occurs more than once, "the lots which they have received from the king" or from the king's property (εκ του βασιλικου), makes it probable that the Ptolemies had succeeded to large Crown estates from the previous dynasties, or rather had appropriated them on this title, and that these, formerly managed directly by Government officials, were now divided among privileged lot-holders, under fixed conditions.[3] From the group of wills which I found among the Petrie Papyri, it appears that these settlers retained their houses, and probably their city privileges, in

[1] This solution of the difficulty commends itself to me after much controversy, but it is by no means certain. Other suggestions, which I now abandon, will be found in my *Petrie Papyri*, i. p. 42.

[2] *E.g.* P.P. II. [58], where the complainant, though he has a Greek name, was probably a native.

[3] Cf. note on last page.

Alexandria; and this property they bequeathed with
their other chattels as they pleased.[1] The absence of
mention of the κληρος[2] or land lot in almost all these
documents makes us infer that the succession to this
royal gift was regulated by laws beyond the control of
the testator.   The usual trustees of the will selected
are the king, queen, and their children, a polite way of
inviting Government control to carry out the provisions
of the testator.   In no case does a native name appear
in these documents, even among the Epigone.   But,
owing to their limited number, this is possibly (though
I think hardly) an accident.

The whole of this society strikes us as civilised and
orderly.   The Greek of their documents is far the
most correct yet found in business papyri; the
fragments of literature found among their papers are
likewise of the best class; we may therefore confidently
assert that the second Ptolemy had succeeded in
naturalising Hellenic culture in Egypt, or rather in
exhibiting good specimens of it among these settlers,
whose children would be attached to the soil, and
could not but intermarry more or less with the natives.
The existence at this time of settlements of Jews in
Egypt, and even in Upper Egypt, is quite proven by
the existence of the village in the nome called Samareia

---

[1] They not only tell us their military rank, and the *hipparchy*
(we hear of five) to which they belong, but they designate themselves as belonging to one of the demes of Alexandria—Ανδρομαχειος,
Πολυδευκειος, Αιακιδευς, Φιλαδελφειος, Σουνιευς, Ισθμιευς, Μαρωνευς, as
may be seen in the wills and in inscriptions.   There are also men
classed as των ουπω επηγμενων εις δημον, or εις ιππαρχιαν, and yet
soldiers receiving pay and having privileges.   Is this a polite
circumlocution for μισθοφοροι?   Even a παρεπιδημος (P.P. I. xix.)
has the right to bequeath property.

[2] There is one mention of it in the wills, cf. P.P. I. xviii. (1); but
unfortunately the context is lost, so that we cannot tell the connection.   On the other hand, the σταθμος or homestead, granted
εκ βασιλικου, they do bequeath; and to their wives, in I. xvii. (1),
(2).   That the σταθμος was not simply included as part of the
κληρος, and bequeathed with it, appears from the rescript in P.P. II.
viii. (1): Βασιλευς Πτολεμαιος Λυκομειδηι χαιρειν. | των τους κληρους
αφειρημενων ιππεων | οι σταθμοι περιεστωσαν τωι Βασιλει εαν | μη τισιν
ημεις επ ονοματος επιστειλωμεν | διδοναι. ερρωσο L κδ Αρτεμισιου κε.

(its Egyptian name was Kerkesephis, at least in later days), which is mentioned more than once in the Petrie Papyri. We even know of two inhabitants who were retailers of oil—Pyrrias and Theophilos, which are probably Greek translations of Esau and Eldad.[1]

What burdens had these settlers to pay to the State?[2] For we may be sure that the natives had not these only but other taxes laid upon them. Here again the papyri gives us many isolated details, but no adequate materials for any systematic sketch.[3] We are sure that there was at Alexandria a great financial officer over the Exchequer, called διοικητής. But he had under him many local officers, who seem to be called in the Petrie Papyri by the same name. In later days we have the term ὑποδιοικητής, which does not occur here. In the P.P. we have, but rarely, an

[1] This evidence is by no means solitary. There was a Jewish section of the people of Psenuris, concerning whom I found the following (P.P. I. 43):—ενοικουν εν Ψενυρει παντο· | εις τα αποδοχεια της κωμης | παρα των Ιουδαιων και των | Ελληνων εκαστου σωματος < | και τουτο λογευεται δια | Δι[. . .]ιου τοι επιστατου. I commend this fragment to Willrich, who has only quoted the evidence of the P.P. at second hand, and has missed this passage (*Juden u. Griechen*, p. 151). Here is a tax of half a drachma set upon every slave belonging to any Jew or Greek in Psenuris. In one of the wills, dated 237 B.C., a man, whose name is Συριστι Ιωναθας, appears as owing the testator 150 (silver) drachmæ. We have also on the back of a λογος χωρων with assessments of value, dated in the 37th year of Philadelphus, της παρα Σιμωνος ουν σοι αν(τιγραφον) επιστολης απεσταλκα (P.P. II. p. [18]). Hence Simon was an official in the Fayyum in 248–7 B.C. These sporadic, but perfectly unsuspicious bits of evidence are quite conclusive.

[2] According to the rescripts from the Berlin Papyri, numbered 31, 107, 152, 160, 167, 170, Revillout (*Mél.* p. 139) argues that various κληρουχιαι in the Fayyum, in the days of the Antonines, were saddled with the duty of cultivating various fractions of the royal domain which lay around them. This, at all events, shows that there were κληρουχοι there for centuries.

[3] It is a common criticism of my German friends that I have neglected to write the economic history of Egypt under the Ptolemies. Let one of them attempt it himself. The mass of facts we are now recovering from the Roman period may supply us sufficiently for such a history under the Empire; but for Ptolemaic Egypt we are still quite in the dark.

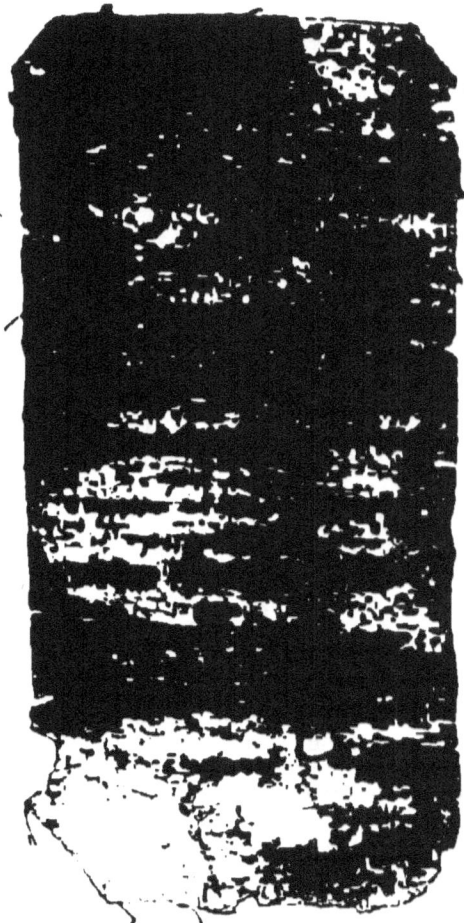

FIG. 24. A business letter of 240 B.C.

Transcription.

Δωροθεος Ηροδωρωι
χαιρων γιινωσκι μι
τρυγησοντα τηι θ
τοῦ Παυνι καλως οὑν
ποιησις αποστυλας
τηι ἡ
τινα δι ιταπολωθη
τηι ιγχυσιι
ςιι τον γινομινον
γλιυκους η γραψαι μοι
πωι συνταςους
ιρρωσο LΣ παυνι Δ

ἐπιμελητής, whose functions seem much the same,[1] and whom I take to be a temporary officer acting for the διοικητής. But in the list of local officers addressed by the Crown in the Revenue Papyrus (col. 37) none of these names occurs, and the only διοικητής mentioned in the course of that legislation is the head controller in Alexandria. The constant repetition of such names as Apollonius make it impossible to infer identity of the officers in various papyri by the coincidence of names. But in the Revenue Papyrus list there is mentioned a set of special officers under one Satyrus, and these may possibly have been ἐπιμεληταί. We come next to the *œconomus*, an officer frequently mentioned in all our

[1] P.P. II. xx. 2nd col. line 3.

groups of papyri, to whom falls much of the financial working of each district—whether *nome* or division (μερίς) of a nome. The whole conduct of the oil monopoly in the Revenue Papyrus is entrusted to him as the responsible officer. But in that papyrus, and in it alone, there is associated with him his secretary (ἀντιγραφεύς), who is no mere clerk, but the deputy or *alter ego* of the œconomus, when the latter is absent. What the relations of these officers were to the Chief διοικητής at Alexandria can be fairly guessed; but what they had to say to the local διοικηταί I cannot say. Nor were these the only co-ordinate officers; there were also the Crown secretaries (βασιλικοι γραμματεις), who are frequently mentioned, but whose functions I cannot distinguish from the rest. Under them all, for the management of each village or parish, we have nomarchs and toparchs, also τοπογραμματεις and κωμογραμματεις, and these seem usually to have been natives. All this was mere civil administration; each nome had also a strategus, originally the chief military authority, but in course of time usurping civil powers; under him a chief policeman (ἀρχιφυλακιτης) with subordinates to keep the peace and insist upon order. The Revenue Papyrus even mentions ἡγεμόνες, who were probably the infantry officers commanding local garrisons, and some other authorities of a special kind, such as Libyarchs. Seeing that the legal affairs were not under any of these people, but settled either by judges of assize for the natives (if not by native courts) or by a special tribunal of Greeks mentioned in the Petrie Papyri (I. xxvii.-viii.), we have a wealth of officials which produce on our minds mere perplexity. To unravel the system of government from these details seems to me as yet impossible. It is likely that the system of Greek officials was set up without abolishing the local customs and courts of the natives; but these latter were encouraged to appeal to the Greek courts, and in course of time did so habitually. We have a large number of documents drawn up in the two languages, Greek and demotic, and it is to these that the so-called decipherers of demotic are beholden for their very doubtful successes.

Passing now to the taxes levied by this host of officials, we have not yet found any complete list of them, but can gather from various documents a surprising number, which may any day be increased by new discoveries. I cannot find in the papyri of this period any mention of a λαογραφία or poll-tax upon all the natives, and suppose that it was not yet instituted. Of the ἀπογραφή or census returns made by each householder we have various specimens. But the burdens on land seem to have been very heavy, not only in Egypt, but in the neighbouring Hellenistic lands. The Crown seems to consider the landholder as a mere occupant on the *metayer* system, wherein half the profits belong to him, the other half to the Royal Exchequer. Indeed I think it likely that the occupant did not secure 50 per cent. of his produce. One-sixth, as we know abundantly from the Revenue Papyrus, was due to the temples, and was absorbed during this reign by the Crown. The curious fragments xxxix. in the Petrie Papyri (vol. II.) contains notices of all manner of small taxes (φυλακιτικον, χωματικον, ιατρικον, λειτουργικον, and others, such as αλικη ανιππιας (?) βυρσης), and to these is added the irregular benevolence or *aurum coronarium* called στεφανος, which was not only levied upon the accession of the king, but also upon the occasion of his visit to a particular district in that district.[1] In addition to all these small imposts there was the

[1] This seems to be the interpretation in P.P. II. xxxix. (*e*) of στεφανος, followed by αλλου παρουσιας, "for another gift for the king's visit." But I confess this interpretation of the whole matter is still very problematical. The curious reader will do well to look at E. Revillout's very confused note (*Mélanges*, 1895, p. 310) for further conjectures, and promises of future explanations, and compare this with the merely tentative conjectures put forward by the decipherer in the P.P. II. xxxix., with the particular caution that he did not profess to have explained it. But M. Revillout is not himself if he is not scurrilous. He proposes to translate ανιππιας by *horse transport*, and παρουσιας by *the present year*! So much for his Greek.

revenue from mono-
polies such as that
of oil, carefully
guarded by minute
enactments such as
those in the third
part of the Revenue
Papyrus. The far-
mers are compelled
to sow a certain
proportion of their
farms in sesame or
croton or flax ; the
preparation and sale
of the produce is
watched by Govern-
ment officials,
farmed out to tax-
farmers, and their
profits carefully
superintended. The
Ashmolean papyrus,
recently published
by me (*Trans. Royal
Irish Acad.* vol. xxxi.
part vi. 1898), shows
still more clearly
that the whole crop
was supervised, and
in this particular
case, the growing of
κνηκος (a thistle or
artichoke) for oil,
specially enforced.
The toparch or ko-
m o g r a m m a t e u s
seems to have kept
a register of every
acre in his district
and its treatment.

IV—7

FIG. 25.—Fragment of Hom. *Il.* xi. 502-37. (From the Petrie Papyri I.)

Note.—Very interesting in that it contains the ends and beginnings of several lines wholly unknown in our later texts. The same curious phenomenon has been found in other fragments of the 3rd cent. B.C. by Mr. Grenfell (cf. his Papyri, vol. ii.).

Probably the Nitrian desert, with its peculiar products, was also worked by the Government.

But all these details bring us no nearer to any estimate of the actual revenue of the Crown, which made the king of Egypt the richest of the sovereigns then known. There seems to have been a system of farming out the collection of almost every tax ; even the local banks, which were not Crown establishments, were farmed out to lessees. By this means the Crown officials were saved much trouble, especially in the frequent case of taxes paid in kind, some of which, such as wheat, were stored in State granaries, and used for payments and pensions ; others of perishable quality must have been realised in money by the tax-farmers, and the result controlled. In the case of the oil monopoly our great difficulty is to understand why any man should have undertaken the thankless office of tax-farmer, without any possibility, so far as we can see, of large direct or indirect profits, and I incline more and more to the belief that this was a burden forced in some way upon wealthy citizens by the Crown. There are not wanting indications in the Revenue Papyrus that bidders at the auction of the contracts for farming taxes were not always to be had. In such cases the arrangements in the case of oil provided that that the *œconomus* and his deputy could deal directly with the cultivators, as they were bound to do, in case of the failure or unpunctuality of the tax-farmers. All importations of oil from Syria were strictly forbidden, and there are curious regulations even forbidding the melting down of lard so as to make it pass for oil. The olive, afterwards well known and flourishing in the Fayyum and at Alexandria, was evidently not yet domesticated in Egypt. The vine appears in old Pharaonic pictures, and in many Ptolemaic descriptions of property about Thebes, but we wonder that the climate was suited to it. Here again the slope of the Fayyum formed a remarkably favourable locus for vineyards.

We may now affirm with some confidence that as soon as Ptolemy was bereaved of his wife (L 15 of his reign) he associated in the crown his eldest son Ptolemy, who afterwards succeeded. The earlier form of dating seems to have been " in the reign of Ptolemy, son of Ptolemy," Arsinoe never being formally associated in the Government, though she issued coins in her own name. From L 15 to L 27 the formula, which I was the first to find, is, "in the reign of Ptolemy, son of Ptolemy, and of his son Ptolemy." From the year 27 onward it changes to " in the reign of Ptolemy, son of Ptolemy Soter."[1] It has been a subject of much discussion why this last change took place. I still hold it to be connected with the crown prince's residence at Cyrene, from that time on. Magas, after a reign of fifty years, had died, leaving as his heir a young princess, Berenike, not yet grown up. Her mother, the Syrian Apama, desired to obtain a Macedonian prince as the future prince consort, and so Demetrius the Fair, son of Demetrius the Besieger and an Egyptian princess, came to Cyrene. But, owing to his intrigue with Apama, he was put to death, and Ptolemy hastened to send his son to occupy the vacant prospect, no doubt with the assent of an Egyptian party in Cyrene. It seems to have been inconsistent with his duties as associated prince of Egypt to hold this foreign position, or else the jealousy of the Cyrenæans refused to accept him as crown prince of Egypt, but only as the accepted suitor of Berenike. At all events, the strange fact is established, explain it as we may.

Towards the Syrian side the ageing king endeavoured to extend Egyptian influence. He negotiated a marriage between his daughter Berenike, sister of the crown prince, and the king of Syria, Antiochus Theos, who rejected his wife Laodike and her sons for the sake of the brilliant connection and enormous fortune now offered to him. But though the princess, who was not

---

[1] There seems to be one remarkable exception, which makes the whole argument uncertain. In P.P. II. viii. (1) B, we have quite distinctly βασιλειοντος Ητολεμαιου του Ητολεμαιου σωτηρος L ια (possibly ιδ) μηνος Διου. But this is probably the mere rehearsal of a former decree, with the formula of dating adapted to later days.

young (over thirty), was accompanied by stores of Nile water to ensure fertility, and though she did promptly produce an heir, the hopes of Egyptian influence were ruined for the time by her murder, which her father just lived to hear.   In another direction he had given subsidies to Aratus of Sicyon, to work the Achæan League against Antigonus, king of Macedon, thus showing the widespread and various ramifications of his foreign policy.   But his brilliant and varied life was coming to a close.   He died in March 246 B.C., probably a little over sixty years old, leaving to his mature and able son a splendid empire, a full treasury, and a brilliant court.   Up to the end of his life he seems to have been contemplating new honours to Arsinoe, and at some time of his reign, probably when he sought to extend his foreign commerce by friendship with the Romans, he commissioned his architect, Sostratos of Cnidos, to build the beacon tower with a light for mariners, which, occupying the E. point of the island Pharos, gave this name to the whole genus of lighthouses.   Strabo, who saw it, speaks of the material as white or limestone marble, and

Fig. 26.—Philotera? (Vatican).

A companion statue to those of Ptolemy II. and Arsinoe, but the name and titles have unfortunately been polished off the ridge running down the back of the figure, where they had been engraved.

the design as many roofed (πολυώροφον), by which he probably means many-storeyed, like those campaniles in Italy which have many roofs one over the other, gradually diminishing in size.[1] Josephus says it could be seen by approaching sailors 300 stadia (33 miles) out to sea. The king permitted the architect to make the dedication in his own name—a thing which seemed so odd to the subjects of the later kings that a story was invented to account for the curiosity. The architect was supposed to have covered his own dedication with a perishable cement upon which he engraved the king's name as dedicator. Lumbroso (*Egitto*, pp. 118 *seq.*), with his usual acuteness, has seen through the imposture of the story, but he gives too much weight to the words of Strabo describing the inscription : ἀνέθηκε Σώστρατος Κνίδιος, φίλος τῶν βασιλέων, τῆς τῶν πλωιζομένων σωτηρίας χάριν, ὡς φησιν ἡ ἐπιγραφή. As we now know that the title "Friend of the King" was not in use under Ptolemy II., this point has been added by Strabo, and the real epigram only attested the last fact. Here Strabo is in perfect agreement with Lucian's report of the text : Σώστρατος Δεξιφάνους Κνίδιος Θεοῖς Σωτῆρσιν ὑπὲρ τῶν πλωιζομένων. I see no reason to doubt the accuracy of this account. Lumbroso quotes from a translation of the Arab traveller Makrizi (*loc. cit.*) that the inscription faced north, *i.e.* seaward, and consisted of letters of lead let into the stone (no doubt gilt), each letter being a cubit high and a span wide.

This splendid guide to the narrow entrance was not a sign of open welcome. Very strict regulations were enforced as regards entering and leaving the port, and a passport was imperatively required even for the latter in Strabo's day, probably in continuation of the precautions devised by the first Ptolemies.

I have already spoken of Ptolemy's relation to his heir and crown prince and of the marriage of his daughter Berenike. Strack thinks (*Dynastie der Ptolemäer*, § 3) that Arsinoe II. was never formally associated in the Government, in spite of her deification and the coinage with her name and image and even her thronename. In the year after her death, at all events, she

---

[1] Such are also many of Wren's spires in London and elsewhere.

and her husband had been established with a cult as Brother Gods (cf. P.P. I. xxiv. (2)), and I am not at all confident that we shall not some day find the formula, " In the reign of Ptolemy, son of Ptolemy, and of Arsinoe, Brother Gods." At all events, the formula which we do know lasted from L 15 to L 27 of the reign, when two events occurred which caused a change. Ptolemy Soter was formally deified under that title, and the heir-apparent was sent as viceroy to Cyrene, and betrothed to the heiress of that territory.

These official relations tell us little or nothing concerning the domestic relations of the king and his children. Concerning Ptolemy, Berenike, and their brother Lysimachus there is absolute silence among the anecdotists. Neither love affairs nor adventures are recorded of any of them. Justin calls the crown prince Tryphon, which may have been his original name. His education was conducted by the lights of the Museum, and his tastes were serious, if we may judge from the learned epigram of Eratosthenes, to be discussed hereafter, and the utter silence regarding any love affairs or mistresses either during his long celibacy—he did not succeed to the throne and marry till he was over thirty—or during his reign. His individuality is perfectly unknown to us.

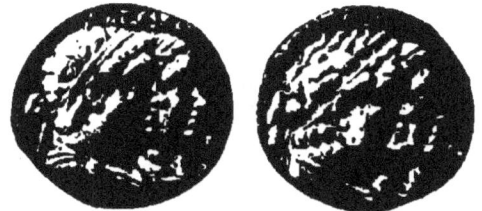

FIG. 27.—Coin with the Gods Adelphi on obverse and the Gods Soteres on reverse.

CHAPTER IV

FIG. 28.—Cartouches of Ptolemy III.

AUTHORITIES.—In addition to the general histories and the commentary of S. Jerome on Daniel xi., which contains Porphyry's views, we have two important inscriptions (the Canopus stone and the throne of Adule), translated below, besides a few dedications—all to be found in the Appendix to Strack's *Ptolemies.* Our Greek historians are almost silent on this reign. But a great mass of most interesting home documents have been obtained from the paper boards of mummy cases, and published under the title *The Petrie Papyri*, 2 vols. and an appendix, in the Cunningham Memoirs, VIII. and IX. of the Royal Irish Academy. These documents, wills, contracts, letters, etc., most of them dated, throw great and unexpected light on the condition of the Fayyum under Ptolemy III. Cf. the chapters on this period in *Greek Life and Thought from Alexander to the Roman Conquest* (2nd ed. 1897). The great building text inscribed on the walls of the temple of Edfu, and published by Dümichen, with a translation in the *Z. für Ægypt.* 1871, gives us important facts for all the succeeding reigns.

THE opening of the reign of Ptolemy III. (Euergetes) was one of the most stirring moments in the history of

the dynasty.   His sister, recently married to the king
of Syria, and successful in producing a prince, was set
upon by the partisans of the former queen and her
growing sons, who took advantage of the death of the
king (apparently at Ephesus) to attack her and her
infant and murder them, after a short siege, at her
palace in Daphne.[1]   The first duty of the new king of
Egypt was to avenge this bloody deed.   But he did not
start upon this adventure before marrying the princess
Berenike of Cyrene, long betrothed to him, and only
awaiting his coronation to become his royal wife.   For
then only (as I have already explained) would her children
be legitimate heirs to the throne.   We still have, in the
Coma Berenices, which Catullus translated from Callimachus, a court poet's version of what he thought
important in this crisis.   The bride-queen had dedicated a lock of her hair in the temple of Arsinoe
Aphrodite with vows for the safe return of her husband.
The lock had disappeared, and was cleverly discovered
by the court astronomer, Conon, among the stars,
whither it had been translated by the goddess.   As
there were still anonymous constellations, and the
astronomers were then mapping out the heavens, this
translation was not only convenient for science, but for
the courtiers.[2]

Another scrap of contemporary evidence, of a very
different character, was found by me among the Petrie
Papyri (II. xlv.).   It contains the narrative of a soldier
or officer who took part in the opening campaign.   It
appears that Ptolemy's fleet first attacked the coasts of
Asia Minor, so as to seize the treasure-forts in Cilicia,
and also to interrupt the communications between the
headquarters of the Syrian queen Laodike and her son,
which were at Ephesus (or in that neighbourhood),
and the capital Antioch.   Presently either this or
another fleet advanced along the court of Palestine to
Posidion, and then to Seleukia, at the mouth of the
Orontes, which fortress fell into Egyptian hands with-

---

[1] Justin, as cited presently.
[2] Cf. Aratus, *Phænomena*, 370 *seq.*

out a struggle, and remained in their power for many years. The march up to Antioch was a mere triumphal procession, for the Egyptian party in that city had regained their ascendency after the murder of the queen, and now the whole population must have dreaded the vengeance of the Egyptians.

The sequel of the campaign is only known to us from three sources: the king's own boastful inscription

FIG. 29.—A fragment from the Papyrus of 246 B.C. on Third Syrian War (the entry into Antioch). Cf. Petrie Papyri, II. xlv., for transcription and commentary.

copied at Adule (near Suakim) by the monk Cosmas, and so only preserved; the statement of S. Jerome, borrowed from Porphyry; and the abstract of Justin. (1) "The great king Ptolemy, son of king Ptolemy and queen Arsinoe, Brother Gods, children of king Ptolemy and queen Berenike, Saviour Gods, the descendant on his father's side from Herakles, son of Zeus, on his

mother's from Dionysus, son of Zeus, having inherited
from his father the royalty of Egypt and Libya and
Syria and Phœnicia and Cyprus and Lycia and Caria
and the Cyclades, set out on a campaign into Asia with
infantry and cavalry forces and a naval armament and
elephants both Troglodyte and Ethiopic, which his
father and he himself first captured from these places,
and, bringing them to Egypt, trained them to military use.
But having become master of all the country within the
Euphrates, and of Cilicia and Pamphylia and Ionia and
the Hellespont and Thrace, and of all the military
forces and elephants in these countries, and having
made the monarchs in all these places his subjects, he
crossed the river Euphrates, and having brought under
him Mesopotamia and Babylonia and Susiana and
Persis and Media, and all the rest as far as Bactriana,
and having sought out whatever sacred things had
been carried off by the Persians from Egypt, and
having brought them back with the other treasure
from these countries to Egypt, he sent forces through
the canals "—and here the text breaks off.[1]

(2) The text of S. Jerome, commenting upon the vague
and obscure verses 7 and 8 of the eleventh chapter of
Daniel, is as follows :—" Berenice being murdered, and
her father Ptolemy Philadelphus having died in Egypt,
her brother, himself also a Ptolemy called Euergetes,
succeeded as the third king, of the stock of that root,
in that he was her brother ; and he came with a great
army, and entered into the province of the king of the
North, *i.e.* of Seleucus called Callinicus, who with his
mother Laodice was reigning in Syria, and abused
them and obtained so much as to take Syria and Cilicia,
and the upper parts across the Euphrates, and almost
all Asia.   And when he heard that in Egypt a sedition
was in progress, he, plundering the kingdom of
Seleucus, carried away 40,000 talents of silver, and
precious cups and images of the gods, 2500 ; among
which were those also which Cambyses, when he took
Egypt, had brought to the Persians.   Finally the

[1] Cf. C.I.G. 5127, or Strack, *Ptolemäer*, No. 38.

Egyptian race, being given to idolatry, because he had brought back their gods after many years, called him Euergetes. And Syria he himself retained ; but Cilicia he handed over to his friend Antiochus to govern, and to Xanthippus, another general, the provinces beyond the Euphrates."

(3) Justin's account (lib. xxvii.) is longer but still more unsatisfactory, because he epitomises Trogus without grasping more than vague notions of the subject. After speaking of the murder of king Antiochus Theos by Laodike and her son Seleukos, and the resolution to murder the Egyptian queen Berenike, who had taken refuge in her palace in Daphne (by Antioch), he proceeds : "When it was announced to the cities of Asia (*Asiæ civitatibus*) that she and her infant son were besieged, in consideration of her ancestral dignity they felt pity at so undeserved a misfortune, and all despatched succour. Her brother, too, Ptolemy, alarmed at the danger of his sister, hurried from his kingdom with all his forces. But before the arrival of help, Berenike, who could not be captured by force, was deceived by treachery and murdered. Universal indignation ensued. And so, when all the cities which had revolted could have prepared a great fleet, forthwith alarmed at this specimen of (Laodike's) cruelty, and in order to avenge her whom they had meant to protect, they went over to Ptolemy, who, unless he had been called home by a domestic sedition [internal revolution] would have taken possession of all the kingdom of Seleukos." The following chapter gives an account of the succeeding wars and truces between the king of Egypt and the two young Seleukid princes, so confused, that nothing can now be made of it.[1]

We may, however, infer from corroborative inscriptions that though the Egyptian king was completely victorious, he did not desire to appropriate the whole vast kingdom of Syria, still less to become a new Alexander, but did desire to hold the whole of Cœle-

[1] Cf. the conjectures of Droysen, iii. 1. 384 *seq.*

Syria, including Damascus and the port of Antioch, and to control the sea up to the Hellespont and the coasts of Thrace. It was in this latter policy that he found opposition not only in the rival Seleukid princes, whom he weakened by setting them up one against the other, but in the commercial Greek cities of Asia Minor and probably in Rhodes, which feared the results of so powerful a regent of the Levant. But they were only able to limit, not to abolish, his sovereignty over these countries. So far only are we concerned with his foreign policy.

The effects of these brilliant wars upon Egypt itself are now to be considered. A quantity of treasure was brought home from Asia, but this, of course, went into

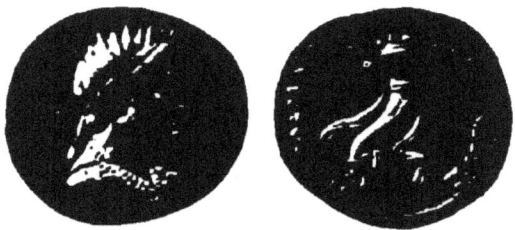

FIG. 30.—Coin of Ptolemy Euergetes I.

the royal purse. Still it enabled the king to meet great public wants from that private purse. It transpires from a solitary allusion in the Petric Papyri (II. p. 99), that he brought back captives not merely for the purpose of exchange or sale, but to settle them as cultivators of the land, probably of the Crown land. This shows that he sought to increase the population of Egypt. His care to discover and restore the lost gods of Egypt was a policy pointed out to him by the records of both his father and his grandfather. But what they could only do to a trifling extent, his victories enabled him to do wholesale.

How came it, then, that he should be compelled to hurry home from Asia by a *domestica seditio*? I do not for a moment believe, as Droysen does (iii. 403), that by this phrase is meant a revolt of Cyrene. Why should such a revolt be called by so misleading a name?[1]

If we compare the Adule inscription, dating from about the king's fourth year, with the decree of Canopus passed in his ninth, we shall remark at once the contrast of style. In the former the king is a Greek hero, descended from Herakles and Dionysus, who sets out to conquer Asia without any better reason than mere glory. In the latter he is the son and grandson of Egyptian deified kings, whose main merits are his benevolences to the gods of Egypt, and whose wars are carried on in defence or promotion of the prosperity of Egypt. The bringing back of the gods of Egypt from Persia is the only feature common to both. If, as Letronne and Revillout maintain, the Canopus inscription was originally drawn up in Greek, the argument would be even stronger to show that the whole attitude of the king is changed. We know that in the following year he began one of the greatest of extant temples, that of Edfu in Upper Egypt. It seems likely that the change was induced by the "domestic sedition" which recalled him from Asia ; and this again may have been induced by the threatened famine

---

[1] Droysen bases his inference on the statement of Polybius (x. 22), that two philosophers from Megalopolis, Ekdemos and Demophanes, after assisting in the *liberation* of several Peloponnesian cities from their tyrants, were invited to Cyrene, where they became distinguished for directing the people and preserving their liberty. ἐπιφανῶς προύστησαν καὶ διεφύλαξαν αὐτοῖς τὴν ἐλευθερίαν. This expression is contrasted with the ἠλευθέρωσαν of the previous sentence, and clearly means that by ordering the internal government, and putting an end to intestine quarrels, they enabled the Cyrenaean cities to maintain their communal independence under Ptolemy's rule. I have elsewhere (*Hermathena*, xxii. 393 *seq.*) shown how in this age democratic constitutions and internal independence were constantly associated with the control of an outside *Benefactor* or king. All the cities of Cyprus, for example, were democracies controlled by kings. In the case of Cyrenaean cities, as soon as there was internal disorder, Ptolemy's officers and garrisons at once assumed direct control ; while there was peace and order they were probably kept as much out of sight as possible.

to which the Canopus stone makes allusion as having happened some time before (ποτε).

The most reasonable combination of the scanty facts seems to be this: During the king's long absence, perhaps in his third year, occurred the threat of famine, from the failure of the normal inundation. We can imagine both priests and people complaining that their king was far away wasting the wealth and population of Egypt upon foreign expeditions. Perhaps he had given lands to many foreigners, and so diminished the scope of native industry. This discontent may have been exacerbated by hunger, and the king may suddenly have learned that while subduing foreign nations he might lose his own before his return. and

FIG. 31.—Coin of Berenike II. (from Cyrene).

after the first burst of jubilation as a Greek conqueror was over, he may have studied the national question more carefully, and resolved that for the future he must pay greater attention to national needs and sentiments. We never again find any Ptolemaic inscription similar to that of Adule. In later days such ·a document would have been an insult to the nation ; perhaps it was so even then. The reason for which the king set it up in this far country we can only conjecture. He can hardly have returned from Babylon by the sea route round Arabia. Such a voyage, though then undertaken by adventurous traders, was out of the question for a sovereign and his army. But he showed great interest in the elephant-hunting to the south, and may even have spent some time in this outlying province as crown prince.

At all events, after his return we hear of no more expeditions to Syria or even the Levant, but only of home policy and of the management of foreign enemies by diplomatic means. Mr. Floyer, in his researches through the eastern desert of Egypt, has found traces of stations dating from this king, possibly established for mere hunting parties. For at this time the camel was not yet introduced as a beast of burden into Egypt, and so the vegetation of the desert was much richer. Mr. Floyer was the first to show the fatal consequences to the flora of the desert produced by the camel. There are also two scraps of evidence from early papyri which may be thought to prove that the king continued to pay attention to his frontier on the Red Sea. The first is in the Grenfell Papyri, vol. I. ix., which mentions payment for a mercenary crew (πληρωμα) employed in the Red Sea ; dated in L 8. The second, dated L 24, —I think of this reign,—is the curious letter I have printed in the P.P. II. xl. (a), which speaks of a party of Egyptians,

FIG. 32.—Græco - Egyptian bronze statuette (Alexandria). (From the Petrie collection.)

probably soldiers at Berenike, whose supplies were brought to them by an elephant transport which had been wrecked. The writer consoles them by telling them that help by land is prepared and going to them. But how can we fit these isolated facts into the king's general history?

We come now to consider the circumstances of the decree of Canopus, which is fortunately preserved to us in two almost complete copies, as well as in a much damaged copy now in the Louvre. Its object is to add to the divine honours already accorded to the king and queen as Benefactor Gods, and to assign divine honours to their infant daughter, who died suddenly during the sitting of the conclave of priests.

We shall begin by giving a complete translation of the document.[1]

" In the reign of Ptolemy son of Ptolemy and Arsinoe, Brother Gods, year 9, Apollonides son of Moschion being priest of Alexander and the Gods Adelphi and the Gods Euergetæ, Menekrateia daughter of Philammon being Kanephoros of Arsinoe Philadelphos, on the 7th of (the month) Apellaios, but of the Egyptians the 17th of Tybi. DECREE. The chief priests and prophets and those who enter the inner shrine for the robing of the gods and the feather-bearers and the sacred scribes and the rest of the priests who came together from the temples throughout the land for the 5th of Dios, on which the birth-feasts of the king are celebrated, and for the 25th of the same month, on which he received the sovereignty from his father,[2] in formal assembly on this day in the temple of the Benefactor Gods in Canopus declared :—Since king Ptolemy son of Ptolemy and Arsinoe, Brother Gods, and Berenike, his sister and wife, Benefactor Gods, are continually performing many great benefits to the national temples, and increasing

---

[1] It was first published (1866) in hieroglyphic and Greek, the former very inaccurately (says Wilbour), by the discoverer Lepsius, who had not observed the demotic version round the edge of the stone ; since that partially by Wescher in the *Rev. Arch.*, and completely in a cheap and handy 8vo form by Reinach and Rösler. The most recent reprints are in my *Empire of the Ptolemies*, pp. 226 *seq.*, with a brief commentary (not here repeated), and by Strack in his *Dynastie der Ptolemäer*, No. 38, who has also given the variants of the duplicate copy in the Gizeh Museum. These I had carefully noted independently in 1895. My commentary takes account of the transcript and translation of the demotic version by E. Revillout in his *Chrestomathie démotique*, with the Greek in parallel columns.

[2] It seems to me certain, that from all absence of any mention of an enthronement at Memphis in the temple of Ptah (a fact stated over and over again on the Rosetta stone in the case of Ptolemy V.) that this king and his two predecessors did not condescend to any specially Egyptian coronation.

the honours of the gods, and in every respect take
good care of Apis and Mnevis and the other renowned
sacred animals with great expense and good appointments ; and the sacred images carried off from the
land by the Persians, the king having made a foreign
campaign, recovered into Egypt, and restored to the
temples from which each of them had been carried
away ; and has kept the land in peace, defending it
with arms against many nations and their sovereigns ;
and afford [1] (*sic*) good government to all that dwell in
the land and to all others who are subject to their
sovereignty ; and when the river once failed to rise
sufficiently and all in the land were in despair at what
had occurred, and called to mind the disasters which
had occurred under some of the former kings, when it
happened that the inhabitants of the land suffered from
want of inundation ; (they) protecting with care both
those that dwelt in the temples and the other inhabitants,
with much forethought, and foregoing not a little of
their revenue for the sake of saving life, sending for
corn for the country from Syria, Phœnicia, Cyprus, and
many other lands at high prices, saved the dwellers
in Egypt, thus bequeathing an immortal benefaction,
and the greatest record of their own merit both to this
and future generations, in requital for which the gods
have given them their royalty well established, [2] and
will give them all other good things for all time. WITH
THE FAVOUR OF FORTUNE: It is decreed by the priests
throughout the country : [3] to increase the pre-existing
honours in the temples to king Ptolemy and queen
Berenike, Benefactor Gods, and to their parents the
Brother Gods, and to their parents the Saviour Gods,
and that the priests in each of the temples throughout
the country shall be entitled in addition priests of the

[1] The plural nom. (king and queen) is here silently resumed.

[2] The order of the words makes ευσταθουσαν a second predicate,
so that it may mean "have granted that their royalty be well
established," perhaps an indication that the reverse case was a
threatening possibility.

[3] κατα την χωραν might also mean *on the spot*, but then it would
have been supplemented by some word such as *assembled*.

IV—8

Benefactor Gods, and that there be inserted on all their documents, and added to the engraving of the rings which they wear, the priesthood of the Benefactor Gods, and that there be constituted in addition to the now existing 4 tribes of the community of the priests in each temple another, to be entitled the fifth tribe of the Benefactor Gods, since it also happened with good fortune that the birth of king Ptolemy, son of the Brother Gods, took place on the 5th of Dios, which was the beginning of many good things for all mankind ; and that into this tribe be enrolled the priests born [1] since the first year and those to be entered among them up to the month Mesore in the 9th year, and their offspring for ever, but that the pre-existing priests up to the first year shall remain in the tribes in which they were, and likewise that their children shall henceforth be enrolled in the tribes of their fathers ; and that instead of the 20 Councillor priests chosen each year from the pre-existing 4 tribes, of whom 5 are taken from each tribe, the Councillor priests shall be 25, an additional 5 being chosen from the 5th tribe of the Benefactor Gods ; and that the members of the 5th tribe of the Benefactor Gods shall share in the holy offices and everything else in the temples, and that there shall be a phylarch thereof, as is the case with the other tribes. AND since there are celebrated every month in the temples feasts of the Benefactor Gods according to the previous decree, viz. the 1st and 9th and 25th, and to the other supreme gods are performed yearly national feasts and solemn assemblies, there shall be kept yearly a national solemn assembly both in the temples and throughout all the land to king Ptolemy and queen Berenike, Benefactor Gods, on the day when the star of Isis rises, which is held in the sacred books to be the new year, and is now in this 9th year kept on the 1st of the month Payni, on which

---

[1] Krall (*Studien*, etc., ii. 49) points out that the hieroglyphic text of this word γεγενημενοις reads: [the priests] " whom the king has inducted into the temples," thus confessing the supremacy of the crown. Lepsius' bracketing of και and δε is here misleading.

the little Bubastia and the great Bubastia are celebrated, and the gathering of the crops and the rise of the river takes place ; but if it happen that the rising of the star changes to another day in 4 years, the feast shall not be changed, but shall still be kept on the 1st of Payni, on which it was originally held in the 9th year, and it shall last for 5 days with wearing of crowns and sacrifices and libations and the other suitable observances ; AND in order that the seasons may correspond regularly according to the establishment of the world,[1] and in order that it may not occur that some of the national feasts kept in winter may come to be kept in summer, the sun changing one day in every four years, and that other feasts now kept in summer may come to be kept in winter in future times, as has formerly happened, and now would happen if the arrangement of the year remained of 360 days, and the five additional days added ; from now onward one day, a feast of the Benefactor Gods, shall be added every four years to the five additional days before the new year, in order that all may know that the former defect in the arrangement of the seasons and the year and the received opinions concerning the whole arrangement of the heavens has been corrected and made good by the Benefactor Gods.

"And since it happened that the daughter born of king Ptolemy and queen Berenike, Benefactor Gods, and called Berenike, who was also forthwith declared queen, being yet a virgin, passed away suddenly into the ever-lasting world,[2] while the priests who came together to the king every year from the country were yet with him, who forthwith made great lamentation at the

[1] There is evidence that this excellent reform was not adopted by the priests generally, so that it is an anticipation of our reformed calendar, made in Egypt, but not adopted in Europe for many centuries.

[2] The form of the sentence would lead us to think that she died in her earliest infancy, but this seems not to be the case, for there is a green vase extant with the inscription θεων ευεργετων Βερενικης βασιλισσης αγαθης τιχης (Strack, No. 48), which is referred to this princess.

occurrence, and having petitioned the king and queen, persuaded them to settle the goddess with Osiris in the temple in Canopus, which is not only among the temples of first rank, but is among those most honoured by the king and all in the country [1]—and the procession of the sacred boat of Osiris to this temple takes place yearly from the temple in the Heracleion on the 29th of Choiach, when all those of the first-class temples contribute sacrifices upon the altars established by them on both sides of the way—and after this they performed the ceremonies of her deification and the conclusion of the mourning with pomp and circumstance, as is the custom in the case of Apis Mnevis. IT IS DECREED : to perform everlasting honours to queen Berenike, daughter of the Benefactor Gods, in all the temples of the land ; and since she passed away to the gods in the month Tybi, in which also the daughter of the Sun in the beginning changed her life, whom her loving father sometimes called his diadem, some-times his sight, and they celebrate to her a feast and a boat-procession in most of the first-rank temples in this month, in which her apotheosis originally took place—[it is decreed] to perform to queen Berenike also, daughter of the Benefactor gods, in all the temples of the land in the month Tybi a feast, a boat procession for four days from the 17th, in which the procession and concluding of the mourning originally took place ; also to accomplish a sacred image of her, gold and jewelled, in each of the first and second rank temples, and set it up in the (inner) shrine, which the prophet or those of the priests who enter the adytum for the robing of the gods shall bear in his arms, when the going abroad and feasts of the other gods take place, in order that being seen by all it may be honoured

---

[1] This statement evidently refers to the dedication of which the gold plate was once in the British Museum, but has now disappeared, namely : βασιλευς Πτολεμαιος, Πτολεμαιου και Αρσινοης | Θεων Αδελφων, και βασιλισσα Βερενικη, η αδελφη | και γυνη αιτου, το τεμενος Οσιρει. Apparently then he had added to the enclosure round the temple.

and worshipped as that of Berenike, queen of the maidens ; AND that the diadem placed upon her image shall differ from that set upon the head of her mother queen Berenike by two ears of corn, in the midst of which shall be the asp-shaped diadem, and behind this a suitable papyrus-shaped sceptre, such as queens are wont to hold in their hands, about which also the tail of the diadem shall be wound, so that from the disposition of the diadem the name of Berenike shall be signified according to the symbols of the sacred grammar ; and when the Kikellia[1] are celebrated in the month Choiach before the second cruise of Osiris,

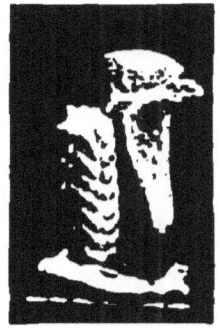 

FIG. 33.—The head-dress of the young Berenike (two sides, asps and ears of corn). (From the M'Gregor collection.)

the maidens and the priests shall prepare another image of Berenike, queen of maidens, to which they shall perform likewise a sacrifice and the other observances performed at this feast, and it shall be lawful in the same way for any other maidens that choose to perform the customary observances to the goddess ; and that she shall be hymned both by the chosen

[1] We know nothing of the Kikellia, but it seems to me probable that there were some duties established for maidens coming of age to this deified princess—at least, if my restoration of the Grenfell Papyri I. xvii. line 11 be correct, ενηλικοι δε | [ημεις γενο]μεναι τα καθηκοντα τελη θεαι Περενικηι κυρι | [αι παρθενων] εδωκαμεν εν τωι λ I., etc. It is an objection, but not a strong one, that if so, κυρια is substituted for ανασσα, the term in the decree.

sacred maidens and by those that are in service to the gods, putting on them the several diadems of the gods whose priestesses they are wont to be ; and when the early [1] harvest is at hand, the sacred maidens shall offer up the ears which are to be set before the image of the goddess ; and that the singing men and the women shall sing to her by day, in the feasts and assemblies of the remaining gods also, whatever hymns the sacred scribes, having composed, may hand over to the teacher of choirs, of which also copies shall be entered in the sacred books ; and when the rations (of corn) are given to the priests out of the sacred property, when they are brought to the whole caste, there shall be given to the daughters of the priests from the sacred revenues, (counting) from whatever day they may be born, the maintenance determined by the councillor priests in each of the temples (?) in proportion to the sacred revenues ; and the bread served out to the wives of the priests shall have a peculiar shape, and be called the bread of Berenike.   But the overseer and high priest appointed in each of the temples and the scribes of the temple shall copy this decree on a stone or bronze stele in sacred writing, both in Egyptian and in Greek, and shall set it up in the most conspicuous place in the first, second, and third rank temples, in order that the priests throughout the land may show that they honour the Benefactor Gods and their children, as is just."

I think that the notice in S. Jerome is correct, namely, that the title *Euergetæ* was specially conferred upon the king and queen early in their reign, not at their coronation.   He says it was after Ptolemy's return from Asia, and in consequence of the restored images of the gods ; in any case, it was most probably the προτερον γραφεν δογμα of line 33.   I also infer from the silence of the decree regarding the building of temples, that this part of the king's activity came later in his reign, certainly after his title of Euergetes, which

---

[1] Our two texts have respectively (A) προωριμος, (B) πρωιμος.   In neither is the meaning clear.

appears in most of the temple inscriptions, but not in the pompous Adule text, nor in the dedication at Philæ.

The wording of the concluding directions concerning the distribution of bread to the priests and their daughters seems to me intentionally vague, and the king's interference in the temple property, of which we know so much in the previous reign, is carefully hidden. Yet this additional claim on the temple revenues for the *bread of Berenike* must surely have been a concession from the crown for what they had sequestrated from the national church property.

I have already argued in another place (*Emp. Ptol.* p. 226) against Letronne and Revillout, that this decree, being a purely Egyptian and priestly affair, was, in the first instance, drawn up in demotic, and then transcribed and translated into hieroglyphics (the archaic and ceremonial script) and into Greek. The longer I examine it, the less can I understand any other order in the composition.

For the rest of the acts of the king, both home and foreign, we have but scanty information, and still scantier dates. We know of his founding and adorning many Egyptian temples, but the succession in which he did so is difficult to determine. The text of Canopus, seeing that neither the title *Gods Benefactors* nor the royal children are mentioned, may have been the earliest. That recently discovered by Captain Lyons over the north portal of the great hall of columns at Philæ, begun and well-nigh completed by Philadelphus, may be the next, seeing that while children are mentioned, the title *Euergetæ* is not.[1] There are still remains of a small temple at Aswan, begun by this king, and of course in purely Egyptian style. A very similar temple, containing an account of his cam-

---

[1] Here is the text : βασιλευς Πτολεμαιος βασιλεως Πτολεμαιου και Αρσινοης θεων αδελφων και βασιλισσα Βερενικη η βασιλεως Πτολεμαιου αδελφη και γυνη και τα τουτων τεκνα τον ναον Ισει και Αρποκρατηι. This text, cut deeply over the doorway, and the letters gilt, was discovered by mere cleaning of the dust from the surface.

paigns, was set up at Esneh, but destroyed in this
century by an enterprising pasha.

FIG. 34.—Pylon of Ptolemy III. at Karnak.

The pylon or pylons at Karnak, where the king is
said to be represented in a semi-Greek costume, are

totally undated, but may have come later in his reign.
The one fixed point is the foundation of the great
temple of Edfu, commenced, according to the explicit
chronological account still preserved in hieroglyphics
on the temple, in his tenth year, shortly after the
decree of Canopus. Thus the building of temples
to the national gods all over Egypt occupied the
attention of the king. Quite exceptional and remarkable is the dedication of a Greek temple to Greek
gods by Greek priests recently found near Alexandria
(Ramleh), and now in the museum of that city:
"on behalf of king Ptolemy, son of Ptolemy and
Arsinoe, Brother Gods, and of queen Berenike, wife
and sister of the king, Benefactor Gods, Kleon and
Antipater, priests of Zeus (have dedicated), the altars
and sacred enclosure, and the land appertaining to it,
to the Brother gods, Olympian Zeus, and Zeus the god
of confederacies."[1]

This curious document naturally leads us to say a
word upon the king's foreign relations, which I have
treated more fully in another place. We know that
he had a garrison, like his predecessors, at Thera; he
appointed officers to manage his naval supremacy in
the Ægean; he played off several Greek politicians
against one another, and against his dangerous rival
Antigonus of Macedonia, by large subsidies, but not,
so far as we hear, by sending out great fleets. It is
the quarrels of the Greek patriots, and the good fortune
that the lives of three of them—Agis and Cleomenes,
kings of Sparta, Aratus, president of the Achæan
League—are given us by Plutarch, which disclose

---

[1] After the usual formula, which I need not repeat, comes: και
Θεοις | Αδελφοις Δυι Ολυμπιωι και Δυι | Συνωμοσιωι τους βωμους | και τα
τεμενη και την συν ' κυρουσαν αυτοις γην Κλεων | και Αντιπατρος οι
ιερεις | του Διος. The first και is evidently misplaced, and should
come after αδελφοις. The epithet Συνωμοσιος applied to Zeus is
very curious, and does not occur elsewhere. The substantive
means a conspiracy, but also (less frequently) a mere confederacy
sanctioned by oaths. This dedication refers therefore, possibly,
to some confederation of Greek coast cities and islands with
Ptolemy, such as that of the Cyclades.

to us how the Egyptian king was the figure in the background, controlling Greek patriotism (as the king of Persia had often done in olden days) by diplomacy, enforced by large doles and bribes.

He set up votive monuments at Olympia, particularly a statue to king Cleomenes. At no time was the Museum of Alexandria more flourishing and famous, especially for science, which seems to have had especial attractions for this king. The reform of the calendar above mentioned, and the appointment of the famous Eratosthenes as librarian and educator of his children, attest this honourable taste in the king. Whether he was indeed of the free and easy manners implied by the long story in Josephus of the adventures of his name-sake, the successful tax-farmer of Syria, may be doubted. I am more inclined to give some weight to this story, than are most of my German critics.[1]

The king's energy seems to have waned before he attained old age, and when he died, after twenty-five years' reign (221 B.C.), he can hardly have been more than sixty-three years old. His death is variously attributed to disease, and to the wickedness of his son, whom Justin openly accuses of parricide. But the former view is to be preferred, for reasons which will appear in the sequel. The king left three children, his heir, Magas, and a young daughter named Arsinoe. His wife Berenike II. and his brother Lysimachus also survived him. His empire and its dependencies were never in a more flourishing condition.

The last acts we know in his life do not concern Egypt, but his foreign policy. He had long been supporting Aratus of Sicyon and his Achæan League as a counterpoise to the king of Macedonia, who threatened to take possession not only of Greece, but also of the islands under Egyptian sway. Finding Aratus expensive and treacherous, he sought an abler and more effective ally in king Cleomenes of Sparta, who seemed likely to combine all Greece under the

[1] Cf. *Empire of the Ptolemies*, pp. 216 *seq.*, and Willrich, *op. cit.* § 4.

old historic sovereignty of Sparta. But after a long campaign, Antigonus Doson of Macedonia managed to arrange matters with Ptolemy, who withdrew his subsidies, so that Cleomenes was obliged to fight the battle of Sellasia (221 B.C.), which he lost, and was obliged to fly to Egypt, where he was kindly received at court by the ageing and now perhaps dying king. The powerful Antigonus died suddenly soon after his victory, and so relieved Egypt of a dangerous neighbour.

During this war, we cannot tell the exact date, Rhodes was visited by a terrible earthquake, which half-ruined the city, threw down the great Colossus, and threatened all the Hellenistic world with commercial failures, owing to the collapse of the banks. Ptolemy came forward loyally, with all the neighbouring kings, to relieve the distress of the great trading city, and promised as his gift "300 talents of silver, a million artabæ of corn, ship timber for 10 quinqueremes and 10 triremes, consisting of 40,000 cubits of squared pine planking, 1000 talents of bronze coinage, 180,000 pounds of tow (for ropes), 3000 pieces of sailcloth, 3000 talents (of copper) for the repair of the Colossus, 100 master-builders with 350 workmen, and 14 talents yearly to pay their wages. Besides this, he gave 12,000 artabæ of corn for their public games and sacrifices, and 20,000 artabæ for victualling 10 triremes. The greater part of these goods were delivered at once, as well as one-third of the money named" (Polybius, v. 88). The other donors were Antigonus (who died before Ptolemy), Seleucus of Syria, etc. The next king of Egypt seems to have carried out the obligations unfulfilled at his father's death.

If we take up the documents recovered from the Fayyum, and seek from them the inner life of at least one province of Egypt, we find in them no considerable change from those already cited under Philadelphus' reign. New officials have replaced the old; there is not in the correspondence so much talk of organising the nome; but there are the same sort of

complaints from native workmen, that they are disappointed in supplies, or in being relieved, and these
complaints seem always met by the order to see that
they are removed, not by any harsh refusal, far less by
the exhibition of force.   There were no doubt hardships
remaining: there are several petitions from people
imprisoned, and kept there without trial; but the old
tyrant's jeer, "Ye are idle, ye are idle, get you to
your labours," is no longer the language of the Crown
or of its officials.   Among these latter we begin to find
(though exceptionally) natives, such as Phaies the
œconomus, and possibly under the Greek names of
such officials are hidden others who assumed them as
translations of their native names.

Still the king and court did not dream of understanding or learning Egyptian.   The famous Eratosthenes
was specially brought to instruct the prince royal, and
we hear no more of attempts to translate foreign
documents or ancient records of the subject race, such
as had been the fashion under Philadelphus.   The
scientific turn of the king, shown by his attempted
reform of the calendar, is further exhibited in the
extant poem addressed to him by Eratosthenes,
who solves a geometrical problem, and dedicates the
solution with flattering words to the king and the
crown prince.[1]

Thus what evidence we possess—it is indeed miserably scanty—shows us this remarkable king turning
from a successful warrior into a good-natured but
lazy patron of politicians, of priests, and of pedants.
His character is lost to us.   As it appears through
the mist, we seem to feel that it was rather his circumstances than his character that made him great; and
yet the moral soundness of his life,—scandal never
touched him,—compared with the looseness of Ptolemies
before and after him, makes us feel that the want of

---

[1] This poem was first vindicated and explained in a remarkable
article by Wilamowitz ("ein Weihgeschenk des Eratosthenes,"
Gött. G.A. for 1895); and for Eratosthenes' other scientific work,
cf. Susemihl, or my *Greek Life and Thought*, p. 545.

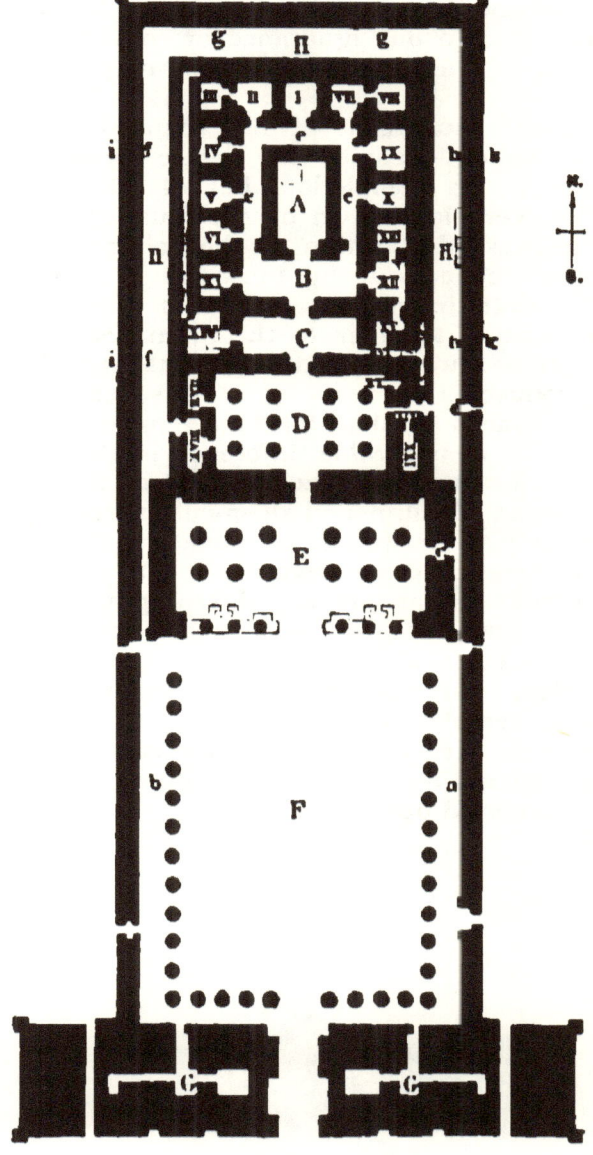

FIG. 35.—General Plan of the Temple of Edfu.
(A B C D, and the chambers surrounding them, are the work of Euergetes I.)

expression and colour in his life, as we know it, may be merely due to our ignorance or to the neglect of those vulgar anecdotists who seek only for piquant details.

The great monument of his reign is the temple of Edfu, which occupied the whole dynasty of the Ptolemies in its completion, but of which the plan and lines were laid down by the founder in 236 B.C. It is the great declaration of the solidarity of internal policy carried out by these kings ; and shows, I think, that in matters religious they were one and all content to defer to the great corporations of native priests, whose fixed traditions and hereditary ideas produced that unity of style so remarkable in this, and indeed in all, Ptolemaic temples.   There is, of course, a considerable difference in the decoration from that of older work, such as that of the Ramessid era.   Instead of huge and deep-cut hieroglyphics we have a far greater wealth of much smaller and more ornate writing, covering the walls as with a rich pattern. If the increase in the quantity of writing had caused the gravers to seek out information and give us historical statements, the change would have been by us highly appreciated.   But alas ! the long inscriptions on these Ptolemaic temples only exaggerate the old vice of dealing with hardly anything but honorary titles, and the commemoration of the various dignities and divine favours conferred upon the kings.

CHAPTER V

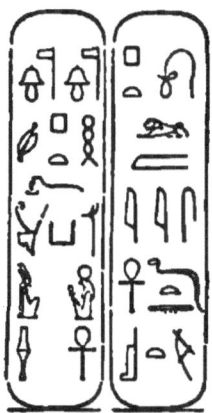

Fig. 36. Cartouches of Ptolemy IV.

AUTHORITIES.—In this chapter our main ancient authority is
  Polybius, who begins his formal history at the moment of
  Philopator's accession. There is also much in Josephus and
  in the 3rd Maccabees upon this reign, as well as in Plutarch's
  Life of Cleomenes. Inscriptions and papyri are as yet scarce
  from this period; but the former will be found in Strack's
  Ptolemäer, a few of the latter in the end of vol. ii. of the Petrie
  Papyri.

THE fourth Ptolemy succeeded (222 B.C.) in the heyday
of youth, with his education completed by the greatest
masters, to a great empire, a full treasury, and peace
at home and abroad. Yet, in the opinion of our Greek
authorities, Polybius and Strabo, no member of the
dynasty was more criminally worthless, none so care-

less, none so fatal to the greatness and prosperity of
Egypt.

As I have already shown in another place, the evidences from temples at home and inscriptions abroad
leave upon us no such impression. But Polybius is an
authority not to be put lightly aside. Certain it is
that Ptolemy IV., surnamed Philopator, succeeding
about the age of twenty-two,[1] was for the first few years
of his life under the influence of the able but unscrup-
ulous Sosibius, who planned the murders of his brother
Magas and of the queen-mother Berenike, not without
misgivings and fear of the mercenary soldiers, on account
of which he humoured king Cleomenes, as being their
natural leader. Polybius (v. 36) speaks as if this king
had even been conscious of the foul plot. But when
Sosibius died, or lost his influence, Philopator fell
under the domination of a Greek mistress, Agathokleia,
who, with her brother, Agathokles, controlled the youth,
mismanaged the government of the country, and raised
him up enemies on every side. I even conjecture that
they kept him from marrying, in the hope that Agathokleia might produce a child to become an heir to the
throne. It was not till this hope was disappointed that
they permitted his marriage with his sister Arsinoe.

The political atmosphere, which seemed so clear at
the king's accession, soon clouded over. In both
Macedonia and Syria, instead of steady or insignificant
kings, there succeeded at the same time young and
ambitious men, Philip V. and Antiochus III., in his
youth justly called the Great ; and it was very plain
that either of them would soon begin to question the
right of Egypt to control the Ægean and the coast of
Palestine up to Seleukia. Philip was kept very busy

---

[1] His parents were married in 246 B.C., immediately upon his
father's accession ; but his sudden departure for Syria makes it
likely that he did not beget a son till his return, probably in his
third year. Had he left his young wife *enceinte*, and had this
son been born in his absence, I think it very probable the poem of
Callimachus (the *Coma Berenices*) would have contained some
allusion to it. I suppose then that Philopator was twenty-two,
not twenty-four, as the historians assume.

with Achæan and Ætolian affairs; but Antiochus,
though a youth of but twenty-one, and beset by a great
revolution in his Eastern provinces, a mighty pretender
in Asia Minor (his uncle Achæus), and a still more
troublesome grand vizier, Hermeias, who desired to
control him as Sosibius controlled Ptolemy, overcame
or adjourned all these difficulties, and set to work to
recover Cœle-Syria and Palestine from Egyptian control.
Meanwhile Ptolemy had done nothing to justify his
position but murder his brother Magas, immediately
upon his accession, and his uncle Lysimachus. Polybius
speaks of the party of Magas as if there had been
some movement in Egypt to keep the young debauchee
from the throne. He then devoted himself, says
Polybius, to drunkenness and wantonness, and neglected all his public business, even allowing his
ministers to insult the governors of outlying provinces,
who were holding them faithfully for Egypt.

The affair of the Spartan Cleomenes, whom the
young king received as a sort of legacy from his
father, was of little importance to the history of Egypt,
though Plutarch and his predecessors in Greek history
have made a fine and affecting tragedy of the exile's
failure and death. He was living at Alexandria, hoping
against hope to receive a commission from the Court
to go back and raise Greece against Macedonia, now
that the great Antigonus Doson was dead and the
kingdom in the hands of an untried stripling. It is
said that Euergetes had this intention, but the new king
would attend to no foreign affairs, and Cleomenes was
reduced to idling and walking the quays of Alexandria
in hopeless indignation. Very naturally he did not
bridle his tongue, and Sosibius, who knew how dangerous he was in a city full of Greek mercenaries, had him
shut up in a palace which was really a prison. From
this Cleomenes and his friends broke loose, and tried to
call the Alexandrians to liberty, committing, moreover,
a few murders in the streets. The citizens looked at
them with amazement, and slunk into their houses in
great apprehension of the consequences. So the little

party of thirteen Spartans committed suicide, and no vengeance was left to Ptolemy but to assassinate their families. Danger to his throne there was none from this noble but Quixotic adventurer.

The attack of Antiochus was a very different matter. In the first place, the fortress of Seleukia on the Orontes, which had been the keystone of the Egyptian possession of Cœle-Syria, was taken partly by force, partly by fraud (219 B.C.) ; then Theodotus, Ptolemy's general in Syria, turned traitor, and so Tyre and Ptolemais were lost. Nicolaus, the new general sent to defend Palestine, was defeated ; and it was only by long diplomatic discussions, and the solicited interference of mediating Greek cities, that the advance of Antiochus was delayed for at least a year. This policy of delay was absolutely necessary to Egypt, for, according to Polybius, Ptolemy had altogether neglected the defence of the country, and there was no army ready to fight. Sosibius and Agathocles set to work with vigour to mend this defeat ; but it astonishes us to think that in three years after the death of Euergetes, Egypt was already in such a helpless condition. It is more than

FIG. 37.—Ptolemy IV. (From bronze ring in the possession of Mr. Petrie.)

likely that the old king, growing weak and slothful with years or with failing health, was more to blame than his son. He evidently trusted in his later years to diplomacy and to bribery to maintain his interests abroad, and he may have thought the maintenance of a mercenary army too expensive, when it seemed a mere luxury. Thus the fourth Ptolemy may have succeeded to a kingdom without an army, and was certainly not the man to set to work with vigour to renew the defences of Egypt. Polybius turns aside to describe with considerable detail the preparations made by Sosibius to meet the emergency, and how a great army was gathered and trained at Alexandria, while the envoys and mediators from Syria were only allowed

to come as far as Memphis, which was indeed on the
high road from Syria to Alexandria, but was separated
from it by 90 miles of river.[1]

The task of the Egyptian ministry was twofold:
first, to gather from Greece, Thrace, Crete, Asia
Minor as many mercenary forces as was possible;
secondly, to make what use they could of the home
forces of Egypt. The former was a mere matter of
money; for the latter they obtained from Greece three
military men, trained in the wars of Antigonus Doson
and his predecessor Demetrius II., who took in hand
the mass ($\pi\lambda\tilde{\eta}\theta\upsilon\varsigma$) of the natives, and, wholly disregarding the old native caste of $\mu\alpha\chi\iota\mu\omega\iota$ and its armour, reformed the recruits into a Macedonian phalanx, trained
with the sarissa, and taught to understand and obey
Greek or Macedonian words of command. There was
already a force of cavalry available from the household
troops and those settled in the country, as we know
from the Fayyum papyri. To these were added Libyan
cavalry, which had probably been organised at Cyrene.
The whole of this force amounted to 3000, which, allowing 700, which Polybius gives, for the household cavalry
of Alexandria, and perhaps 500 for the Libyans, leaves
1800 as the probable number of cavalry soldiers settled
in the country. But there were also 4000 Thracians
settled both as $\kappa\alpha\tau\omega\iota\kappa\omega\iota$ and $\epsilon\pi\iota\gamma\upsilon\upsilon\iota$, which were united
with 2000 Galatæ, specially imported, in one force.

This exposition assumes that the text of Polybius
(v. 64-5) has been confused by the excerptor, and so
misunderstood. There appear to be two phalanxes
mentioned, one under Andromachus and Ptolemy of
25,000 men, another native, under Sosibius, of 20,000.
From the subsequent account of the battle of Raphia, it
seems clear that there was only one Egyptian phalanx,
that of the natives, and that it was commanded (as was
that of Antiochus) by two commanders. The former
passage, then, merely refers to the *training* of the single
phalanx, which afterwards appeared under Sosibius'

[1] Historians have not appreciated that the only high road from
Alexandria into Syria and Palestine lay through Memphis.

command, and probably amounted to 20,000 men. Two phalanxes in the same line of battle are an unheard-of thing in Hellenistic warfare.[1]   On another point Polybius, or at least the excerpt, keeps silence.   At the battle there were seventy-three "Libyan" elephants on the Egyptian side.   This was the force which Philadelphus and Euergetes had collected by their elephant-hunting in Abyssinia during the previous fifty years. At Philadelphus' great pageant, described above (p. 70), there had been a conspicuous absence of war-elephants. We now know, from an inscription preserved by the late Mr. Wilbour (Strack, *Ptolemies*, No. 56),[2] that Philopator also sent out expeditions to obtain elephants, possibly during the very preparations which we have been describing.

I had formerly (*Empire of the Ptolemies*, p. 250) inferred that the ill-success of the African elephants at Raphia must have stopped the troublesome hunting for them in the far south country, but this inference has

---

[1] From this point of view, then, Mr. Shuckburgh's translation of the passage, which I have quoted elsewhere (Greek *Life and Thought*, p. 434; *Empire of the Ptolemies*, p. 252), requires correction; and so do the figures in the subsequent passage of Polybius (v. 79), where Ptolemy's infantry is summed up as 70,000. It was really only 50,000, viz. not $\bar{\mathrm{M}}$, but $\overset{\mathrm{E}}{\mathrm{M}}$.   I also propose to amend the senseless πρῶτον μὲν γὰρ κατὰ γένη καὶ καθ' ἡλικίαν διελόντες ἀνέδοσαν ἑκάστοις τοὺς ἐπιτηδείους καθοπλισμοὺς ὀλιγωρήσαντες τῶν προτέρων αὐτοῖς ὑπαρχόντων, μετὰ δὲ ταῦτα συνέταξαν οἰκείως, etc., λύσαντες τὰ συστήματα καὶ τὰς ἐκ τῶν πρότερον ὀψωνιασμῶν καταγραφάς into πρῶτον μὲν γὰρ οὐ κατὰ γενη ἀλλὰ καθ' ἡλικίαν, etc., or καθ' ἡλικίαν δέ.   The γενη refers to the Hermotybians and Calasirians mentioned by Herodotus, and of which Revillout has found quite a late mention.   Thus I translate : "for first dividing the πλῆθος of the soldier caste, not by their [two] classes, but according to age, they gave to each its suitable weapons, without any regard to the arms of the natives, and then drilled them suitably to the present need, abolishing their former organisation, and the muster-rolls based upon their former receipt of pay."   We know from Papyrus 63 of the Louvre and elsewhere that the μάχιμοι received monthly allowances in kind as well as some share of land.

[2] Mr. Hall has pointed out very justly that even this inscription, which commemorates the second expedition of Lichas, must date from the days after Raphia, and even after 212 B.C., as it mentions Arsinoe III. *as queen*.

been proved false by Mr. H. R. Hall (of the British Museum) by the light of a newly-found inscription (published in *Class. Review* for June 1898), which is a dedication on behalf of king Ptolemy and queen Arsinoe, Gods Philopatores, and of their son Ptolemy, etc., to Ares Euagros, by Alexander, son of Syndikos of Oroanna, who was sent out together with Charimortos, the general, to hunt elephants, and by Apoaris, son of Miorbollos the Etennean, the captain ($\eta\gamma\epsilon\mu\omega\nu$), and the soldiers under him. The mention of the infant Ptolemy, not born till 210 B.C., shows that even after Raphia this outlying occupation of soldiers continued. Charimortos was an Ætolian mercenary otherwise known to us from Polybius; the others Pisidian mercenaries, probably chosen as skilled in slinging, to meet the formidable archery of the natives, of which we hear from Strabo (cf. the facsimile of this text on p. 138).

After many delays and discussions, the two armies, making a leisurely and deliberate approach, met at Raphia in southern Palestine, near Gaza, where a pitched battle was fought, which Polybius describes with minuteness but not with clearness. Before the battle the commanders rode along their respective lines, especially exhorting their phalanxes, in which they evidently placed their confidence.[1] Ptolemy was accompanied by his young sister Arsinoe, who excited great sympathy among the soldiery. This is told with emphasis in the 3rd book of Maccabees, and may be copied from some fuller account of the battle than that of Polybius. The elephants were stationed on the two wings of each army and in advance of the cavalry, so that they began the battle. While the conflict was raging, Antiochus, commanding his own right wing against Ptolemy in person, rode round the elephants and turned Ptolemy's flank, which was thus defeated, and the king driven behind his phalanx. But while Antiochus went in pursuit of the broken wing, the

[1] This is, in all the wars of the Diadochi, a marked feature in contrast to Alexander. With him heavy cavalry was always the deciding arm. Now infantry was again superior.

same manœuvre was carried out against his left wing
by Echecrates, who did not go too far in pursuit.
There were left the two phalanxes in the centre, of
which the Egyptian was encouraged by the presence
of the king and his sister.   In the charge which ensued
the Syrian phalanx broke and fled, leaving Ptolemy
victor in spite of the defeat of his left wing and the
rout and capture of almost all his elephants.   For
it was now found upon trial in action that African
elephants would not face the Indian (Polybius, v. 81).
But how Ptolemy's elephants were carried off by the
vanquished Syrians, or why their victorious elephants,
over a hundred in number, did nothing to retrieve the
battle or to shake the Egyptian phalanx, the historian
does not tell us.   So far then his account is incomplete.   But we hear enough to understand why the
hunting after Troglodyte elephants seems to have been
gradually abandoned.

We are told that Ptolemy, probably astonished at his
own success, was content with it, and made easy terms
with Antiochus, retaining Palestine, but not Seleukia,
and requiring no war indemnity.   As he spent three
months going about the cities of Phœnicia and Palestine
as victor, I believe the story in 3rd Maccabees that he
went to Jerusalem, and insolently entered the Holy of
Holies.   The exaggerations of the story, and the fit
which seized the king, may be the writer's invention.
But it is clear that from henceforth Philopator and the
Jews were at variance, and that the latter were persecuted or discouraged in Egypt in various ways.   This is
the reason why they have blackened his memory and
assailed his character in this curious book.   Nevertheless, for the rest of his life Philopator secured to
Egypt the quiet possession of the Syrian provinces,
nor did Antiochus attempt the conquest of them till
the king was dead and his son, an infant, upon the
throne.   We cannot but feel that the Syrian was not
restrained by oaths and treaties, but by the knowledge
that the Egyptian government was not of the character
ascribed to its king—weak, slothful, and improvident.

Probably the lesson. taught to Antiochus by the native Egyptian phalanx was a very serious one.   If the Fellahs could be taught to stand and fight, even in masses, with pikes, they formed a force which in those days was thought the heart of a good army.

On the other hand, we know from an extract of Polybius (v. 297) that this weapon cut both ways. The natives learned their strength, and began to meditate a revolution under leaders of their own; and it was not long till they found one. It is most unfortunate that Polybius was not more explicit concerning the formation of the phalanx by the three experienced soldiers already mentioned.

Meanwhile, the accounts of the king's private life and the internal management of the country seem not to have been consistent.   He is said by Revillout, on the evidence of demotic papyri, not to have been invested with the title God Philopator till after his fifth year of royalty, viz. after, and probably in consequence of, the victory at Raphia.   But Revillout has already in other cases misled himself and others by arguments from demotic deciphering and arguments from the omission of a royal title in a business document.   I, therefore, here question the correctness of his inference.   Of the fifteen extant Greek inscriptions which mention the king, only one (Strack, 53) omits the title, the other fourteen have it, though one of them, mentioning his son, omits his queen (57).   Is it likely that if the five first years of his reign (out of seventeen) were spent without the title, this would be so?   The antecedent probabilities are strongly against it.   Wilcken (art. "Arsinoe III." in Pauly-Wissowa) refers to Poole's *Coins* for support of Revillout's view, but I cannot find anything in the confused series of these coins which could be called an argument on that side.   It is also stated by Lepsius, and by Revillout from the evidence of demotic papyri, that though Ptolemy Soter was long since deified, he does not appear in the list of associated gods with Alexander and the later Ptolemies till this reign; also that the special cult of Soter at

Ptolemais is now first mentioned. In the latter case, at all events, I consider the *argumentum ex silentio* quite inconclusive.

Having at last been permitted to marry his sister Arsinoe, who brought him an heir in 210 B.C., she too was set aside and privily murdered by the machinations of Agathocles. The king spent his time not altogether in drinking, but in literary amusements. He even wrote a tragedy called *Adonis*, and built a temple to Homer as the king of poets, thus evidently favouring the literary and æsthetic studies of the Museum.

But if we were to assume that he therefore neglected the national religion, we should greatly err. We do indeed hear of his particular devotion to Dionysus in

FIG. 38.—Coin of Arsinoe III. (Philopator).

the 3rd Maccabees, and possibly he may have formed some guild or society in honour of that Greek god, but we have the other policy upon far better evidence, that of the historical text on the great wall of Edfu. "So was the temple built, the inner sanctuary being completed for the golden Horus, up to the year 10, Epeiph the 7th day, in the time of king Ptolemy Philopator. The wall in it was adorned with fair writing, with the great name of His Majesty and with pictures of the gods and goddesses of Edfu, and its great gateway completed, and the double doors of its broad chamber, up to the year 16 of His Majesty. Then there broke out a revolution, and it happened that bands of insurgents hid themselves in the interior of the temple," etc. The building was interrupted for

nearly twenty years.   But what can be plainer than
this text, that the building of the Edfu temple was
being carried on steadily till the last year but one of
the king's life?   Nor is this evidence isolated.   At
Luxor his cartouche is found on various buildings,
showing that if he did not there erect buildings, he
at least decorated them, and desired his name to be
identified with them.   On the opposite side of the river
he certainly founded the beautiful little temple of Dêr-
el-Medineh, which was completed by his successors.

FIG. 39.—Dêr-el-Medineh.

Moreover, at Aswân he attempted the completion
(which he seems not to have accomplished) of the small
temple begun by his father.   This work, then, is on the
same line of policy as that at Edfu.

But, higher up, the evidences of his activity are still
more curious and important.   Not only does his name
appear on various parts of the complex of temples at

Philæ, but the recent researches of Captain Lyons have disclosed a ruined temple of Ar-hes-Nefer on the east

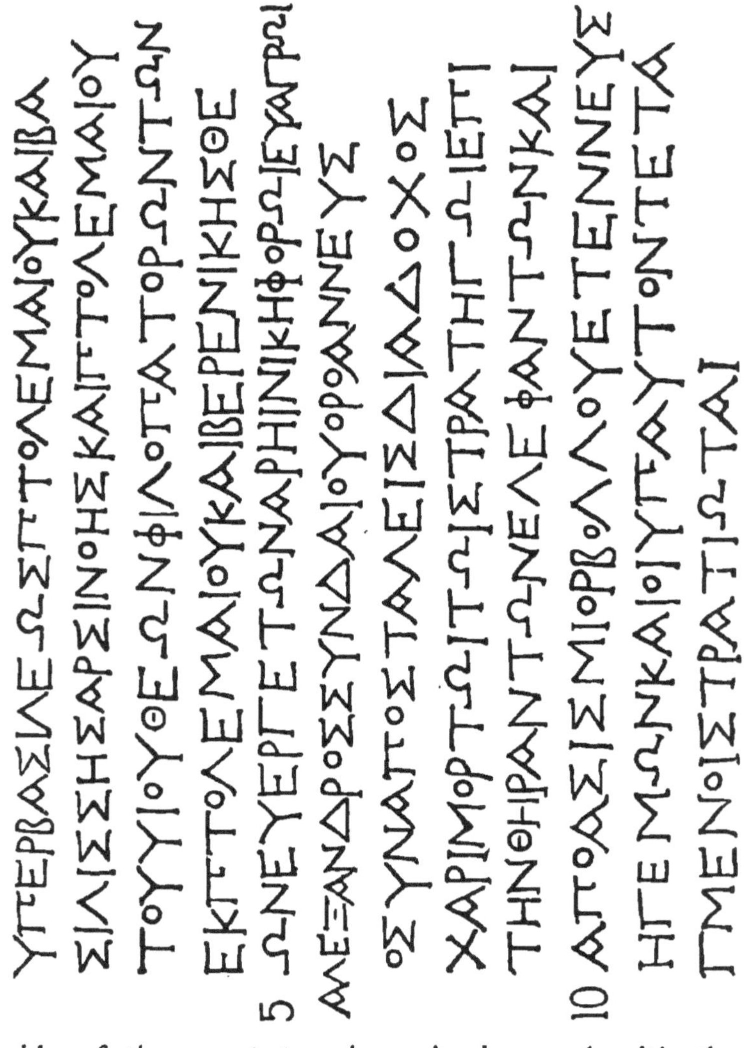

ΥΠΕΡΒΑΣΙΛΕΩΣΠΤΟΛΕΜΑΙΟΥΚΑΙΒΑ
ΣΙΛΙΣΣΗΣΑΡΣΙΝΟΗΣΚΑΙΠΤΟΛΕΜΑΙΟΥ
ΤΟΥΥΙΟΥΘΕΩΝΦΙΛΟΠΑΤΟΡΩΝΤΩΝ
ΕΚΠΤΟΛΕΜΑΙΟΥΚΑΙΒΕΡΕΝΙΚΗΣΘΕ
5 ΩΝΕΥΕΡΓΕΤΩΝΑΡΗΙΝΙΚΗΦΟΡΩΙΕΥΑΓΡΩΙ
ΑΛΕΞΑΝΔΡΟΣΣΥΝΔΑΙΟΥΟΡΟΑΝΝΕΥΣ
ΟΣΥΝΑΤΟΣΤΑΛΕΙΣΔΙΑΔΟΧΟΣ
ΧΑΡΙΜΟΡΤΩΙΤΩΙΣΤΡΑΤΗΓΩΙΕΠΙ
ΤΗΝΘΗΡΑΝΤΩΝΕΛΕΦΑΝΤΩΝΚΑΙ
10 ΑΠΟΛΞΙΣΜΙΟΡΒΟΛΛΟΥΕΤΕΝΝΕΥΣ
ΗΤΕΜΩΝΚΑΙΟΙΥΠΑΥΤΟΝΤΕΤΑ
ΓΜΕΝΟΙΣΤΡΑΤΙΩΤΑΙ

FIG. 40.—Elephant-hunters' Inscription (Brit. Museum).

side of the great temple.   As is usual with these Ptolemaic temples, several   monarchs built several

chambers. Of these the inmost and earliest (D) was
built by Philopator, the entrance-hall to it (C) by the

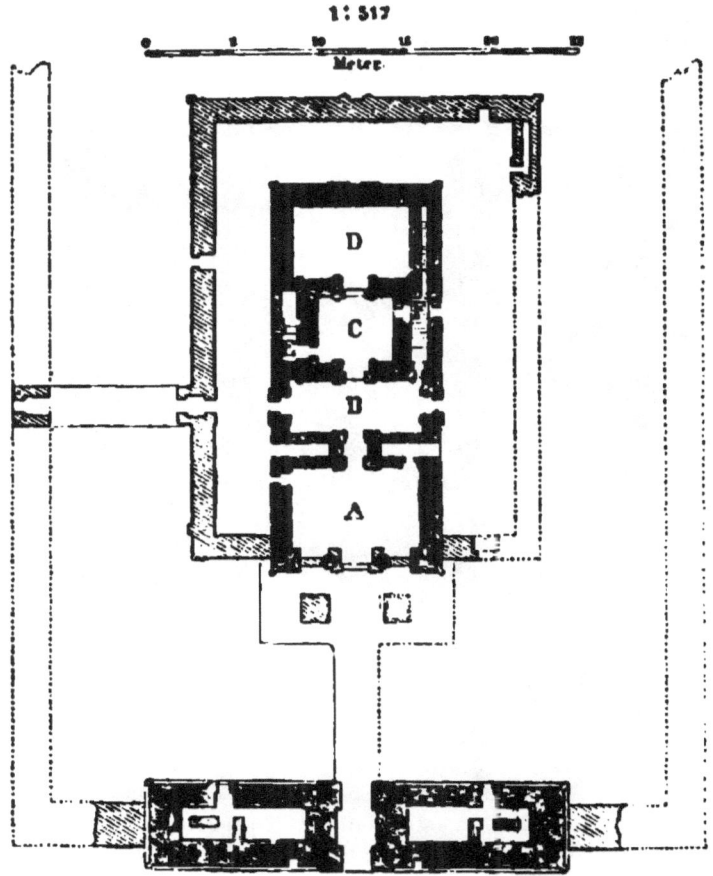

FIG. 41.—Temple of Dakkeh.

Nubian king Ergamen, but unfinished, while his work
is partly defaced, partly enlarged and finished by
Ptolemy V. This combination is peculiarly instruct-

ive, because there was already known at Dakkeh in
Nubia, some 50 miles higher than Philæ, a similar
temple where analogous building was carried out by
Ergamen and Philopator in the reverse order, the outer
hall by the king of Egypt, the inner shrine by Ergamen,
the pronaos by Ptolemy IX., while both this and the

FIG. 42.—Inscription of Ergamen.
(From the Temple of Ar-hes-Nefer, Philæ.)

temple at Philæ show additional work of the Emperor
Augustus.   The combination shows (1) that Ergamen
was a contemporary, not of Philadelphus, but of Philopator, as I had already asserted from the form of his
cartouche ; [1] (2) that the relations of Egypt and Nubia
were then friendly, and ceased to be so during the next

[1] *Empire of the Ptolemies*, p. 273.

reign. It is probable that the easy-going Philopator made some concessions of independence to Ergamen, who then consented to recognise the king of Egypt as his suzerain. For this Ergamen, as we know from Diodorus, was a prince educated in Egypt, who overthrew a priestly tyranny which had dominated the country, and made himself real master of the land between the two Cataracts. Yet neither Ptolemy II. nor III. seems to have attempted any subjugation of this country.

At all events, while all this evidence of building in the upper country is quite consistent with the statement on the temple of Edfu, that the revolution did not break out till the sixteenth year of the reign and survived it for years, it seems not so with the statements of Polybius, that a long and cruel civil war occupied Egypt during the king's life, and that it was put down by Polycrates (evidently the same man who had commanded the Egyptian and Libyan cavalry at Raphia). If such a revolt had occupied even the middle country, how could Ptolemy have spent great sums of money in building temples at Philæ and in Nubia? There is but one way out of the difficulty if we adhere to our faith in Polybius, and this is, that the long and sanguinary revolt, put down by Polycrates, only occupied Lower Egypt—most likely the cities of the Delta. I think a comparison of the two passages in Polybius [1] with the Rosetta stone, which speaks of the early revolt under Epiphanes being one of old standing, points to two separate revolts under Philopator, one settled by Polycrates, and only in Lower Egypt, the second embracing Lower and Upper Egypt, and raging at the time of his death. Nor does either seem to have been as serious as the historian implies, for all the foreign possessions and relations of Egypt remained on the same footing as they were under the great Euergetes. On this point our evidence, though sparse and disjointed, is perfectly consistent, and to my mind quite sufficient.

But before I pass on, it is worth mentioning that

[1] Polybius, v. 107, saying εὐθέως ἀπὸ τούτων; and xiv. 12, saying ὀψὲ δέ ποτε.

we have from Alexandria, on the site of the new bank, plaques of gold, silver, copper, and stone commemorating the building of a temple to Sarapis and Isis, Saviour Gods, and king Ptolemy and queen Arsinoe, Gods Philopatores.[1] The other inscription, from Naucratis, set up by Komon, son of Asklepiades, the controller (œconomus) of Naukratis and its surroundings, does not go quite so far, though it gives the king more high-sounding titles: "on behalf of king Ptolemy, the great God Philopator, Saviour and Victorious, and on behalf of his son, to Isis, Sarapis, Apollo." Another (Strack, 54) dedicates on behalf of the Gods Philopatores a temple to Demeter, Kore, and *Justice*, a curious dedication—apparently a personification of the king's justice, as appears from Mr. Grenfell's Papyri (ii. p. 30, line 8).

This may be called the Hellenistic side of the king's religion. Dedications to him at Lesbos and Sestos show that his sway still included these regions. There is every reason to believe that, in regard to Rhodes, he carried out loyally the great generosities promised by his father on the occasion of the disastrous earthquake at the close of Euergetes' reign. The Athenians, according to Polybius, disgraced themselves by their constant flatteries of this king. Had he been a mere idle debauchee, who took no notice of any foreign affairs, they would surely not have thrown away their flattery upon him. "The Athenians," says Polybius, "having recovered their freedom from Macedon, took no part in Hellenic affairs ; but, under the guidance of Eurycleides and Mikion, were effusive to all the kings of the Hellenistic world, and particularly to Ptolemy, and tolerated all manner of complimentary decrees and proclamations, taking small account of public decency on account of the tendency of their leaders." Towards the end of his life (207 B.C.) the king sent an embassy to mediate between Philip and the Ætolians. When the Romans were in great difficulties in the Hannibalic war, which lasted almost all the king's reign, and kept

[1] *Empire of the Ptolemies,* p. 73.

them from interfering in Hellenistic affairs, they still sent a polite embassy to Ptolemy, to maintain their hereditary friendship with him and secure from him supplies of corn.[1] When the Capuan Decius Magius, who opposed Hannibal and was sent by him to Africa, was driven by a storm to Cyrene, he took refuge at the statue of Ptolemy—then a safe asylum—at Cyrene, and so was brought to Alexandria. But when liberated by Ptolemy and offered a passage to either Rome or Capua, he preferred to stay at Alexandria with the procurer and asserter of his liberty (Livy, xxiii. 10). All these scattered items are so consistent that I cannot but feel convinced further evidence, when found, will corroborate it. Even in the great riot after his death, when his infant son was put upon the throne, the conspicuous loyalty of both army and people to this son, and the utter absence of railing at the dead king, show that he was not personally unpopular at Alexandria.

Against all this evidence of a favourable, or at least of a neutral, kind, we have Polybius' strong and utter condemnation of the king, copied from some very explicit source, from which he has also taken his long and graphic account of the riot at Alexandria following upon the king's death. The concurrent statements of Strabo, of Plutarch, and of Justin are probably mere reflections of the same evidence, and without independent value. Justin even adds the crime of parricide to that of matricide, without any likelihood of its truth. How are we to treat this remarkable conflict of evidence?

It will not serve us to argue that while the king was notoriously idle and worthless, all public affairs were in the hands of that "subtle old baggage" Sosibius, his minister. For, in the first place, Sosibius did not survive through the whole reign. He had nothing to do with the murder of Arsinoe, though Polybius in one place (xv. 25) distinctly says he had. But the historian's own account of the riot accompanying the new king's accession, which was mainly caused by indignation at

[1] Polybius, ix. 44.

the queen's murder, says not one word of Sosibius' share in it, which the perpetrators would before all things have urged on behalf of themselves when pleading for their life.   Moreover, in this very scene, the younger Sosibius (his son) appears as a person of consequence, and indeed the chief man in Alexandria. Hence his father must have been dead before the long-concealed murder of Arsinoe.

As regards Agathocles and his party, they were clearly the worst possible ministers of Egypt; while those who administered for the infant Epiphanes were excellent and able men.   How comes it, then, that Philip V. of Macedon and Antiochus the Great did not venture to attack the debauchee Philopator and his debauchee administration, while they pounce upon the infant Epiphanes, with his able ministers, and attempt to dismember his kingdom ?   There is but one answer : Philopator was felt to be a power personally, while the infant Epiphanes was not.

Surely, then, we must suspend our judgment, and inquire diligently into the sources of this part of Polybius' history, for he could not speak at first hand of this king, as he might of Ptolemy IX., and therefore must have reproduced some earlier author.   Of these we know by name two, Kallixenos of Rhodes and Ptolemy of Megalopolis.[1]   The former described the vast ship and the state *dahabiyeh* built by Philopator, in a passage quoted at length by Athenæus (v. 37 *seq.*) ; the other, who had administered Cyprus long and faithfully for Philopator and for Epiphanes, in his old age, says Polybius, came to Alexandria, where he lived a dissolute life, and wrote memoirs of Philopator.   Polybius seems to me to infer the worthless old age of the man from the character of his book.   And yet this was probably the source which has blackened the name of Philopator.   Polybius is no more infallible in his judg-

---

[1] If this Kallixenos be the same person that described the pomp of Philadelphus (above, p. 70), how can he have been *eye-witness* of this scene, and of the huge vessel of Philopator, as Susemihl (i. 905) seems to think ?

ment or free from prejudice than Thucydides, though both have that seriousness of style which averts suspicion. It is more than probable that the fate of Cleomenes and his family in Egypt (dangerous visitor though he was, and not unlikely, as people thought, to seize Cyrene) rankled deeply in the Hellenic mind, and gave Philopator the reputation of being a vulgar Oriental tyrant in contrast to the noble Spartan king.

There is also something, too, to be said concerning the hostility of the Jews. I believe that the 3rd Maccabees, with all its absurdities, is so far no invention, that this king set himself to limit the influence of the Jews in Egypt. They took their vengeance upon him, as they have ever since been wont to do upon their enemies, by influencing the judgment of men against his character. It was done secretly, but persistently, till the romance of the 3rd Maccabees merely brought together the many adverse traditions which they had caused to grow up at Alexandria.

But if all these considerations are subject to doubt, and will be questioned by other students of the evidence, there is no reason to underrate the statement of Polybius that this reign marked a great change in the treatment, and consequently in the spirit, of the natives. They had been armed and drilled; the main fortunes of a decisive battle had been entrusted to their phalanx, and they had come out victorious. Hitherto the caste of the warriors ($\mu\alpha\chi\iota\mu\sigma\iota$) seems to have been disregarded by the dynasty, and whatever natives accompanied the armies of earlier Ptolemies were only employed in the service of the real army. But now they were the real army, and why should foreign settlers occupy the best lands, the best posts, all the advantages of court favour, to their exclusion? Hence arose the two dangerous revolts: the first, as I have shown, in Lower Egypt, put down after several years of desultory but of sanguinary and cruel war; the second in Upper Egypt, beginning some years later, but handed down to the new king as a disastrous

legacy.[1] When Philopator died, all his Hellenistic
empire was intact and apparently at peace. The upper
provinces of Egypt and Nubia were in revolt, and
completely beyond his control. His heir, though associated in the throne already, was an infant of five years
old, his affairs in the hands of selfish and criminal
favourites, who only sought to secure their own wealth
and importance.

These villains, of whom Agathokles and his sister,
the king's mistress, were now chief, had taken care to
murder Queen Arsinoe, who was young and vigorous,
and who, if the king's life was clearly on the wane,
was looked to throughout Egypt as the natural regent
and protectress of the infant heir. She was in some
way removed from sight, so that her murder might not
quickly become public.[2] Probably the king was known
to be dying and his demise expected, but the death of
Arsinoe came as a shock upon the people of Alexandria.

Polybius gives us at great length (evidently quoting
from some very anecdotic local historian) the details of
the great riot which ensued when Agathokles produced, with many sham tears, the urns containing the
ashes of the king and queen. It very soon transpired
that she had been murdered, and it was her sad fate, her
bravery, her ill-treatment by the king and his minions,
her early death, when she would have at last attained
her just authority, that roused the grief of the populace

[1] It would be inestimable if we had some private documents of
this reign. But the papyri contain nothing which throws light
upon it. Singularly few are dated at this epoch—possibly one
among the Petrie Papyri (II. xlvii.), but it is a mere contract, and
has no allusion to the state of the country.

[2] It seems to me very odd that Philammon, the actual murderer,
who is not appointed to the government of Cyrene till after the
oath of allegiance is administered to the new king, should be
described as having arrived from Cyrene two days before the
riot and murder of Agathokles, when he also is torn in pieces by
the mob. I cannot but suspect that he had been appointed
Libyarch some time, and possibly even committed the murder at
Cyrene, whither the queen may have been sent. This would
account for the letter directed to him on the subject, which
Deinon saw and did not intercept (Polybius, xv. 26a).

and their fury at her murderers. But every mob wants
leading, and so the revolution (if so we can call it)
hung fire, till the "Macedonians," as the household
troops were called, took the matter up. At first they had
received Agathokles only with jeers and contempt, but
when he proceeded to rid himself of those among them
who were inciting Tlepolemos, the governor of Pelusium,
to assume control of Alexandria, and one of them,
Moeragenes, escaped naked from the chamber of torture
and took refuge in their camp, they also rebelled, insisted upon having the child king surrendered to them
by Agathokles, and, disregarding all his entreaties to
have the bare spark of life in him spared, handed him
and his family over to the mob, who tore them in
pieces. A similar fate befell Philammon, the actual
murderer of Arsinoe, who had just returned from
Cyrene.

FIG. 43.—Græco-Egyptian Head (bronze).
(From the Petrie collection.)

CHAPTER VI

FIG. 44.—Cartouches of Ptolemy V.

AUTHORITIES.—Polybius, Livy, and the general histories (as before). The Rosetta stone (decree of Memphis) is the principal home document.

WHEN the riot was over, the young king was put under the protection of the younger Sosibius, apparently a respectable and loyal person, and there was associated with him Aristomenes, who had indeed risen to notoriety by his gross flattery of the elder Sosibius, but who turned out in the sequel an able and trusty minister. So far the child was in good hands; but the control of the army, and even of the treasury, was in the province of Tlepolemos, a successful mercenary, not desirous, indeed, of ousting the king, but absolutely thoughtless and frivolous when he was not commanding forces in the field, and lavish of the public purse to Greek embassies, to the Dionysiac guilds of actors, and

148

to the household troops. This reckless extravagance led to his downfall at the hands of the other ministers, though the details are not known to us. Probably the affair was managed in like manner as the deposition and death of Skopas, to be mentioned presently. These mercenary leaders (now chiefly Ætolians) were from henceforth a standing menace to Egypt. Indeed they had been so in older times, as in the case of Sheshonk.

But other dangers soon gathered about the unfortunate country, both from without and from within. We know from the arguments in the great Turin Papyrus [1] that a revolt in the upper provinces prevailed in the very first year of this reign, and it does not appear that the forces sent to quell it returned for years to Thebes, their original station. Indeed, from this time onward, Ombos, higher up the river, appears to have become the principal garrison town to guard the Thebaid.[2] This revolt must have been an extension of that which had begun in the last year of Philopator, but which apparently did not affect the particular forces to which the plaintiff's father had belonged.

The king of Macedon and the king of Syria entered at once upon an unholy alliance to divide the possessions of Egypt among themselves. Philip made a naval raid against the islands and coast cities which acknowledged Egypt as their suzerain. Antiochus began a campaign against Cœle-Syria and Palestine, to recover the conquests from which he had been ousted by the defeat at Raphia. There was no decent excuse or pretext for this policy of plunder. But the royal villains seem to have delayed in some inexplicable way to make their attack, while there was an open rebellion in the upper country, and a new one had broken out, or was threatening to do so, in Lower Egypt. The campaigns of

---

[1] Ed. A. Peyron (*Trans. Turin Acad.* 1827), I. p. v. 27 : τον εαυτου πατερα μετηλθαι εκ της Διοσπολεως μεθ ετερων στρατιωτων εις τους ανω τοποις εν τηι γινομενηι ταραχηι επι του πατρος του βασιλεως θεου Επιφανοις· και εφη, αναλογιζομενων των χρονων, απο μεν του Επιφανοις ετη κδ, etc.

[2] Cf. Turin Papyrus II. 39.

Philip against the Egyptian cities in the Ægean, and of
Antiochus into Palestine, do not appear to have actually
taken place for three years after the young king's accession.   Philip was encountered by the Rhodians and
Attalus of Pergamon, who gave his fleet so rough a
handling that his further action against Egypt was
paralysed.   Antiochus was at first held in check by
Skopas, the Ætolian general sent out by the Egyptian
Government, and was unable to dislodge him from
Cœle-Syria till the great battle of Panion in 198 (the
king's sixth or seventh year).

But by that time a new power had arisen in the
affairs of the East.   The Romans, who had sent a
friendly embassy in 201 B.C. to announce their victory
over Carthage and their thanks for the neutrality of
Egypt, were now apprised of the whole situation and
of the great straits in which their old ally was situated.
Though it is not true that the Egyptian ministers
begged the Romans to take charge of the kingdom,
or that M. Lepidus was appointed the king's tutor
and lord at Alexandria,[1] it is true that the Romans
not only crushed Philip's power at Cynoscephalæ
(197 B.C.) and cured him of all hankering after the
flesh-pots of Egypt, but they at last interfered actively
to prevent Antiochus from continuing his successes
against Egypt.   He was obliged to meet their intervention by stating that his quarrel with Egypt was
over, for that he was about to join an alliance with
that kingdom which would satisfy the claims of
both parties.   He accordingly betrothed his daughter
Cleopatra to the young Ptolemy in 198 B.C., with a
promised dowry of half the revenues of Cœle-Syria
(S. Jerome, *ad D.*), or of this and Palestine (Josephus).

Thus Aristomenes, after six years of sore trouble
and anxiety, brought his sovereign out of foreign difficulties by the help of Roman intervention.   But still the
risks from foreign condottieri and from internal revolt
remained.   Skopas came home from Syria, and, despite
his defeat, played the great man at Alexandria.   But the

---

[1] On this point cf. *Empire of the Ptolemies*, p. 296.

minister was too strong for the freebooter, and having summoned him in vain, and then arrested him, to bring him before the Privy Council,[1] ordered his execution. There remains to be considered the most important part of all these disturbances, I mean the rising of the natives against the young sovereign and his ministers. Of this we have two widely different accounts, both of them sadly brief—one, that of Polybius ; the other, that in the Rosetta inscription.

This latter was certainly decreed in the king's 9th year, but whether it corresponds to his formal coronation, or was a subsequent affair, is yet under discussion. We know that the young king was produced with a crown on his head by Agathocles, as soon as his father's death was made known. We know that he was betrothed to the Syrian princess about 198 B.C., shortly after the battle of Panion, when he was twelve or thirteen years old. Allowing a little time for the affairs of Skopas and his execution, we hear that Aristomenes proceeded to the ἀνακλητήρια or proclamation of the king's majority (and so his release from regents or guardians). This has usually been identified with the solemn progress to Memphis, when he entered into the temple of Ptah. I hesitate to do so. The ἀνακλητήρια, mentioned again in the case of Philometor, was the Hellenistic ceremony celebrated at Alexandria. The Egyptian proclamation at Memphis was a very different matter, and probably followed upon the other, but was no doubt considered the only legitimation by the priests, just as in our days a religious marriage follows upon the civil in many European states, which require the latter, while society or the Church ignore it in comparison with the other. The wording of the decree of Memphis, to which we shall now come, seems to me to imply not only a previous decree that the king should receive the title of the god Epiphanes Eucharistos (*manifest and*

---

[1] Polybius tells us he invited the distinguished Greeks on embassy to Alexandria, and especially the Ætolians, to be present at the inquiry, thus courting the consent of these people to the justice of his proceedings.

full of favour), but that he had been formally crowned in the Egyptian fashion. Here is the text. To reproduce the Egyptian style was difficult enough to the Greeks. In English it may well be deemed impossible.

"In the reign of the young [1]—who has also received his royalty from his father—lord of crowns, glorious, who has established Egypt, and is pious towards the gods, superior to his foes, that has set up the life of men, lord of the 30 years' feasts, even as Hephæstos the Great;—of the king, like the sun, a great king of the upper and lower country; of the offspring of the Gods Philopatores, whom Hephæstos (Ptah) has approved,[2] to whom the sun (Ra) has given the victory, the living image of Zeus (Amon), son of the sun, of 'Ptolemy living for ever beloved of Ptah,'[3] in the 9th year, when Aetos, son of Aetos, was priest of Alexander, and the Gods Soteres, and the Gods Adelphi, and the Gods Euergetes, and the Gods Philopatores, and the God Epiphanes Eucharistos;[4] Pyrrha daughter of Philinos being Athlophoros of Berenike Euergetis, Areia daughter of Diogenes Canephoros of Arsinoe Philadelphos, Eirene daughter of Ptolemy being priestess of Arsinoe Philopator, the 4th of the month Xandikos, according to the Egyptians the 18th of Mecheir. DECREE. The chief priests and prophets and those that enter the holy place for the dressing of the gods, and the feather-bearers and sacred scribes, and all the other priests who have come together to the king from the temples throughout the country to Memphis,

---

[1] The reader who compares this with the opening of the Canopus decree will at once see what progress Egyptian ideas and style have made in the interval (238-196 B.C.); the Greek copy is now a slavish translation of the Egyptian. The Greek text is printed with a commentary in *Empire of the Ptolemies*, pp. 316-327.

[2] This refers to the solemn and private visit paid by the king to the inner shrine of Ptah for his coronation.

[3] This is the rendering of his name-cartouche.

[4] He had therefore already obtained this title, and association in the worship of his predecessors.

for the feast[1] of his reception of the sovereignty,
that of Ptolemy, 'the everliving beloved of Ptah, the
God Epiphanes Eucharistos,"[2] which he received from
his father, being assembled in the temple of Memphis
on this day, declared : Since king Ptolemy, etc., the
son of king Ptolemy and queen Arsinoe, Gods
Philopatores, has much benefited both the temples
and those that dwell in them, as well as all those that
are his subjects, being a god sprung from a god and
goddess (like Horus, the son of Isis and Osiris, who
avenged his father Osiris), being benevolently disposed
towards the gods, has offered to the temples revenues
in money and corn, and has undertaken much outlay
to bring Egypt into prosperity, and to establish the
temples, and has been generous with all his own
means, and of the revenues and taxes which he
receives from Egypt some he has wholly[3] remitted
and others he has lightened,[4] in order that the natives
and all the rest might be in prosperity during his
reign; but the debts to the crown, which they in Egypt
and in the rest of his royalty owed, being many in
number,[5] he has remitted ; and those who were in
prison, and under accusation for a long time back, he
has freed of their charges ; and has directed that the
revenues of the temples and the yearly allowance given
to them, both of corn and money, likewise also the
proper share to the gods from vine land, and from
parks,[6] and the other property of the gods, as it was

---

[1] Hence this πανηγυρις was not the actual Egyptian coronation,
which took place after his victory in the 8th year, but its *commemoration* in the 9th.

[2] I shall indicate this recurring cartouche-name by "etc."

[3] I suppose εις τελος means no more than this. "Has merged
into the τελος, or state revenue from other sources" is possible so
far as the Greek goes.

[4] This lightening is said to be expressed in the demotic version
by "gave them the control of," viz. gave back the collection of
them to the priests.

[5] Not 'remitted to the πληθος of priests,' as it is usually rendered ;
cf. below, line 29, οντα εις σιτου τε και αργυριου πληθος ουκ ολιγον.

[6] We now know that this απόμοιρα amounted to one-sixth, and
had been seized by the crown, as a yearly gift to Arsinoe Phila-

in his father's time, so to remain ; and directed also,
with regard to the priests, that they should pay no
more for their right of consecration (τελεστικόν) than
what they were assessed up to the first year in his
father's time,[1] and has relieved the members of the
sacred caste from the yearly descent (of the river) to
Alexandria, and has directed that the pressgang for
the navy shall no longer exist;[2] and of the tax of byssus
cloth paid by the temples to the crown[3] he has remitted
two-thirds ; and whatever things were neglected in
former times he has restored to their normal condition,
having a care how the traditional duties shall be duly
paid to the gods ; and likewise has he apportioned
justice to all, like Hermes the great and great.[4] AND
he has ordained that those who come back[5] of the
warrior caste, and of the rest who went astray in their
allegiance in the days of the confusion, should, on their
return,[6] be allowed to occupy their old possessions ;
and he provided that cavalry and infantry forces should

delphus.   The priests, whether truly or falsely, imply that it had
been restored to the temples.   A Petrie papyrus (II. xlvi.), dated
the 2nd and 4th year of Epiphanes, speaks of this tax as
paid to Arsinoe and the Gods Philopatores, so that the statement
of the priests is probably false ; but see Revenue Papyrus, p. 121,
and Mr. Grenfell's note.

[1] This very puzzling phrase εως του πρωτου ετους επι του πατρος
αυτου may possibly mean during that part of the king's first
year, in which his father was still alive — the odd months of the last
reign always counting into the first year of the new sovereign.
Probably Philopator had made some concessions just before his
death.

[2] συλληψιν των εις την ναυτειαν may also mean the right of seizing
whatever is wanted for the navy.   But the word ναυτεια is not
known in this sense, and the demotic version, which is said to
indicate some compulsory service, has no equivalent for it.

[3] We now know from the Revenue Papyrus (cols. 98, 99) that
there was a tax on the sale of this cloth.

[4] I have not altered this truly Egyptian phrase, which often
occurs in the form *great great*.

[5] Lit., who come down the river, probably from the insurgents
in Upper Egypt, perhaps at Edfu, who were at this time by no
means subdued.

[6] It might be inferred from the D.V., which makes the word
future (according to Revillout) that we should read καταπορευσομενοις.

be sent out, and ships, against those who were attacking
Egypt by sea and by land, submitting to great outlay
in money and corn, in order that the temples, and all
that are in the land, might be in safety ;[1] and having
gone to Lycopolis, that which is in the Busirite nome,[2]
which had been taken and fortified against a siege with
a lavish magazine of weapons and all other supplies,
seeing that the disloyalty was now of long standing
among the impious men gathered into it, who had
done great harm to the temples and all the dwellers in
Egypt, and encamping against them, he surrounded it
with mounds and trenches and remarkable fortifications ;
but when the Nile made a great rise in the 8th year
(of his reign), and was wont to inundate the plains, he
prevented it, having dammed from many points the
outlets of the streams, spending upon this no small
amount of money ; and having set cavalry and infantry
to guard them,[3] he presently took the town by storm,
and destroyed all the impious men in it, even as
Hermes and Horus, the son of Isis and Osiris, formerly
subdued the rebels in the same district ; and the mis-
leaders of the rebels in his father's day, who had
disturbed the land, and ill-treated the temples, these
when he came to Memphis, avenging his father and
his own royalty, he punished as they deserved at the
time that he came there to perform the proper ceremonies for his reception of the crown ;[4] and he

[1] Whether this refers to the campaigns of Skopas in Palestine
seems to me doubtful ; it seems to mean guarding the frontiers
with a large force.
[2] There was another town in Upper Egypt (the Thebaid), on
the site now known at Siout.
[3] I.e. The dams ; or it may be, owing to the inundation being
kept off, that he set his army to invest the rebels, who had hoped
the rising Nile would raise the siege.
[4] The repeated mention of this solemn enthronement at Memphis
in Egyptian fashion marks a new and great concession to the
priests and the national feeling. It is quite certain that neither
the second nor third Ptolemy had any such ceremony, almost
certain that neither the first nor fourth had. They posed as
Hellenistic kings, ruling over an inferior race. Now we have a
very different story.

remitted what was due to the crown in the temples
up to his 8th year, being no small amount of corn
and money; so also the fines for the byssus cloth not
delivered to the crown, and of those delivered the cost
of having them verified,[1] for the same period; he also
freed the temples of (the tax of) the artaba for every
aroura of sacred land, and the jar of wine for each
aroura of vine land; and to Apis and Mnevis he gave
many gifts, and to the other sacred animals in Egypt,
much more than the kings before him, considering
what belonged to them [the gods] in every respect; and
for their burials he gave what was suitable lavishly and
splendidly, and what was required for private shrines,
with sacrifices and festivals and the other customary
observances; and the honours of the temples and of
Egypt he has maintained according to the laws;
and the temple of Apis he has adorned with rich work,
spending upon it gold and silver and precious stones,[2]
no small amount; and has founded[3] temples and
shrines and altars, and has repaired those requiring
it, having the spirit of a beneficent god in matters
pertaining to religion, and finding out the most honourable of the temples [or sites], renewed them during
his sovereignty, as was becoming—in requital for all
of which the gods have given him health, victory, power,
and all other good things, his sovereignty remaining
to him and his children for all time. WITH PROPITIOUS
FORTUNE: It seemed good to the priests of all the
temples in the land to increase greatly the existing
honours of king Ptolemy, etc., likewise those of his
parents, the Gods Philopatores, and of his ancestors,
the Gods Euergetes and Gods Adelphi and Gods Soteres,
and to set up of the everliving king Ptolemy, etc., an
image in the most holy place of every temple, which

---

[1] This clause is quite obscure to us, as we do not know what
δειγματισμος means. The demotic version is said to be, "the
complement for pieces of cloth kept back," which implies a
different reading.

[2] Both H.V. and D.V. give for this *corn*, a curious variant, if
Revillout be credible in his rendering.

[3] D.V. "amplified."

shall be called that of Ptolemy, the avenger of Egypt,
beside which shall stand the leading god of the temple,
handing him the emblem of victory, which shall be
fashioned [in the Egyptian] fashion;[1] and the priests
shall pay homage to the images three times a day, and
put upon them the sacred adornment (dress), and perform the other usual honours such as are given to the
other gods in the Egyptian festivals; and to establish
for king Ptolemy, etc., a statue and golden shrine in
each of the temples, and to set it up in the inner
chamber with the other shrines; and in the great
festivals, in which the shrines go abroad, the shrine
of the God Epiphanes Eucharistos shall go abroad with
them. AND in order that it may be easily distinguishable now and for all time, there shall be set upon the
shrine the ten golden crowns of the king, to which
shall be applied an asp, as in the case of asp-formed
crowns, which are upon other shrines, but in the centre
of them shall be the crown called Pschent, which he
assumed when he went into the temple at Memphis to
perform in it the ceremonies for assuming the royalty;
and to place on the square surface round the crowns,
beside the afore-mentioned crown, golden phylacteries,
[on which shall be inscribed] that it is (the shrine) of
the king, who makes manifest (ἐπιφανη) the upper and
lower country.   And since the 30th of Mechir, on
which the birthday of the king is celebrated, and
likewise [the 16th of Paophi[2]] in which he received
the royalty from his father, they have considered name-
days in the temples, since they were the occasions of
great blessings, a feast shall be kept in the temples on

---

[1] From the 40th line onward the fracture at the right side
becomes more serious, and invades the text, so that words, not
always certain, have to be supplied to fill up the construction.
But there can be no doubt regarding the general sense. I have
therefore not thought it worth while to indicate each of the gaps
at the close of the lines. All the English reader requires is to be
assured of the substance and of the sense, and that no modern
idea has been imported into the text.

[2] This date is recovered from the duplicate of the hieroglyphic
text from Damanhour.

these days in every month, on which there shall be
sacrifices and libations, and all the ceremonies customary
at the other festivals [some words lost], and to keep a
feast to Ptolemy, etc., yearly (also) in all the temples
of the land from the first of Thoth for 5 days; in
which they shall wear garlands, and perform sacrifices,
and the other usual honours; and that the priests
(. . .) shall be called priests of the God Epiphanes
Eucharistos in addition to the names of the other gods
whom they serve, and that his priesthood shall be

FIG. 45.—Bronze statuette.
(Petrie collection.)

entered upon all formal documents (and engraved on the rings
which they wear [1]), and that
private individuals shall also be
allowed to keep the feast and set
up the afore-named shrine, and
have it in their houses, and perform the customary honours at
the feasts, both monthly and
yearly, in order that it may be
published that the men of Egypt
magnify and honour the God
Epiphanes Eucharistos the king,
according to the law. This decree
to be set up on a stele of hard
stone, in sacred and native and
Greek letters, and set up in each
of the first, second, and third
(rank) temples at the image of
the everliving king."

The first word of caution to the reader is not to
regard this document as absolutely trustworthy because
it is very formal, and solemnly inscribed on stone.
Fortunately, however, there must be some limits to
falsehood, and had the priests, for example, copied from
earlier documents (as they were wont to do) that this
king had brought back the Egyptian gods from Asia,
the Greek version at all events would have excited

[1] This gap is filled up from the parallel passage in the Canopus
decree of Ptolemy III.

ridicule. So also they could hardly claim remission of taxes in Greek, which the king had not really remitted. The whole text, however, points to a compromise whereby the crown thought to conciliate the priest-hood, and so limit or overcome the disloyalty now rampant throughout the country. The Edfu building text seems explicit that the revolution which broke out in Upper Egypt in the 16th year of Ptolemy IV. did not terminate till the 19th year of the present king, when he crushed it and entered his name upon the temple.

With this agrees the conclusion of an excerpt of Polybius, that the king was kept from having any per-sonal part in the local wars by the jealousy of his general Polykrates, though the king was now in his 25th year (which corresponds to his 19th year of sove-reignty). But the details which precede this statement are so like the statements of the Rosetta text, that I cannot accept two wars so correspondent, the one con-cluding in the 8th the other in the 19th year. Here is the excerpt: "When Ptolemy, king of Egypt, besieged Lycopolis, the dynasts of the Egyptians, terrified at what happened (*i.e.* the damming operations above de-scribed), submitted to the king's parole. But he used them badly, and fell into great dangers. What happened was very like the conjuncture when Polykrates sub-dued the revolters [in his father's time]. For Athinis and Pausiris and Chesuphos and Irobastos, the only survivors of the dynasts, bowing to circumstances, came to Sais, to submit themselves to the king's honour. But Ptolemy, having broken his faith, dragged the men naked after his chariot, and then put them to death with torture. Having then come to Naukratis with his army, and having received the mercenary force which Aristonikos had hired in Greece, he sailed with them to Alexandria." Then follows the sentence about Polykrates' dishonest policy to the king. There seems to me no way out of the difficulty but to sever this passage into two separate notices, one referring to Epiphanes' early civil war in the eastern Delta, the

other, with the names of the insurgents, to the long
war of the upper country, settled in his 25th year.
For surely there were not two captures of Lycopolis, or
the capture of the two Lycopolises. I think then that
the former part of the passage gives Polybius' account
of the affair mentioned in the inscription.

At all events, with the solemn progress to Memphis,
and the decree, Epiphanes' difficulties for the time were
over. The Syrian princess Cleopatra, betrothed to
the young king some years previously, was conducted
with great pomp as far as Raphia in 193 B.C., and
married to him when he was about 17. Her dowry of
the revenues of Cœle-Syria (including Palestine, according to Josephus) was very great, but gave rise to political complications in the sequel. The provinces were

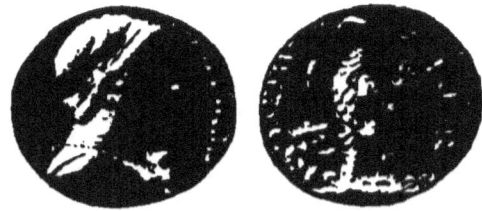

FIG. 46.—Coin of Ptolemy V.

certainly held by Syrian troops, and permanently lost
to Egypt. Upper Egypt and Nubia were not recovered
from their long revolt till the king's 19th year (as the
Edfu text tells us). We now know from the recently
excavated temples of Arhesnefr and Imhotep at Philæ,[1]
which had been begun by his father and Ergamen
conjointly, that he not only considerably enlarged and
completed them, but that he mutilated the cartouches
of Ergamen upon their walls, thus showing that he
reconquered Philæ from the Nubian power, and also
held it long enough and peaceably enough to carry out
considerable work there.

Meanwhile Ptolemy and his wise minister took care
to court the favour of the Romans in their wars

[1] By Captain Lyons in 1896.

with Philip of Macedon, with the Ætolians, and with Antiochus the Great. But though the Romans made polite speeches, they declined all Egyptian offers of help, nor did they restore to Egypt the cities of the Ægean which had been under the control of the fourth Ptolemy. Neither did they, in punishing Antiochus after the battle of Magnesia (190 B.C.), think of giving back Palestine and Cœle-Syria actually to the king. We hear that the Syrian Cleopatra was an able and devoted wife, and did what she could to keep up Egyptian influences in the lost provinces.

It was an attempt to undertake the reconquest of them which cost Epiphanes his life. When asked whence he would draw the necessary means for a foreign war, which in Egypt the king always waged at his own expense, he replied, giving a new sense to the famous saying of Alexander the Great, that his wealth consisted in the number of his *friends* (φιλων). What Alexander had said in a loyal sense meant a policy of plunder in Epiphanes. For we know with tolerable certainty from the strong negative evidence of earlier documents, together with the appearance during this reign of a whole system of titles, comparable to our modern peerages, that ranks of nobility were instituted by either Philopator or Epiphanes,[1] and it is a very certain inference that these honours were paid for. With a despot like Epiphanes, not to solicit them may have been a danger, and so the official classes may have been mercilessly taxed by being compelled to accept these titles. Such is the explanation I have already offered for the facts as I discovered them. It is an interesting problem to discover how far these titles were derived from Alexander's court, how far from old

[1] So far I can find no clear evidence of either of the titles των φιλων or των διαδοχων in the inscriptions of Philopator, and I hesitate about the supplying of these words to fill gaps in his inscriptions (*i.e.* Strack, No. 60) where των δ[occurs, whereas both certainly occur in one of Epiphanes (Strack, 7-). It is nevertheless possible that both Strack's 60 and another from Thera, which H. von Gärtringen has sent me, attest the origin of the titles in the earlier reign.

Egyptian heraldry; for we know that here a very elaborate system of official titles, amounting to the honours of a peerage, also existed. There is a most interesting stele (demotic) commented on by Krall (*Studien*, ii. 48), describing the honours of one Petubastis, son of Psiphtah and of *Berenike*, in the close of the reign of Ptolemy Alexander (108 B.C.), in which the series of titles does not seem to be at all identical with the Greek titles we know. This man was (I quote from Krall's authority) "scribe of the Doublehouse (palace, $\beta a\sigma. \gamma\rho a\mu$?), scribe of the king's accounts ($\upsilon\pi o\delta\iota o\iota\kappa\eta\tau\eta s$?), scribe of Ptah and Arsinoe Philadelphos in the whole 4th and 5th Phylæ (of priests), scribe of decrees and papyrus rolls," and some more titles. There may then

FIG. 47.—Another Coin of Ptolemy V.

have been an Egyptian peerage distinct from the Greek, and yet this man's mother was probably of the dominant race.

Turning to the character of this king and his government of Egypt as we have it in our scanty authorities, we hear on the one hand that he was a very athletic young man, and fond of field sports, on the other that he was cruel, and grew tyrannous with increasing age, so that he even put to death his wise and valuable minister Aristomenes, who spoke to him with too much freedom. But on the whole, apart from the misfortunes of his sudden accession as a child and his long minority, I think he is hardly to be blamed for the sore diminution of the Egyptian empire during his reign. For the Romans had come upon the Eastern stage after the

battle of Zama, and the loss of his island empire
through Philip's invasion was made permanent by the
sentimental phil-Hellenism of the Romans, together
with the great power of the Rhodian League.   Even
with the ablest monarch I hardly think that the empire
of Philadelphus and Euergetes could have been kept
intact.   The loss of Cœle-Syria and Palestine might
perhaps have been avoided, had the late king's ministers
treated their Syrian officials and commandants better.
But the child Epiphanes, with mercenaries to help him,
was no match for the able and enterprising Antiochus.
Worst of all, the great experiment of arming the natives
had turned out disastrously.   The old nobility of the
land, which was not extinct, saw its chance of reasserting a national policy against the grasping and the
greed of the "Greeks," as the mixed army of invaders
is generally called.   They were not going to fight for
the Ptolemies and be debarred from all the honours of
the Court and the Government.   Epiphanes was therefore thrown back upon the use of mercenary troops.

The long struggle with the natives, the loss of
Upper Egypt through almost all his reign, the cutting
off of the taxes of the Ægean cities, the squandering
by Tlepolemos and Skopas—all these causes produced
great financial difficulties, of which some traces still
remain.   It was even maintained by Revillout, · on
the evidence of his demotic papyri, that the silver
standard of coinage existing up to the reign of Philopator was replaced in the end of his reign or during
this by a copper standard.   This is now conclusively
shown to be false.   There were both silver and copper
standards, or at least in the earlier times many official
payments were made in copper, and without discount,
for 24 obols to 1 tetradrachm (stater) was the recognised
equivalent.[1]   Even in the days of financial distress,
such as the present, the discount charged on copper
payments was only about 10 per cent. and many payments were made now and even much later in silver.

[1] On these questions of currency cf. Mr. Grenfell's able refutation of Revillout's theories in App. III. to the Revenue Papyrus.

But it is probable (again from demotic papyri) that the εγκυκλιος εικοστη, or 5 per cent. tax on all sales, of which the Government receipt became conclusive evidence of the sale, was introduced by this king, to aid his shattered finances. Still the Egyptian crown estate and revenues remained enormous, and the later kings remained the wealthiest in the known world.

FIG. 48.—Dedication of Temple of Imhotep by Ptolemy (V.) and Cleopatra (I.), Gods Epiphaneis.
(Discovered and photographed by Captain Lyons at Philæ, 1896.)

CHAPTER VII

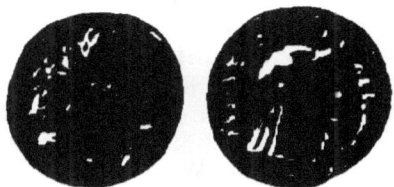

FIG. 49.—Coin of Cleopatra I. as Isis,
with Sarapis on the obverse.

AUTHORITIES.—In addition to those already cited which cover the
whole period, such as Strack, etc., we have to guide us in
this chapter many excerpts of Polybius, who often refers to
the Egypt of this period, the commentary of S. Jerome on
Daniel xi., and the epitomes of Livy's lost books, xlvi. *seq.*
Then there is a wealth of papyri both at the British Museum,
the Louvre, at Leyden, at Turin, which happen to refer to
these two reigns. The publication of many of these documents has been revised and amended by E. Revillout in his
Revue Egyptologique (seven years' issue), and in his recent
Mélanges, but without any facsimiles of the Greek, which,
when taken in connection with his proposed emendations,
warns us that his reading of Greek is not to be trusted. Still he
has contributed greatly to our knowledge of these documents.

CLEOPATRA was left with several young children ; as
the deified queen, called for dignity's sake sister as well
as wife of the king, she was the natural regent. But
her eldest son, whom we know from several inscriptions
to have been associated in the throne during his father's
life, and who had even assumed the title of Eupator,
reigned so short a time that he is ignored by all the
historians, and has only recently been recovered by the
hieroglyphic and demotic texts deciphered by Lepsius, as
well as by the much more recent corroboration of the
Greek papyri published by Mr. Grenfell. In several

lists he is placed between Epiphanes and Philometor, and though we know nothing whatever about him, we are bound to enumerate him (as VI.) in the list, as did the official public in Egypt until the end of the dynasty. But for practical purposes his next brother Philometor, who was now about seven years old, was the successor to the vacant throne.[1]

The queen was a prudent woman, and the neighbouring Hellenistic sovereigns were so busy with their own affairs that Egypt was left in external peace. Nor do we know anything of the internal state inconsistent with it. But I think it quite likely that this Syrian queen, whose interest it was to recover the provinces, of which the revenues were her dowry, in real earnest for Egypt, introduced at her court those foreign officials (especially Jews) whom we see in power during her son's reign. They had long been settled and active in the country. Now they began to creep into office. So it was also with the natives. It seems to me certain that the new titles of nobility were from the first obtainable by natives; if, as I believe, they were sold by Epiphanes, rich natives could buy them, so they begin to find their way into Government offices, even of high trust. But no event of any striking kind happened during the rest of the queen's life, except the sudden and romantic advent of Antiochus IV. (Epiphanes) to the throne of Syria. This was sure to portend trouble to Egypt.

We do not know the date of Cleopatra's death, but it seems nearly to have coincided with the formal proclamation of the young Philometor as king in 173 B.C. To this ceremony there came embassies of congratulation from all the Hellenistic States,[2] also from the Romans *renovandæ amicitiæ causa*, for it appears that the treaties of alliance of Rome with these and other kings

[1] Strack (p. 197) thinks that as he is called the twin brother of Apis in a hieroglyphic text, he was born at the same time as the Apis bull, in 186 B.C.; in any case not before 188.

[2] We have no account surviving of the Egyptian enthronement of this king at Memphis, but may confidently assume that such a ceremony, quite distinct from the Alexandrian accession, did take place.

only lasted for the current reign, and required renewed sanction from each new occupant of the throne. The young king was still under tutors, probably set over him by his mother,—the eunuch Eulæus, who even marks the coinage of this moment, and the Syrian Lenæus. These men are accused of having prompted the boy-king to make an attack upon Syria. The most obvious reason would be the cessation of the payment of Cleopatra's dowry, which the Syrians held to be only her personal estate, while the Egyptians claimed that it was a permanent cession to Egypt.

We may run briefly over the complex quarrels and proposed arbitrations of the next three or four years, as they are indeed of great importance to Alexandria and

FIG. 50.—Ptolemaic Coin with head of Sarapis, common to many of the kings.

the dynasty of the Ptolemies, but of comparatively little to the real history of the country. It is remarkable that among all the people mentioned in the dispute about Cœle-Syria, as arguing the case for Egypt, not a single native appears. The whole interests of the country are entrusted to Greek embassies which happen to be at Alexandria, to the Rhodians, ultimately, and with effect, to the Romans. Antiochus IV. was able to secure the provinces in dispute before the Egyptians were ready, and when the contending hosts ultimately met near Mount Casius, completely defeated Philometor, and, seizing Pelusium, advanced up the river, and was even formally crowned by the priests at Memphis. Meanwhile the young king, flying in despair

to Samothrace, seems to have been taken on the sea,
and brought a prisoner to Memphis. Antiochus
appeared to have now conquered the country, and even
issued a copper coinage as king ; but Alexandria was
not subdued, and the people set the next brother upon
the throne.   His sister, Cleopatra II., who seems even
then to have been already married to her eldest brother,
seconded him loyally, and this boy of fifteen showed his
vigour in organising resistance to the victorious Syrian,
whose army was unable to take the capital.   Antiochus
accordingly retired, leaving Philometor formally king
at Memphis.   He may have thought that he had thus
established a civil war in the country, which he evidently intended to control ; but his schemes resulted
in the brothers making friends, it is said through
their sister's good offices, and combining again against
Antiochus.   Even this, however, would not have
availed.   Antiochus again defeated their forces by
land and sea, and was about to resume the siege of
Alexandria, with every prospect of success, when the
Romans, who had just crushed King Perseus of
Macedon at Pydna, and therefore had their hands free,
sent Popilius Lænas to Egypt, with peremptory orders
to stop Antiochus.   The "circle of Popilius" was
drawn round the invader, and he was obliged, sore
against his will, to submit.

But on his way home (167 B.C.) he discharged his ill-
temper, and perhaps other griefs, in his famous persecution of the Jews.   I believe that they had in some
way delayed his advance, and thwarted him so that
his conquest, which seemed quite certain, was delayed,
and then baulked by Roman interference.

It was clearly at this moment, when the friendly
Ptolemies had lost all chance of recovering Palestine,
and when the Hellenising party at Jerusalem were
supported against the orthodox by the Syrian king
with fire and sword, that Onias, the high priest,
took refuge with many followers in the "land of
Goshen," and received from Ptolemy VII. and Cleopatra II. a settlement at Leontopolis, afterwards called

the "place of Onias," and still apparently marked in
tradition as the "mound of the Jewish maiden" (cf.
Memoir vii. of the *Egypt Exploration Fund*).   Presently,
when the temple at Jerusalem was horribly defiled, Onias
obtained leave to build near Heliopolis, in the nome of
Arabia, a Jewish temple to Jehovah, and there set up a
service for the Jews of Egypt, which lasted till Roman
times, and was a great grief to the faithful of Jerusalem,
by reason of its successful rivalry.   But, however hate-
ful to the faithful in Palestine, it was loyally attached
to the Ptolemies, and Onias seems to have rendered
important services to Philometor and still more to
Cleopatra in after years.   In spite of many exaggerations and falsehoods about it—a text in Isaiah (xix.
18 *seq.*) is even held by some to have been forged in
to support it—the main facts are not disputed, and add
one more item to the indications that this king, like
some of his predecessors, was very friendly to the Jews,
and recognised their high and sterling qualities.[1]   We
now turn to internal affairs.

The first problem which now faces us is the co-
existence of not only two, but three sovereigns.   The
younger brother had been elected king while Philometor
was practically the prisoner of Antiochus Epiphanes at
Memphis, and it seems that with him the young queen
Cleopatra II. was raised to a co-regency which had not
been accorded to any preceding queen, not even to
Arsinoe Philadelphos.   From henceforth she appears
in all solemn datings with her brother-husband, "in
the reign of king Ptolemy and queen Cleopatra, Gods
Philometores"; presently is added, "and of their
children."   So far the matter is clear enough, though
we may wonder that so great a novelty as the formal
associating of the queen with her husband should either
have been so long avoided—considering the former
remarkable queens—or introduced without a word of
notice from historians.   Strack, to whom this important observation is due (*op. cit.* p. 32), can only infer

[1] Cf. H. Willrich, *Griechen und Juden*, cap. iii., the best part of
his very unconvincing tract.

that it took place about 170 B.C., and notes that hereafter Livy usually speaks of the *reges Ægypti*, Ptolemy and Cleopatra.

But what place had the younger brother? It seems now pretty certain that he did not assume the title of Euergetes, or marry his sister, upon his sudden accession, but that he counted as one of the Gods

FIG. 51.—Ptolemies VII. and IX. and Cleopatra II., from Temple at Dêr-el-Medineh.

Philometores. When the difficulties of the invasion were surmounted by the circle of Popilius, and Antiochus sent home, it does not appear to me that, though he afterwards counted his sovereignty as beginning with the twelfth year of his brother (169 B.C.), he was ever actual king with him—*gleich berechtigt*, as Strack calls

him—at Alexandria.   He was not enthroned according
to the Egyptian customs at Memphis till after his real
accession in 146 B.C., as Diodorus expressly tells us.
Among the dedications of this time, only one mentions
the three sovereigns together, and there the younger
is spoken of as king Ptolemy, the God Philometor,
brother of king Ptolemy and queen Cleopatra.[1]   In
all the rest, some of which must surely date from the
so-called joint reign, we only hear of Philometor and
Cleopatra.[2]   In the immediately succeeding acts which
we know, Philometer alone is active ; his brother had
no doubt royal prerogatives and insignia, but no em-
ployment except to plot against the king in Alexandria.

The following six years, those of the " triple
sovereignty," were much disturbed by internal troubles.
An excerpt from Diodorus (F.H.G. II. viii. *seq*.) tells
us that a certain Dionysius, surnamed Petosiris, an
influential man at court, and far the most important
of the natives, attempted to produce a revolution by
spreading reports that the elder prince was plotting
against the younger's life.   Here we suddenly, and for
the first time, find a native in a high position at court.
Petosiris, surnamed Dionysius, would probably be a
more correct description, for we find in many papyri
the habit of calling natives by a second (Greek) name.
The time had not yet come when a Greek would assume

---

[1] This is the interpretation I prefer for the curious Cyrenaic
inscription (Strack, 86).   I do not know what evidence Eisenlohr
has (Baedeker, *Upper Egypt*, p. 124) for attributing a doorway to
the joint reign of the two kings.   I cannot remember a case of the
three cartouches together in any of the temples I have visited.
Nor is there any evidence of the triple reign to be found in the
coinage.   There is therefore no support whatever in contemporary
documents for the explicit statements of the Hellenistic historians.

[2] I cannot believe that the curious dates L ς and L ζ which occur
in B.M. Pap. XXII., regarding the payment of the Twins Thaues
and Taous can be meant for years of the joint reign.   On the
back of that very papyrus the proper dates, L ιζ and L ιθ (of Philometor), are given.   They must be some date noting the establishment of this special service, or some record in the temple.
Nevertheless, the other interpretation has the sanction of Wilcken
(*Gött. Gel. Anz.*, 1894, p. 720).

a native name to escape persecution.[1] Philometor
quieted the threatening riot by appearing in royal
robes with his brother, and Petosiris was driven out
to the suburb Eleusis, there to excite the disorderly
mercenaries.   Here, again, Philometor promptly
attacked and overcame the danger, and then Petosiris turned to the natives, among whom he had more
success, and caused a new and dangerous revolt.

Whether this be the revolt in the Thebaid, mentioned
in the following extract of Diodorus, which the young
king also put down by a vigorous campaign, ending
with the storming of Panopolis (now Akhmîn) in Upper
Egypt, we cannot tell. But Panopolis, over against
Ptolemais,[2] the great Greek city in Upper Egypt, seems
a very curious selection of a stronghold by the native
insurgents.   The large number of inscriptions, com-

[1] In the history of the conflicts between the English settlers and
the natives in Ireland during the seventeenth century, an epoch
not without many striking analogies to that we are treating in
the text, there are frequent instances of the adoption both of
English names by the Irish, and, what is more to the point, of
Irish names by the English, by way of conciliating the dominant
sentiment which threatened a minority of either race in a lawless
and turbulent society.

[2] We have traces of some special relations of this king to
Ptolemais; in fact that he added to the two pre-existing eponymous priesthoods there, that of the founder Soter (to which
Epiphanes had added his name) and the canephorus of Arsinoe
Philadelphos, a third for himself and his mother, quite early in
his reign, then one for his wife, then (before his L 28) the whole
series of the preceding kings. These facts, made out by Lepsius
from Egyptian datings, are corroborated by Mr. Grenfell's discoveries (Greek Papyri, i. p. 23), whose note is very curious. But
I cannot as yet see any importance in these exaggerations of
ceremoniousness. No doubt the Greek priests at Ptolemais made
some profit out of the transaction, and so it implies liberalities on
the part of Philometor. More we cannot infer from the facts,
even if they do not arise from negligences and ignorances on
the part of the scribes. Thus in the Leyden Papyrus N, col. 2, 4,
dated 105 B.C. (Cleopatra III. and Alexander), we have : εν δε
Πτολεμαιδι της Οηβαιδος εφ ιερεων του μεν Σωτηρος των οντων και ουσων
εν Πτολεμαιδι, where the scribe manifestly omitted the other
Ptolemies by oversight or laziness. The actual text tells that
here; but does not this case show us how dangerous are the
arguments *ex silentio*?

memorating dedications to this king, his wife, and their children, found about Syene, and even at Debot in Lower Nubia, suggest that he must have at one time

FIG. 52.—Colonnade of Ptolemy VII. at Kalabshe (Nubia).

visited the upper country, and asserted his sway over the Nubian kingdom. This is the only period in his life when we can positively assert that he visited the

Thebaid, and therefore it may be in these six years (169-3 B.C.) that he reconquered and pacified the upper country.[1] But there is room for such an expedition, though it does not seem likely, in his after years, and it is also possible that the dedications were made without implying an actual visit from the king. The most important of them is first made accessible by Strack, No. 95. Though its provenance (it is now in Paris) is not stated, it must certainly have come from Syene. The gods commemorated in it are those of that place, as we may see from Nos. 108 and 140 in the same collection. The identification of Egyptian with Hellenic gods is in all of them very interesting. We have Ammon = Chnoubis, Hera = Satis, Hestia = Anoubis, Dionysus = Petempamentis. The dedication to the king and queen and children is made on behalf of Boethos τον Νικοστρατου Χρυσαορεως (a place in Caria near Stratonicea), who was not only αρχισωματοφυλαξ and στρατηγος, but also founder of two towns, Philometoris and Cleopatra, in the "30 schœni" district of Lower Nubia. But the actual dedicator is Herodes, son of Demophon, from some town such as Pergamon or Kyzikos (the termination—ηνος only is preserved), who has all the modern titles of nobility, των διαδοχων, ηγεμων επ ανδρων, then φρουραρχος Συηνης, and governor of the upper country,— now comes a greater novelty,— prophet of Chnoubis, and archistolistes of the temples in Elephantine, Abaton, and Philæ, thus combining native religious functions with his governmental duties.

[1] Our only explicit authority, the Edfu building text, says that the king's work there was done partly in his 16th year and taken up again in his 30th. So it does not settle the difficulty. It is not unlikely that the well-known Greek dedication (Strack, 88) at Kom Ombo dates from this time, viz. "on behalf of king Ptolemy and queen Cleopatra his sister, Gods Philometores, and their children, this second enclosure (σηκος) is dedicated to the great god Aroeres, to Apollo, and to the co-templar (associated in the same temple) gods, by the infantry and cavalry and the others quartered in the Ombite district, on account of the kindness (of the king and queen) to them." Here are Greeks dedicating a temple in the first place to an Egyptian god, with whom they associate their Apollo as a secondary personage.

He and the priests of the Ptolemies here associated with the god Chnoubo Nebieb assemble in the temple of Satis to celebrate to the royal family a yearly feast and the birthday feast of Boethos, according to the established royal decree.

This extraordinary honour to Boethos seems to imply that he had put in order the province for the king on his own account, and so saved a personal campaign to Ptolemy. At all events, when the latter returned from his campaign, he found Alexandria closed against him by the machinations of his brother, and set off an exile, in beggarly plight, to complain at Rome. The senate treated him with great courtesy, but thought fit to settle the dispute by assigning Cyrene to the younger brother, while restoring Philometor to Egypt. This return to power of the king was celebrated by a decree of Benevolences (φιλανθρωπα) in his 18th year, which seems to have been an act of amnesty to those who served under his brother's usurped government. His successor alludes to this in a rescript, preserved to us in the Louvre Papyrus 63. We also know, from one of the petitions of the twins in the Serapeum, that he and his queen made a solemn progress to Memphis in his L 20 to celebrate his peaceful return. There is also in Louvre Papyrus 62, a strong remonstrance from Dioscorides, the διοικητης, in the name of the king and queen, against the conduct of the tax-farmers.[1] It is remarkable that in this crisis we do not hear one word of the policy or influence of Cleopatra.

The younger brother, still called the God Philometor at Cyrene, was not content. He made pilgrimages to Rome, brought accusations of treachery against the king, and claimed Cyprus as belonging to Cyrene in any fair division of the kingdom. He had his party in Rome, who supported these claims, though not with armed intervention. Philometor, when

---

[1] This document has been republished by Revillout in his *Mélanges*, p. 269, with many odd readings and conjectures, but (as usual) without any photograph of the papyrus to enable us to test his novelties.

pressed to accede, argued, delayed, bribed.   Mean-
time the Cyrenians, whom Euergetes (we may so antici-
pate his Egyptian title for convenience' sake) had left
under an Egyptian viceroy, Ptolemy Sympetesis, revolted.   This is another symptom, and a strange one,
of the rising power of the natives.   For here the
Egyptian viceroy takes the side of insurgent Greeks
and leads them against their king.   Euergetes turned
the forces he had gathered against this rebellion, and
recovered Cyrene, but his invasion of Cyprus was a
failure.   He was defeated at Lapethus, and was even a
prisoner in the hands of Philometor, who was either
too soft-hearted or too much afraid of the party opposed
to him in Rome to put his traitorous brother to death.

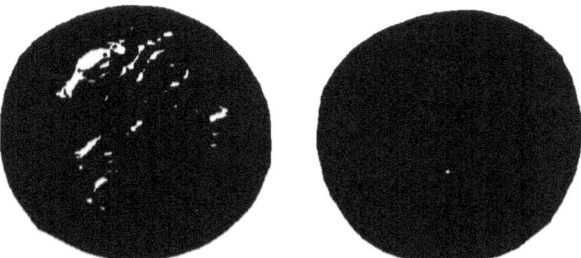

FIG. 53.—Syrian Coin of Philometor.
(Struck when he was at Antioch.)

From henceforth, however (about 156 B.C.), the dis-
contented wretch kept quiet in Cyrene, watching his
opportunity, but either shamed or shackled from making
a new attack.

But it is quite possible that he suborned Demetrius
Soter, now king of Syria, to make an attempt to seize
Cyprus (151 B.C.).   This prince was personally known
to Philometor, and had been kind to him when both
were at Rome, the former as a hostage, the latter as
an exile.   Ptolemy seems to have taken this attempt
so ill, that he set up or prompted another claimant,
Alexander Bala, to seize the crown of Syria, trusting
to the strong unpopularity of Demetrius Soter at
Antioch.   The sequel is preserved to us in two full

narratives, one in 1st Maccabees (caps. x. xi.), the other in Josephus (*Antiq.* xiii. 4). Though the facts do not materially differ, the complexion put upon them is not the same. In the Maccabees Ptolemy is a grasping despot, who seeks to conquer the kingdom of Syria for himself by setting various claimants to fight, and joining the weaker against the stronger. In Josephus this king, who is generally a great favourite with Jewish authors, is a just and temperate man, who even when perfectly successful will not retain a kingdom which properly belongs to others. Although the 1st Maccabees is a far higher authority on this period than Josephus, I incline to believe the latter, owing to the consistence of his account with the fragments of Polybius and Diodorus concerning the king's character.[1] According to this story, the king, having married his daughter in great pomp to Alexander Bala at Ptolemais on the coast of Palestine, was almost assassinated by one Ammonius, whom Alexander, when pressed to interfere, declined or delayed to punish. Ptolemy inferred from this that his son-in-law was privy to the plot, and forthwith set up in place of Demetrius Soter, whom Bala had meanwhile slain in battle, another Demetrius (Nicator), son of the last, to contest the crown. The Princess Cleopatra was transferred from Bala to this prince, as if she were a piece of furniture. She must have been at the moment with her father and his army, not with Bala. Ptolemy and the younger Demetrius then marched upon Antioch, where the populace gladly received the king of Egypt, and crowned him king of Syria. In this he was obliged

---

[1] Polybius, in speaking of Philometor's extreme gentleness and dislike of shedding blood, says that he nevertheless lapsed into the Egyptian vices of ἀσωτία and ῥαθυμία, which brought him into many dangers. Had his dishonest grasping at a kingdom not his own brought about his death in the moment of victory, it is almost certain that the pragmatical historian would have moralised upon this, and charged him with πλεονεξία. I therefore infer that his account of this Syrian war agreed with that of Josephus. Whence the hostile story in the Maccabees came, we do not know.

to acquiesce, till he had persuaded them to accept his new nominee, the son of an unpopular father, as their sovereign.   Meanwhile Bala had gathered an army, and fought a battle with them, in which he was worsted and killed by an Arabian chief during his flight.   But Ptolemy was also thrown from his horse in the thick of the fight, and so badly wounded that he died on the fifth day (146 B.C.), having had the great satisfaction, says Polybius, of seeing his enemy's head.

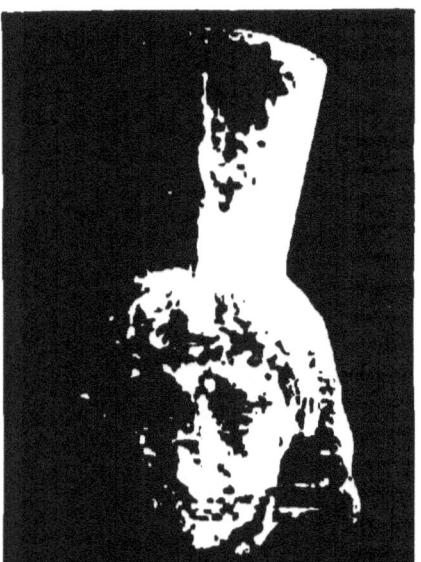

FIG. 54.—Greek head of Philometor. (Probably from Methana in Argolis.)

Thus a stormy and uneasy, but on the whole not unsuccessful, reign came to its close.   The king was but little over 40 when he died. He had shown many high qualities, bravery,   patience, urbanity,   kindliness ; and not even Polybius, who charges him (I know not why) with luxury and effeminateness, denies him these virtues.   There is not a word about concubines, about drunkenness, about cruelty, as is so frequent in this scandalmongering age.   He evidently courted friendly relations with Crete, Argolis, Thera, and other Greek lands, and seems to me not at all so nationalistic as his successor.   But let us see what evidence we have of his internal activity from inscriptions and papyri.

A curious coin, dated in the years 36 and 1 of a king Ptolemy, is referred very generally to this king, and seems to imply that he associated his eldest son in the crown.   Probably he desired to keep his brother out of the inheritance, and made this provision before setting out for his last campaign to Syria.[1] Lists of the deified kings mention an Eupator both before and after Philometor. It is generally assumed that the latter is a mistake for Philopator Neos, who sometimes appears after Philometor in these lists. Strack (p. 48) assumes two Eupators, and places this Philopator Neos after the death of Euergetes II. The question is of little interest to the historian, unless it be to show the strong and religious feeling of officialdom which counted these momentary sovereigns into the permanent list of the deified kings. The God (or Gods) Eupator, the God Neos Philopator take their place in the lists of the next century, like Philadelphus and Euergetes. We have several dedicatory inscriptions to or by Ptolemy and his wife, sometimes with a son or children added, sometimes not, which show that at Antæopolis, Diospolis Parva, Karnak, Esneh, Kom Ombos, Syene, Hesseh (above Philæ), Debôt, this king left his mark. The temple at Debôt is peculiarly interesting ; for not only does it show a Greek inscription of Philometor and his wife (Strack, 87), but it also has texts and cartouches of a native Nubian king, Atkheramon, offering to Osiris, Isis, and Horus. There is also work of the succeeding Ptolemy in this temple. Here, therefore, we have the same sort of relations with a Nubian sovereign as we already noticed in the case of Ptolemy IV. and Ergamen.[2]

The building text of Edfu is very express : "in the year 5, Tybi 1 of Ptolemy Philometor, there was set up the great wooden gate in the hall of the great victor, and the double doors of the second hall ; also the work was taken up again in the year 30 of this king." Both at Karnak and Philæ he did considerable work. Can it be an accident that we have hardly a trace of his building activity in Lower Egypt ? It is quite possible that the natives may have shown him how the upper province had been neglected by his predecessors, and that

---

[1] Cf. the arguments in Strack, p. 37.
[2] Above, p. 140; and see the account in Baedeker, U.E. p. 305.

he chose to heal the long insurrection and its traces
by these benevolences.   But the gap between L 5
and L 30 we can partly supply from the papyri of
Memphis, which are scattered through the museums
of Europe.   There appears to have been a great disturbance in this part of Egypt about the king's 8th

or 9th year (173 B.C.) in connection with the death of Cleopatra
I., and perhaps the war preparations of the regent Eulaeus
against Syria.   This was the
moment when a large number
of Greeks took refuge in the
Serapeum as anchorites,—some
to remain there for life, like
Ptolemy, son of Glaucias, some
to leave it in a year or two,
when the trouble was over.[1]
Whether these people sought
to escape conscription, or the
danger of being massacred by
insurgents, we cannot tell.   The
anchorite Ptolemy always speaks

[1] In the case known to us through
two letters (Pap. Vat. A, and B.M.
Pap. XLII.) which the brother and
the wife of Hephæstion write to him
in his retreat at the Serapeum, it
appears that, owing to some sudden
and great danger, a large number of
men escaped into this refuge, and that
when the rest were let out and came
home, this one remained, to the indignation of his wife and his brother.

FIG. 55.—Egyptian portrait
of Ptolemy VII. (From
Kom Ombo.)

The first intimation they had of his whereabouts was a letter
he sent through a man called Horus.   This is the only Egyptian
name in the affair, unless the wife's name, Isias, may be so
considered.   But the manners and customs seem utterly Egyptian.
She calls herself his sister, whereas she was also certainly his
wife, thus subscribing to Egyptian phrase or fashion.   To take
refuge in the Serapeum was surely also Egyptian, and yet, in
every case we know, Greek-speaking settlers seem to take advantage of it.

with studied reticence of the circumstances which brought him into the seclusion of the Serapeum (συνέβη μοι is his phrase), and yet he boasts that the king shows peculiar favour to men who exhibit this form of piety.   But the whole complexion of these papers shows a fusion of races quite strange to the Petric Papyri of a century earlier.

This Ptolemy fights the case of the Twin acolytes, Thaues and Taus, daughters of an Egyptian neighbour in the village of Psichin (Heracleopolite nome). The officials he petitions, and who long thwart him by shuffling the cards and passing the petition from hand to hand, are Greeks ; but the really responsible controller of the temple stores, who could give out the bread and oil due to the Twins, is Psinthaes, an Egyptian, and he it is who foils the king's good intentions. When the king "got home safe from foreign parts,"— that is to say, was restored by the Romans to his kingdom in 163 B.C.,—he presumably paid a visit in state to Memphis, to worship at the Serapeum, and this was made an occasion for many petitions and requests.   Ptolemy desires to have his younger brother appointed a soldier of the regiment quartered in Memphis, for the sake of the pay ; and after an incredible amount of red-tape the matter is arranged.   Again he complains that in his cell he has been repeatedly subject to raids from Egyptians, who, under pretence of a visitation and search for arms, have treated him with robbery and violence, "because he is a Greek." On the other hand, he or his brother seem to be in concert with the police in watching some criminals in the asylum of the Serapeum, and this may account for his unpopularity.   He ought to have been an aristocrat in that society,—a Macedonian, and originally a cavalry soldier of the Epigone ; but he seems of no more consequence than the ordinary natives.   Apparently the privileged class of κληρουχοι is gone ; we hear instead of κατοικοι or συγγενεις κατοικοι, and we know that Ptolemy was possessed, not of a farm, but of a house and courtyard in a village.   Not only quarrels between Greeks

and natives, but suits among natives, and of wholly
native interests, come before the Greek courts, though
there were Egyptian courts to settle them (B.M. Pap.
III.).   It is interesting that the moments of revolution
are spoken of either as confusion ($\tau\alpha\rho\alpha\chi\eta$) or isolation
($\alpha\mu\epsilon\iota\xi\iota\alpha$), which may imply that then the foreigners and
natives separated into opposed camps, whereas in
ordinary circumstances their mutual intercourse was
quite unrestrained.

CHAPTER VIII

Fig 56.—Cartouches of Ptolemy VII. These are not easily distinguishable from those of his successor, and were probably assimilated intentionally by the priests during the so-called joint reign. The beetle sign (kheper) is said to mark Ptolemy VII.'s cartouches.

AUTHORITIES.—In addition to the histories, of which the ancient are very scanty on these reigns, though there are notices in Polybius and Livy of some value, we have a considerable body of papyri, in the Louvre, in the British Museum, at Turin, and at Rome, which can be utilised to give us some knowledge of Egyptian life at this time.

A BOLD attempt was made by Cleopatra II. to maintain the throne for her young son Eupator or Philopator Neos. But the army of her brother from Cyrene was at hand, while the main forces were still in Syria. Thus, though she may have received loyal support from Onias and the Jews of Leontopolis, a large faction in Alexandria, supported by Thermus, a Roman noble who apparently acted in the interests of Euergetes, and

perhaps invented threats from Rome to coerce the
Alexandrians, insisted upon the king of Cyrene assuming
the crown.   It followed, as a matter of course in those
days, that he should marry his sister, the widowed
queen, and murder the young king who had been
proclaimed by her.   But when we are told that during
his enthronement at Memphis, probably in the following year (145-4) she presented him with a son, whom
he called Memphites, we feel it well-nigh impossible to
accept such stuff.[1]   Formal marriages for state reasons,
without cohabitation, were, as Mr. Petrie tells us,
not foreign to Egyptian history.   During the XXVIth
dynasty Saite kings had married Theban princesses
and hardly ever lived with them.   Such a relation
might be conceivable ; but that a civilised queen should
behave as this Cleopatra is said to have done, or any
civilised man like Euergetes II. could murder this son
of hers publicly during the wedding festivities, then
cohabit with her as if nothing had happened, and by
and by serve up his and her son, Memphites, to her
in morsels as a birthday gift,—these things I refuse to
believe.[2]   What we know on really sound evidence
(Turin Pap. i. p. 9, 21) is that, in his 26th year,
actually the second of his reign, he published an edict
of $\phi\iota\lambda\alpha\nu\theta\rho\omega\pi\alpha$ or indulgences, in which he confirmed
actual possessors of property at his accession, and
protected them from vexatious litigations regarding
their titles.[3]

[1] Revillout's subterfuge, that Philometor, not Euergetes, was
the father of this (posthumous) child, is not supported by any
evidence, and in view of the complicated affairs of Syria, which
occupied Philometor in the end of his life and kept him away from
Egypt, most improbable.

[2] Cf. Justin, xxxviii. 8.   It seems to me not unlikely that this
odd name was chosen by the king to declare his policy, by
contrast to Ἑλληνομεμφίτης, a term of privilege which we find in
B.M. Pap. L., and which implied that a Greek Memphite was
better than a pure one.

[3] Such decrees appear to have been usual at the accessions
of kings ; at least the counsel in the case says they were
numerous in past time.   There was another at the end of this
very reign.

There were, of course, the strongest political reasons why the king of Cyrene, if he were not an outrageous monster, should succeed. He was a titular king in Egypt, of mature age, and fit to deal with the difficulties which threatened the land. The reign of a minor might have been fatal. Not only did he reunite with Egypt the rich severed province of Cyrene, but he certainly commanded friends and interest at Rome, which Cleopatra and her Jews did not. And

FIG. 57.—Cartouches of Ptolemy IX.

These differ but very slightly from those of Philometor, and show many variants among themselves. I have already indicated the only peculiarity which marks those of Philometor.

now Roman favour was more important than ever. Even after the battle of Pydna (167 B.C.) Rome had acquired absolute political sway over the Hellenistic world, and had saved Egypt by her mere command. But behind her political now loomed her commercial monopoly. Her traders had begun to see that the control of the world meant unlimited plunder. Rhodes had been ruined at once. It required twenty years more to destroy Carthage and Corinth, neither of them formidable from any but a commercial view. The

Romans at Delos were to replace both Corinth and
Rhodes; and would not Egypt and its vast wealth
come next under their rapacious grasp?

Such was the situation at the moment of Euergetes
II.'s accession. It was all very well to send the noble
Scipio with his Stoic chaplains to inspect the Eastern
world (*circ.* 143 B.C.), but would future visitors be as
pure and single-hearted? Scipio found the king fat
and puffing (his nickname was *Physkon*), dressed in
too transparent clothes, and whispered, as he went up
to the palace from his ship, escorted by the panting
king, that Alexandria had got at least one benefit from
the visit—it had seen its king taking a walk.

But there is not a word of horror or disgust at any
of his monstrous crimes. Nay, rather the whole
country up to Memphis is represented as teeming with
produce and with population. It is obvious that careful steering of his state was required to keep it from
closer inquisition on the part of the Romans. Presently
came the Gracchan troubles, during which the landed
interests of Italy were shown to be in decadence, and
a bold attempt was made to seize the subject lands for
the pauper farmers of Italy. Then came the bequest
of king Attalus III., whose gift, intended, as I believe,
for a bribe to protect Pergamum, was deliberately
misinterpreted into a bequest of what he had no right
to bequeath.[1] But the war against the claimant of
Pergamum, and the sequestration of its taxes for the
paupers at Rome were no vague signs of what was
likely to follow.

If we believed such people as Justin, we should
rather hold that the king did what he could by his
tyrannies and cruelties to court Roman interference.
Next after his murder of his nephew, his marriage to
Cleopatra II., and the birth of Memphites, we are told

---

[1] This interesting question of bequeathing a kingdom to the
Romans I have discussed in *Hermathena*, xxii. Pergamum was
and remained under the Attalids a nominally sovereign Greek city,
with its own government. The kings were outside the constitution.

that he first violated and then married his niece
Cleopatra III.   Fortunately, Polybius, in his character
of Philometor, has presented to us the fact that the
young princess was already betrothed by her father to
Euergetes.   It seems likely, therefore, that the marriage
with the mother was compulsory, a part of the settlement insisted upon by her party at Alexandria ; the
marriage with the daughter according to his betrothal,
and moreover, in the absence of full brothers, she was
the legitimate heiress to the throne.   It is said that he
divorced the other queen, but there is no clear evidence
for this obvious act.   That he did not cohabit with her
after his new marriage we may assume as obvious.   If
the reader prefers a historical romance to sober criticism,
he will find it in the combinations of M. E. Revillout
(*Mélanges*, pp. 292 *seq.*), who gives us a novelistic
account of the lifelong efforts of the elder Cleopatra,
first to maintain the kingdom for herself and her son
Eupator, who is murdered at the coronation banquet—
for M. Revillout accepts Justin as gospel.   Then she
bears a son by her deceased husband, and waits her
opportunity till the declaration of his majority at the
age of 14.   The new revolution which she excites is
foiled by Euergetes carrying off the prince Memphites,
and sending the pieces of him home to his mother.
How she should have been such a consummate
donkey as to leave the boy in the power of Euergetes, or allow him to be seduced into staying with
him, or, such being the case, how she should have
started a revolt which must secure his death—all
this is left unexplained.   But afterwards, another
son of hers, Philopator Neos, comes upon the stage,
and the old king, by way of amends, associates
this prince in his throne, and reconciles the outraged
queen !

But, speaking soberly, the position of the elder
Cleopatra being maintained as queen, there followed a
peculiarity in the dating of official documents, both
demotic and Greek, which has caused not a little
trouble to the chronologists.   In order to mark that

he was not the actual husband of both ladies, the king
dated as follows :—"in the reign of king Ptolemy, and
queen Cleopatra his sister, and queen Cleopatra his
wife." But this is by no means the only form. A
certain number of documents are dated in the reign of
king Ptolemy and queen Cleopatra, his sister, and their
children, others in the reign of Ptolemy and Cleopatra,
his wife, and their children. Most unfortunately, the
Greek texts to which I refer are not dated, being most
of them mere votive offerings. There are several
demotic documents of the reign which are dated, but
as we are told that the signs for *wife* and for *sister* in
that writing are hardly distinguishable, so also those
for various numbers, these document afford us but
doubtful light.[1] Nevertheless Strack, a very careful

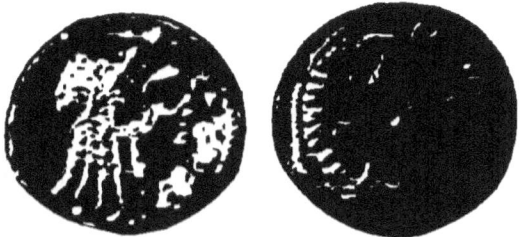

FIG. 58.—Coin of Cleopatra II.

and sober scholar (*op. cit.* pp. 39–41), has taken the
pains to make out a list of these alleged variations,
though he is apparently somewhat staggered at them ;
here is his table (p. 49) of the various changes,
from one wife to two and back again, which
this wonderful Euergetes made, or was compelled to
make, during his 29 years of undisputed reign
(146–117 B.C.) :—

[1] The longer I study this history, the more I suspect the trust-
worthiness of M. Revillout's confident deciphering, never accompanied by autotypes. His fury at these doubts of mine is not
calculated to allay my scepticism.

Euergetes and Cleopatra II.	.	.	145 –141 B.C.
,,	both queens	.	141 –140
,,	Cleopatra II.	.	140 –139[1]
,,	both queens	.	139 –136
,,	Cleopatra II.	.	136[2]–133
,,	both queens	.	133 –131
,,	Cleopatra III.	.	131 –124
Cleopatra II. reigned alone in some parts of Egypt		.	130 –129[3]
Euergetes and both queens	.	.	124 –123
,,	Cleopatra II.	.	123 –121
,,	both queens	.	121 –118
,,	Cleopatra III.	.	118 –116

Surely this is no reasonable history.   That Euergetes II.
first married Cleopatra II., then in a year or two
Cleopatra III. ; that he had grave quarrels with the

FIG. 59.—Coin of Cleopatra III.

former, and tried to oust her from her royalty, but
unsuccessfully—all this I can believe ; and this might
account for three, or at most four, such changes of
official dating.   But the catalogue of a dozen changes
seems to me absurd.   I still adhere to my former view,
namely, that when these changes had been once
decreed, scribes in various outlying parts of the empire

[1] Strack says till 137, but Grenfell Papyri, II. xv., gives both
queens in 139.
[2] Corroborated by the inscription on the temple at Dakkeh
(Nubia).
[3] Grenfell Papyri, II. xix., shows that Euergetes was recognised
as king this year in the Pathyrite nome.

would copy from a document before them without
knowing, perhaps without caring, whether at the
moment two queens or one were to be recognised, and
I think it may be a mere matter of chance which
formula was adopted.

The one serious war between brother and sister
seems to have taken place in 129 B.C. when he fled
with his wife and his son Memphites to Cyprus.   But he
presently regained his hold upon Egypt, which indeed
he seems to have never completely lost, to judge from
protocols (Grenfell, II. xix.), which mention him as
king this very year.   There is, moreover, a Greek
letter of $L \mu$ (130 B.C.) preserved in the Louvre, which
Revillout has printed in his *Mélanges*, p. 295 (Strack,
p. 46), which speaks of Paos sailing up to Hermonthis
with an army to treat the people there as rebels.[1]   There
were, therefore, disturbances both at Alexandria and
in the upper country, but not insurrections against the
crown, so much as civil war, headed by the factions of
the king and his discarded queen.   The well-known
text in Alexandria, commemorating the gratitude of
Soterichos son of Ikadion from Gortyn (Crete), says
that this officer, being governor of the Thebaid, superintended the safety of both the Red Sea shipping and
the caravans from Koptos through the eastern desert, of
precious stones (the emerald of the desert) and spices.
It is dated on the first day of L 41, and implies that
for some time previously this officer was in possession
of the province.   The disturbance at Hermonthis must
therefore have been quite local and transient.

According to our various scraps of information, every
class (save that of the natives) was at some time in
revolt against Euergetes II.   The Cyrenæans, who
had already endeavoured to cast off his yoke, when
he was striving to conquer Cyprus, were massacred by
him, because they spoke too freely concerning his wife

----

[1] Of course I adopt Strack's suggestions as to the correction
of Revillout's more than doubtful Greek.   He should have read
the man's name Εσθλαδας, not Εσθαλδας, an impossible form, and
his curious αναταλειν is probably misread for αναπλειν.

or mistress Eirene. His mercenaries, according to Diodorus, revolted with one Galæstes, who had been a general of Philometor, and had commanded troops at the battle where Philometor fell, near Antioch. He seems to have carried off his contingent to Greece, while the remainder at Alexandria were only saved to Egypt by the loyalty of the general Hierax, who settled their arrears of pay out of his own pocket. Euergetes' Alexandrian subjects frequently revolted, and in these insurrections he so often let loose his mercenaries upon them, that the whole complexion of the population of that capital was changed. We have a fragment from Polybius of great importance upon this point (xxxiv. 14): "Polybius having visited the city is disgusted at the condition in which he found it. For he says that three strata occupy it: the Egyptian and native race, smart and civilised (ὀξὺ καὶ πολιτικόν). Then the mercenary troops, oppressive (βαρύ) and numerous and dissolute; for from old custom they kept armed mercenaries, who had learned to rule, rather than to obey, on account of the worthlessness of the kings. The third stratum was that of the Alexandrians, nor was even this truly a civilised population (πολιτικόν) owing to the same causes, but yet better than the other two, for though of mixed breed, yet they were originally Greeks, with traditions of the general type of the Greeks. But this part of the population having disappeared, chiefly owing to Ptolemy Euergetes Physkon, in whose reign Polybius visited Alexandria, — for Physkon, when revolted against, over and over again let loose his troops on the population and massacred them,—and such being the state of things, to visit Egypt was a long and thankless journey."

This account is very defective, for it omits at least two most important classes, the so-called Macedonian or household troops, which in every home document are clearly distinguished from the mercenaries (μισθοφόροι); and the Jews, who had long been a part of the population, and who under Philometor had attained to places of public trust. This account, however, does insist

upon the disappearance of the Greek population of
Alexandria, and though we may read with a smile the
rubbish of Justin (xxxviii. 8), that the terrified populace
fled for fear of death, and left the king alone with his
servants, the lord of empty houses, so that he solicited
settlers by an edict (*edicto peregrinos sollicitat*), we may
possibly have before us traces of an edict by which
Egyptians and Syrians (Jews) were granted the privileges of Alexandrian citizenship, and the Greek population discouraged and reduced. It is not unlikely
that if there ever was such an edict, the king took pains
to invite Roman trading people to settle at Alexandria.
Inscriptions found at Delos seem to attest that he
made a Roman, Marcus, one of his peers. Two texts
(Strack, 115, 118) mention the gratitude of a class
called $\tau\omega\nu$ $\epsilon\nu$ $A\lambda\epsilon\xi\alpha\nu\delta\rho\epsilon\iota\alpha\iota$ $\pi\rho\epsilon\sigma\beta\upsilon\tau\epsilon\rho\omega\nu$ $\epsilon\gamma\delta\sigma\chi\epsilon\omega\nu$, among
the $\xi\epsilon\nu\sigma\iota$ of that city. Another (113) expressly thanks
him for his protection of Roman shippers and merchants
at the capture of Alexandria (either at his accession, or
at the recovery of Alexandria, 129 B.C.).

We have, moreover, recovered texts which show that
the Jews were not persecuted, but favoured by this
king. As this evidence is partly new, it is worth giving
here.[1]

There is a stone which professes to be a renewal of
the old inscription $\beta\alpha\sigma\iota\lambda\epsilon\upsilon\varsigma$ $\Pi\tau\sigma\lambda\epsilon\mu\alpha\iota\sigma\varsigma$ $E\upsilon$ | $\epsilon\rho\gamma\epsilon\tau\eta\varsigma$ $\tau\eta\nu$
$\pi\rho\sigma\sigma\epsilon\upsilon\chi\eta\nu$ | $\alpha\sigma\upsilon\lambda\sigma\nu$. Mr. Sayce possesses an ostracon
from Karnak, showing that under this king a Simon
son of Eleazar was tax-collector in Diospolis.

From Athribis in Lower Egypt we have $\upsilon\pi\epsilon\rho$. $\beta\alpha\sigma$.
$\Pi\tau\sigma\lambda$. $\kappa\alpha\iota$ $\beta\alpha\sigma$. $K\lambda\epsilon\sigma\pi\alpha\tau\rho\alpha\varsigma$ $\Pi\tau\sigma\lambda\epsilon\mu\alpha\iota\sigma\varsigma$ σ $E\pi\iota\kappa\upsilon\delta\sigma\upsilon$ $\epsilon\pi\iota\sigma\tau\alpha\tau\eta\varsigma$
$\tau\omega\nu$ $\phi\upsilon\lambda\alpha\kappa\iota\tau\omega\nu$ $\kappa\alpha\iota$ $\sigma\iota$ $\epsilon\nu$ $A\theta\rho\iota\beta\epsilon\iota$ $I\sigma\upsilon\delta\alpha\iota\sigma\iota$ $\tau\eta\nu$ $\pi\rho\sigma\sigma\epsilon\upsilon\chi\eta\nu$ $\theta\epsilon\omega\iota$
$\upsilon\psi\iota\sigma\tau\omega\iota$, also $\upsilon\pi\epsilon\rho$. $\beta\alpha\sigma$. $\Pi\tau\sigma\lambda$. $\kappa\alpha\iota$ $\beta\alpha\sigma$. $K\lambda\epsilon\sigma\pi\alpha\tau\rho\iota\varsigma$ $\kappa\alpha\iota$ $\tau\omega\nu$
$\tau\epsilon\kappa\nu\omega\nu$ $E\rho\mu\iota\alpha\varsigma$ $\kappa\alpha\iota$ $\Phi\iota\lambda\sigma\tau\epsilon\rho\alpha$ η $\gamma\upsilon\nu\eta$ $\kappa\alpha\iota$ $\tau\alpha$ $\pi\alpha\iota\delta\iota\alpha$ $\tau\eta\nu\delta\epsilon$ $\epsilon\xi\epsilon\delta\rho\alpha\nu$
$\kappa\alpha\iota$ $\tau\eta\nu$ $\pi\rho\sigma\sigma\epsilon\upsilon\chi\eta\nu$.

Though it is quite possible that the first of these may
refer to the first Euergetes, and the latter to Ptolemy V. or
VII., I think the probabilities are in favour of Physkon,
who was therefore no persecutor, but a protector of the

[1] Cf. Willrich, *Juden und Griechen*, p. 151.

Jews. This makes the theory that 3rd Maccabees really refers to his massacres, and not those of Philopator, even more improbable than it is in itself.

In Mr. Grenfell's Papyri, I. pp. 74–75, we have other clear evidence of Jews in Egypt; it is the letter of a man to his brother complaining that, having found a suitable mare, and having bought her from a Jew called Danooul, the latter has neither delivered the animal nor has given the money for its journey to the new owner. Mr. Grenfell dates this document in the 2nd century B.C. but it may be quite near the present epoch. In the C.I.G. iii. 4838 c, there are Jewish dedications of which the originals might tell us (palæographically) their date, but they are probably of this epoch. There are also the two texts from Athribis, dedications to a Ptolemy and Cleopatra (probably Philometor), set up by Jews, of which the first just quoted is very curious: "on behalf of the king and queen, Ptolemy son of Epikydes, the controller of the police, and the Jews in Athribis dedicate this *proseuche* (synagogue) to Almighty God."

• We have shown already, in considering the papyri of the middle of the 3rd century B.C., that Jewish settlements had long been existing in Egypt. These new texts referring to the reigns of Ptolemy VII. and IX. are therefore only evidences of an increase in the numbers and importance of the Jews. The seizure of Palestine by Antiochus III., the fierce persecution of the Jews by Antiochus IV.,—the abomination of desolation,—must have sent many exiles from Jerusalem to the old land of Goshen and the flesh-pots of Egypt; now also the persecution of the Greeks of Alexandria, and the encouraging of the rival populations, redounded to the advantage of the Jews.

Hence we are not surprised to hear from the editor of the book of Ecclesiasticus in Greek, that, coming to Egypt in this king's 38th year (133 B.C.) he found the whole Old Testament already translated for the benefit of the Jews in Egypt, especially, as Willrich justly supposes, for the benefit of the religious centre at Leontopolis. How long the process of translating this

great collection of books was in progress, and therefore when it began, we shall never know with certainty.
The Jews themselves, according to the letter called that
of Aristeas, attributed the whole work to the patron-

FIG. 60.—Ptolemy IX, with Two Goddesses (Nishem and Uati).
(From Kom Ombo.)

age of Philadelphus. Some able modern critics, such
as Freudenthal, think it started with Philopator; others,
like Grätz and Willrich, that the impulse was due to
the philo-Judaic policy of Philometor and the new

sanctuary at Leontopolis. I believe it to have been very gradual, and to have reached over all these reigns. It is not at all impossible that the Jews in the remote Fayyum had the Pentateuch translated in the days of the second or third Ptolemy.

But if Physkon favoured the Jews so much, he favoured the natives and their religion a great deal more. His building activity is shown in temples all over Egypt, and as far as Dakkeh in Nubia, nor is there a doubt that if this evidence only remained to us, we should consider him by far the greatest of the Ptolemies.[1] But here again we find a dearth of monuments north of Thebes. There is a solitary allusion in the *Papyrus du Lac Moeris* (ed. Langone) to his activity (with his sister) in the Fayyum. Then we may quote the Edfu text :—

"The completing of the inscriptions carved upon the stone, with the adorning of the walls with gold and colours, with the carpentry of the doors, with the making of the door lintels of good bronze, with the door-posts and locks, and the laying of gold plates on the doors, with the completing of the inner temple-house, lasted till the 18th of Mesore in the 28th year of the deceased king Ptolemy Euergetes II. (IX.) and his wife, the regent Cleopatra—in all 95 years, from the ceremony of the first hammer-stroke to the feast of the formal entrance-procession, the feast of the dedication by his majesty to his divine lord, Horus of Edfu, etc., etc., the great Techu-feast, the like of which has not been from the creation of the world to this day." (Then follows a description of the festivities—sacrifices, feasting, lavish supply of wine and unguents, brilliant lighting, and reckless enjoyment.) "The god of Edfu has taken possession of his adytum (date, year 30, month Payni 9), the feast of the union of the moon-god Osiris with the sun-god Ra which lasts six days, they began the building of the Chent-hall (the great hall of eighteen pillars), and the roof of the lord of heaven.

[1] It is only quite recently that Captain Lyons has found another small temple dedicated to Hathor at Philæ, by this king and his sister. Cf. his *Philæ*, p. 27, and Plate 12.

It was finished in the year 46, 18th of Mesore, 16 years, 2 months, and 10 days after the foundation,

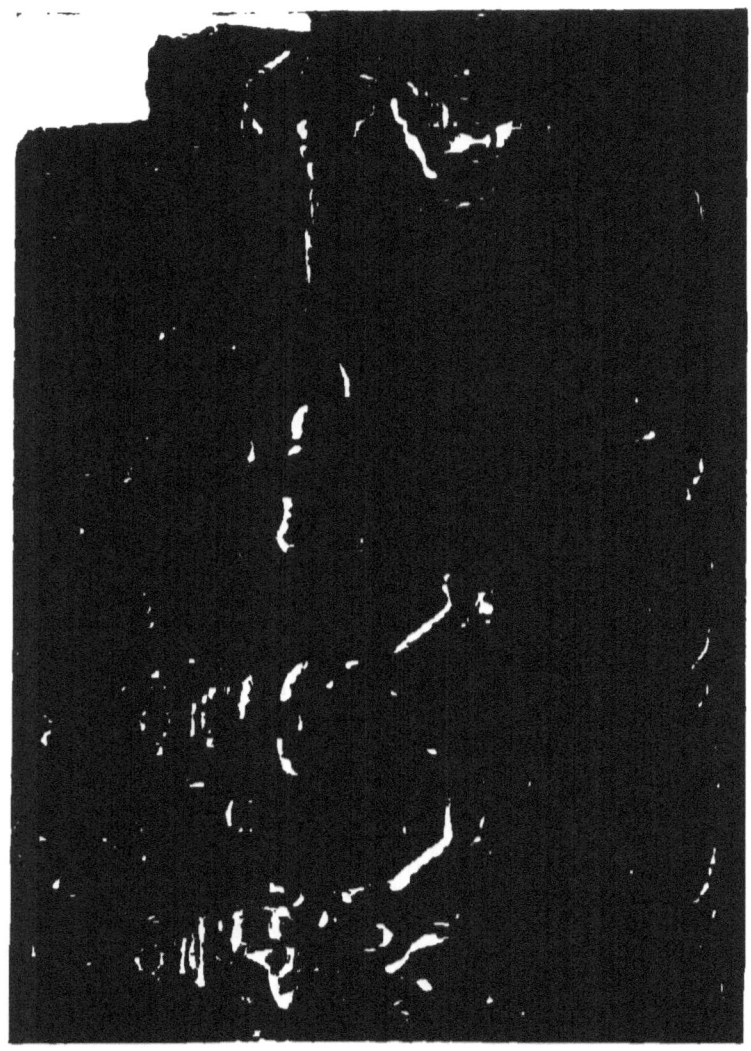

FIG. 61.—Kom Ombo.   Horus bestowing Gifts on Ptolemy IX. and Two Cleopatras.

and the fair feast in this house when the great name of his majesty was inscribed full in the year 48.

"At the close of his life, in the year 54 of this king, on the 11th of Payni, was laid the foundation of the great circuit-wall and the pylons of the entrance. As they were busy with this foundation the king died, and his eldest son succeeded to the throne."

But this does not prove anything very distinctive, for did not every Ptolemy keep working at this great temple, even after it might be regarded complete? We may only note that the activity his government showed in this place lasted up to the very day of his death, and that it was a benevolent policy. This is corroborated by the Aswân stele published by me in *Hermathena*, xxi. (incompletely by Strack, 140, who missed the all-important date L 53, which can be read near the foot of the inscription), where the priests in that place appeal to his successor, quoting certain benevolences granted by the old king in his 53rd year. The counsel pleading in the Hermias case (Turin Pap. i. p. 7) mentions a general indulgence granted to all delinquents up to the 19th of Thoth in the year 53. How universal this edict was, or why it was issued at this moment, we do not yet know. Akin to this is the information given by the Bankes stele (Strack, 103c) in which the king and two queens (probably near the end of their reign[1]) are petitioned by the priests of the great temple of Isis in Philæ to stop the "strategi, and epistatæ, and Thebarchs, and government secretaries, and epistatæ of the police, and all the other officials, and the troops accompanying them, and the rest of their attendants," from making a public house of the temple, and requiring the priests to entertain them. That this was an old practice I have no doubt; the matter was brought to a climax by two circumstances, first, the greatly increased traffic to Nubia and the upper country under this king; secondly, the fact that the natives had

---

[1] This conclusion of Letronne, who found the name of Lochos as governor of the Thebaid in a papyrus dated L 44 (126 B.C.), is approved by Wilcken (*Hermes*, xxii. on the Bankes stele), and is consistent with the king's other benevolences to the upper country in the end of his reign.

only now acquired the boldness to state their grievances
and have them redressed.   The stone of Sehéle (Strack,

FIG. 62.—Screened Colonnade at Philæ (work of Ptolemy IX.).

108) shows us not only the old Egyptian gods of the
cataract, Chnoubis, Satis, Anoukis, etc., assuming the

names of Greek gods in addition to their own, but in
the association or synod of their worshippers, we find
scattered among genuine Greek names (among these
the chief priests of the order) thoroughly native names,
Petearoeris, son of Phanouphis, Psenchnoubis son of
Pellias, Pachnoubis, etc., without any suspicion of
inequality. This case is the more instructive, as the
now ordinary habit of bearing two names, a Greek and
an Egyptian, makes the nationality of people named in
contemporary papyri very uncertain.

The family papers of Dryton, recovered by Mr.
Grenfell (G.P. I. and Pap. cccci. B.M., which I have
published in *Hermathena*, xxi.), give us very curious
information concerning this mixture of names. He
calls himself Dryton son of Pamphilos, a Cretan, and
has several official titles (των διαδοχων και του επιταγματος,
ιππαρχος επ ανδρων); he is married first to Sarapias,
daughter of Esthladas son of Theon, secondly to
Apollonia, a Cyrenæan woman, daughter of Ptolemy
son of Hermocrates. So far we seem to be in strictly
Greek society. But the two sisters of this Apollonia
(G.P. xvii.), one of whom is called Herakleia (the other
Greek name is lost in a fracture), have also Egyptian
names, Semminis and Senapathis, and her five daughters
are called (B.M. cccci.) Apollonia or Senmonthis, Aph-
rodisia or Tachratis, Aristo or Senmonthis, Nicarion
or Thermouthis, the younger Apollonia or Senpelais.
Though their father, who only appears (being of the
older generation) with his Greek name, confines himself to their Greek names in his will, they rehearse
both in a formal legal complaint which they lodge with
the governor of the province regarding an invasion of
their property. It was therefore a usual thing for
Greeks settled in Upper Egypt to be known by native
names, and these were no mere nicknames. I am told
it is universal for English settlers among the Kaffirs
to be called by a native name, which has no relation to
their own, and which they often cannot pronounce
(owing to the clicks). By this all the natives know
them. But here in Egypt the native name is formally

cited in court.   The wife of Dryton, who does business
in lending corn, etc., deals with a society of Persians
of the Epigone, who also appear with double names,
the former being not Persian, but Greek (G.P. xviii
xx. xxiii.).   Sometimes, however, and this too in
formal contracts dated by all the series of the Ptolemies,
these Persians only use their Egyptian names (G.P.
xxvii.).[1]   The influence then of neighbours, of nurses,
of servants, was becoming dominant at this time, and
imposing even upon the aristocracy of the dominant race
a certain use of the native language.   I think the Pap. L.
(50) of the B.M. which the editors refer to the third
century (cf. Add. p. xx) for palæographical reasons,
really belongs to this generation, and represents a
state of things unknown in the earlier time.   It begins:
" To Metrodorus the epimeletes from Apugchis son of
Inarois.   I, a Helleno-Memphite, register according to
the royal injunction published my house and courtyard
in the Hellenion," and he goes on to describe its limits
by his neighbours, one and all of them Egyptian by
name.[2]   Now either this was a Greek oblivious of his

---

[1] Indeed, the Persians who appear in the Leyden Papyri (N, 7
and 8), have such completely and exclusively Egyptian names
that one begins to doubt whether Περσης and Περσινη has not
some quite different meaning.   Nor do they usually appear here
as της επιγονης, which points to a partially foreign origin (cf. a
single case in O, 10, but where the name is still Peteimouthes son
of Horus!)   The curious text in N is as follows:—6 seq. : απεδοτο
Πιμωνθης, ως L λε, etc., και Σναχομνευς, etc., και Σεμμουθις Περσινηι
ως L κβ, etc., και Ταθαιτ Περσινηι ως L λ, etc., μετα του κυριου εαιτων
Πιμωνθου του συναποδομενου, οι τεσσαρες των Πετεψαιτος, των εκ των
Μεμνονεω σκυτεων.   I have left out the personal descriptions, and
set down the mistakes as they stand, viz. Περσινηι for the nom.
and εαυτων for αιτων.   But as for the facts, all the names are
thoroughly Egyptian, their trade is Egyptian, all the neighbours
bounding their holding are Egyptian, and yet the two women
are called Περσιναι without their brothers being called Περσαι.
What are we to make of this?   Possibly their mother was a
Persian woman married to an Egyptian, which is the conjecture
of Leemans.

[2] Wilcken (Gött. G. A. 1894, p. 725), has drawn to light the
citation of Steph. Byz. from Aristagoras of Miletus : Ἑλληνικὸν καὶ
Καρικὸν τόποι ἐν Μέμφιδι, ἀφ' ὧν Ἑλληνομεμφῖται καὶ Καρομεμφῖται,

own Greek name and those of his neighbours, though he belongs to a privileged Hellenistic class and lives in the Greek quarter of Memphis, or else he is an Egyptian living with other Egyptians in the Greek quarter, and admitted to the privileges of the dominant race. I think the latter is the truth, and that accordingly this document dates from the days of Euergetes II. In the Petrie Papyri I found traces of natives assuming Greek names out of policy or convenience;[1] in these later documents the weight of evidence is quite the other way. Here are the words of B.M. xliii. : "Hearing that you were learning the Egyptian language, I was glad for your sake and mine in that now coming to the city you will teach children in ——'s school, and have some means of subsistence for your old age." This may well be contrasted with the note in the P.P. asking for λέξεις to the *Iliad*. I have sought carefully in this period for evidence of the assumption of Greek names by natives, but although I cannot but suppose it still to have occurred, as it surely must have done in earlier days, I have failed to find any evidence.[2]

It is quite possible that the ruin of Macedonia and of Greece may have acted even in Upper Egypt upon the prestige of that part of the population of Egypt, and that the natives may have asserted themselves against these intruders (as they might still be called by a people

therefore probably barracks or camps for foreign mercenaries when first so called. But now, if this Helleno-Memphite indeed lived there, it was wholly peopled by natives.

[1] Cf. *e.g.* the list of retailers in the oil monopoly, who were small people belonging to the villages of the Fayyum (P.P. II. xxviii.). A very few Greek names occur, eight altogether, without any designation of father, so that they may possibly be disgraced Greeks. But I do not think so. Such a thing as a double name, Greek and Egyptian, given to describe a man or woman is perfectly unknown in the P.P. of the third century B.C.

[2] Revillout (*Mélanges*, p. 168) finding demotic contracts where one member of a family is called by a Greek name, "Psechous called by name Heracleides," imagines that this was a privilege sometimes granted to the eldest son of a rich native family by the dominant race. I will make no remark on this curious hypothesis, but note that it is an instance of Egyptians adopting Greek names, which in later times was quite common.

with a long memory) with the knowledge that both races had failed miserably in their conflicts with Rome. In estimating this reign, and its consequences for Egypt, we are thus in the same difficulties that encompass our estimate of Philopator. Our Greek authorities tell us of nothing but the crimes and follies of Physkon,

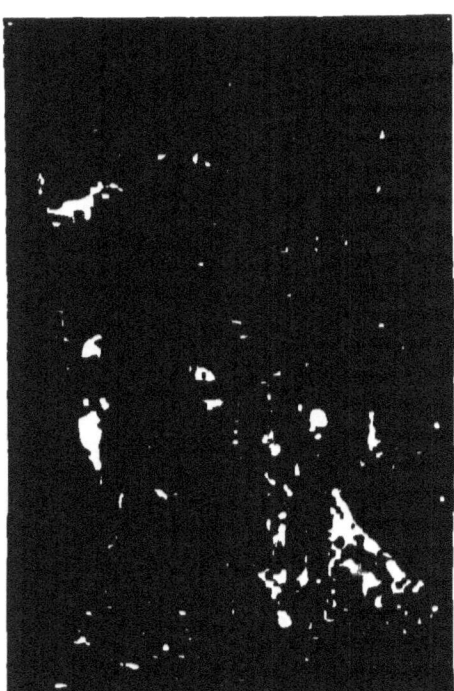

FIG. 63.—Ptolemy IX. making Offerings.
(From Dêr-el-Medineh.)

tempered by Greek distractions of writing memoirs, and of discussions with the learned Greeks of the Museum. All the world, not to say his own nation, are described as filled with horror at his enormities. If we turn to inscriptions and to papyri, which are unusually frequent among the scanty records of the dynasty, we find the king and his queens commemorated in friendly dedications to or by his officers in Delos, in Cyprus, and in Egypt. He extends the commercial bounds of Egypt to the south and east, he keeps Cyrene perfectly still and undisturbed, probably under the viceroyalty of his son Apion. He so far manages to control two ambitious queens, probably at deadly enmity, that at the very close of his life they both appear associated with him in the royalty, as if nothing had happened to disturb the peace of the palace. Throughout the country the legal and fiscal documents still extant show the prevalence of law and order. There was indeed a temporary confusion when the king was exiled and the elder Cleopatra endeavoured to resume the sovereignty in her own name. But even then we have reason to believe that property was not disturbed, that lawless attempts were set right by the ordinary courts in due time; above all, that these courts dealt with perfect fairness between the settlers and the natives. Many of these latter now appear in high official positions. Though there was an order that all demotic contracts should be translated and registered in Greek, this law was not carried out with severity, so as to annul honest transactions among the natives,[1] and there were still native courts and judges before whom those who knew no Greek could plead their claims. But we see a growing and very natural tendency of the natives, even in their own transactions concerning religious customs, such as the embalming of the dead, to come before the Greek courts, and trust to the justice of assize judges sent down by the crown.

A very curious and difficult document, Pap. 63 of the Louvre, which has been edited with his usual ability by Lumbroso, and again recently by Revillout (*Mélanges*, pp. 251 *seq.*, whose knowledge of Egyptian economy is far greater than his knowledge of Greek), gives us some further evidence of the king's care for the interests of the natives. This document, dated at the outset of his reign, is a rambling and wordy circular on the part of the chief financial officer (διοικητης) Herodes at Alexandria to his subordinates, censuring them roundly for their stupidity in not interpreting liberally and justly the existing orders regarding the corvée required from all the inhabitants. This corvée M. Revillout rightly understands to be the cultivating of the crown land. Many complaints had been made by members of the military caste who were doing military and naval duty far from their homesteads that they were still held subject to this duty, when they were not even

---

[1] This appears clearly in the course of the arguments of the case of Hermias against the Choachytæ in Turin Pap. I.

able to till their own farms. Herodes insists that the object of all the royal rescripts was not to ruin the farmers, but rather to obtain the greatest amount of good agriculture on all the land, as well as primarily on the crown estates, whereas this system of stupid oppression defeated its own object. Men became bankrupt and fled for refuge into the asylums of the temples, so leaving both their own and the crown land lying waste. Regarding the corvée of beasts of burden for the same purpose, he desires the strictness to be in no way relaxed. Very interesting is his picture of the military caste (μαχιμοι) throughout the country. The word *all* (he says, line 100) includes those already subject to other state duties, "and the majority of the natives living in the villages, who, being needy, get their living by their labour, not a few also of those on the military roll who get hardly enough to support them from the pay allowed them by the crown, and some even, nay, the majority, of the military caste who are unable to work their land lots from their own resources, but borrow money at high interest on the security of the crop, whom, even if they proposed to aid in the farming of the crown land, no one would trust to carry the seed to the fields." This is a sorry picture of the country, but the writer urges just and liberal treatment of these poor people.

The critics of my former work have spoken of my efforts to rehabilitate this king. I have made no

FIG. 64.—Coin of Euergetes II. with Dionysiac emblems.

such efforts. I have stated fully and fairly the adverse evidence of writers such as Justin and Strabo,—

Polybius, so far as we have him, tells us nothing monstrous of the king,—as well as the favourable evidence of contemporary documents. These latter are of course mainly official, and therefore not likely to allude to any court tragedies. But they could hardly have avoided disclosing any general insecurity or injustice, arising from the oppression of the crown. Apart from the bloody suppressions of riots among the Alexandrian populace,—and this is only asserted by second-hand and late authors,—I can find no evidence of harsh dealing with his subjects on the part of this infamous king.

It is well to observe, before passing on, that in this king's reign there took place a practical change in the dating of documents, of which no ancient historian has left us any notice. Hitherto, in formal dates, the Macedonian and Egyptian months were both given, and these constantly varied in their mutual relation, as the Macedonian were lunar months, with occasional intercalations to make up a solar year, whereas the Egyptian twelve months made up a year of 360 days, to which five days were added. The complications which thus resulted were swept away by the equalising of the Macedonian with the Egyptian months (Dios = Thoth, etc.), so that the mention of the former becomes a mere empty formula.

CHAPTER IX

AUTHORITIES.—In addition to the general histories, we have a recent increase, and a considerable one, to the contemporary documents of these reigns in the great discoveries and acquisitions of Mr. B. P. Grenfell, of which two volumes have already been published (Clarendon Press, 1896, 1897). They are peculiarly rich in documents of Soter II.'s reign. On that of Ptolemy XI. (Alexander) we have several interesting stelæ, one of which is reproduced below, and of which the texts can now be found in Strack. To Ptolemy XIII. (Auletes) we have many allusions in Cicero.

WHEN Euergetes II. died, apparently at the beginning of 116 B.C., he left his empire in a safe and, we may say, a flourishing condition. There was no more question of seizing the Syrian provinces, but, on the other hand, the rival claimants to the Seleukid throne,

one of whom it had been his policy to support against the other during the later years of his life, made all danger of invasion of Egypt to vanish. The king's benevolences in the upper country probably made his sway popular, and there was no external danger then threatening the kingdom from Rome, which was racked by internal disorders. For some reason which we cannot fathom, he bequeathed the important province of Cyrene away from his proper heir to a son called Apion, whom the historians call illegitimate, not knowing that any son except those born of his associated queen in the purple would be so designated by the traditions of the family.[1] Apion can have been no upstart, seeing that he ruled his province in profound peace all his life, bequeathing it to the Romans in 97 B.C. Probably he was the son of the Cyrenæan Eirene, whom the historians call the king's mistress, and worse, but who was most probably a grandee of the old Greek aristocracy in that most aristocratic of Hellenic colonies.

Euergetes is also considered by some (e.g. Strack, p. 178) to have associated in the government of Cyprus another son (by Cleopatra II.!), him who appears as Philopator Neos in many lists,[2] and whom I have represented as the eldest son of his brother Philometor. At all events, this prince never actually succeeded, though if he was really regent of Cyprus with his father, the

[1] The Cyrenaic coinage of this period presents a difficulty. So many coins of Ptolemy X. (Lathyrus) have been found that Mr. Poole (*Coins*, p. lxxx) thinks Apion cannot have succeeded at once, but only after some years' delay. He puts his accession at 107 B.C., the date of the exile of Lathyrus. I feel great hesitation in adopting conclusions inferred from coins only.

[2] The lists (of associated kings in the worship of Alexander, etc., or of the Gods Adelphi, etc., which stand at the head of most official documents) are very unsteady (naturally) about the kings Eupator and Philopator Neos, who never actually reigned. Sometimes these names seem to be interchanged, sometimes one of them is omitted. The only solid argument for the rule of Philopator Neos in Cyprus is the coin of Paphos in the B.M., described by Mr. Poole (*Coins of Ptol.* p. lxxii, and plate xxiii. 4), giving LN and L.A as the years of the old king and his son (cf. Fig. 66).

latter may have intended to bequeath Cyprus to him as
he had given away Cyrene to Apion.   The separation
of these provinces, containing Greek cities, which the
Romans were always disposed to liberate and then to
absorb in their empire, made the homogeneous and
now Oriental kingdom of Egypt much safer from the
rapacious republic.   But whether Physkon had such
far-seeing views we cannot tell.   The other children
with whom we are now concerned were two sons and
two daughters, of whom the eldest pair, contrary to
the practice of crown princes, were married.[1]

The widowed queen, Cleopatra III., however, assumed
the reins of government at once.   And what became
of Cleopatra II., her mother?   She passes away from
the stage of history without a word.   But the very

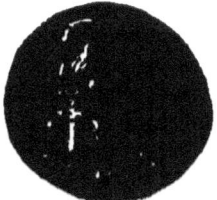

FIG. 66.—Coin of Euergetes II. and Philopator Neos.
(Head of Soter I. on obverse.)

silence about her claims shows that she was dead.   If
she survived her brother, she was surely murdered as
soon as possible by the rival queen, her daughter ; for
though Euergetes managed to live and reign with them
both, when he was gone, Egypt would not contain
them together for one moment.   But though two
regent queens together were impossible, it seems that
the customs of the country would not tolerate even one
without the formal association of the next male heir to
the throne.

The queen urged strongly to have her younger son,
Ptolemy Alexander, raised to this place, either because

[1] This fact gives additional colour to the theory of Strack that
Philopator Neos was an elder son, and designated for the throne.
The marriage of younger sons would not be so strictly supervised.

he was her favourite, or his youth gave her a better chance of exercising the whole power. But the Alexandrians or Macedonians (household troops) would not violate tradition, and the eldest Ptolemy ascended the throne with his mother under the title of Philometor Soter (commonly called Soter II.). That this regulation of the succession was not effected without disturbance in Alexandria is very probable. We did not know till recently that there was also trouble in the Thebaid, —possibly caused by the elder queen and resulting in her death,—for in a complaint of the daughters of Dryton (B.M. cccci.), a respectable citizen of the district, who made his will in the 44th year of the previous reign (G.P. I. xxi.), we hear that after they had succeeded there were καιροι αμειξιας, days when free crossing of the river was dangerous or not permitted, during which their property was invaded by a Greek. This petition is addressed to Phommous as governor of the Thebaid, which he was in the early years of the present reign. There is therefore no room for these disturbances except at the accession of the new king ; for Euergetes' closing years were, as we know, full of favour for this upper country.

Mr. Somers Clarke has suggested to me another evidence of some revolution at this time, which may most reasonably be connected with the same transition. "You will remember," he says in a letter from the spot, "that at Karnak the western pylon, the largest of all, is unfinished ; the exterior of the masses is left in the rough. Entering the court, a vast mound of brick and earth still lies against the south mass. I was long ago convinced that this is not mere accumulation. It has cross walls in it, well built, at right angles with the face of the pylon, and less solid stuff between these walls. It was a scaffold. Now (1896) this mass is being cleared away by De Morgan, and my view is absolutely confirmed. The purpose of the accumulation is clear. The masonry of the great pylon points to a late period, not earlier than Ptolemaic, it might be Roman. All the

IV—14

Ptolemies were busy in adding to these temples. Suddenly the half-finished work stops. The mound of

FIG. 67.—Gate added to Temple of Tahutmes III. at Medinet Habu by Ptolemy X.

scaffolding encumbered the court, and yet so it has remained to this day. Until refuted by better and more direct evidence, I shall consider the unfinished west pylon to be the work of Ptolemy IX., arrested in the days of Ptolemy X."

The disturbance, such as it was, did not last long, for in the second year of the new king (who did not acknowledge the interregnum of his mother) he went on a voyage of conciliation to Syene, and there confirmed the kindnesses of his father in his 53rd year (three years before) in a decree or correspondence with the priests of Abaton, Philæ, and the Cataract, of which part still remains on a stele in the B.M. It is evident that the queen did not accompany him, for her dislike of him was notorious, and she maintained her primacy in the formal protocols, which run, "In the reign of Queen Cleopatra and King Ptolemy, Gods Philometores Soteres," with a common year. But when Justin adds that she compelled the young king to divorce his sister Cleopatra, whom he loved, and marry his younger sister Selene, this probably means that, according to the traditions of the dynasty, children not actually born in the purple did not succeed to the throne. The marriage with Cleopatra would therefore count as morganatic, and her children illegitimate. But when Soter (also nicknamed Lathyros) was expelled by his mother in 108 B.C., she took from him this wife also, who had borne him two sons. This Selene then went to Syria, and married a whole series of Antiochuses, with many wonderful adventures, which do not belong to the history of Egypt. The queen mother also contrived to have her younger son Alexander, who had been sent to Cyprus as governor, probably for safety, declared king of Cyprus in 114 B.C., and from this time onward the policy indicated by Physkon, when he nominated Philopator Neos as his co-regent for this island, took shape, and resulted in a separation of the island from the kingdom of Egypt. But in 108-7 B.C., when Cleopatra and Soter II. had been nine years reigning in Egypt and Alexander six years in Cyprus, a revolution managed by the queen-mother turned out Soter, who was even divorced from his second wife, and brought in Alexander, who reigned with his mother till 101 B.C. (when he murdered her), and afterwards with his wife, Cleopatra-Berenike (IV.), daughter of his elder brother, till 88, when Soter II., who had been first at war with his mother, then in exile, and then, by some unknown arrangement, ruling in Cyprus, in all 19 years, returned to Egypt, resumed sway with his widowed daughter, and remained king till his death in 81 B.C.[1]

Thus we see a going in and out of kings at this period almost as complicated as the going in and out of queens in the days of Euergetes II., and it is painful to examine the labour with which meritorious chronologers—Strack is the most recent and the clearest—have tortured themselves to demonstrate the exact course of these vicissitudes from papyrus records, Apis steles, and Greek chronographers. Matters are further complicated by operations in Syria and Palestine, invasions of that country from Cyprus, and attempted invasions of Egypt, etc., in concert with one of the claimants to the Syrian throne, two brothers of whom were married to the sisters of the kings of Egypt. These ladies show the usual features ascribed to Ptolemaic princesses—great

---

[1] Here is a conspectus of these changes for the reader's benefit :—

PTOL. X. SOTER II. (Lathyros).	PTOL. XI. (Alexander).
1. Joint reign with his mother, B.C. 117-111.	
(a) Whole kingdom, 117-114.	
(b) Egypt only, 114-111.	1. King of Cyprus, 114-108.
2. Sole king of Egypt, 111-108.	
3. King of Cyprus, 108-88.	2. King of Egypt, 108-88.
	(a) Joint reign with his mother, 107-101.
	(b) Sole reign (with his wife Berenike), 101-88.
4. Again king of Egypt (and Cyprus), 88-81.	

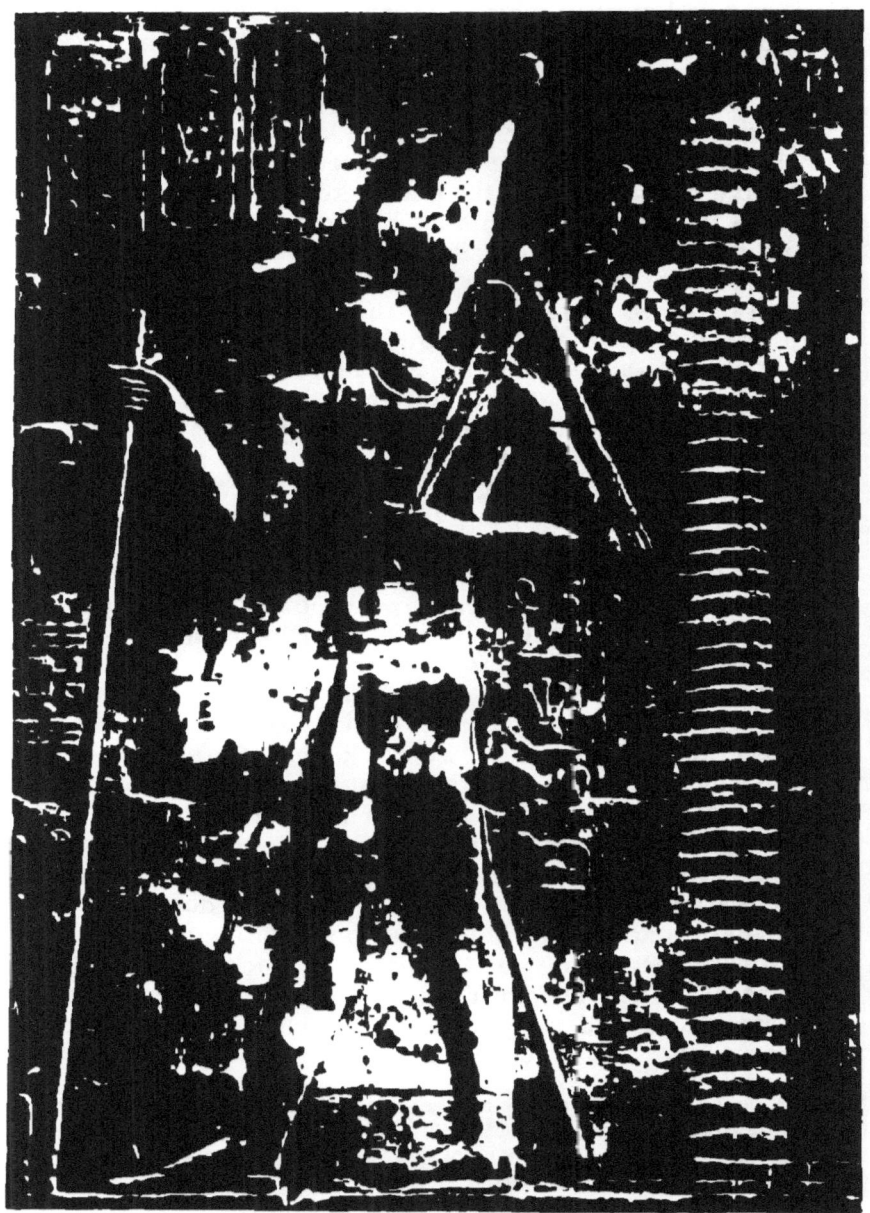

Fig. 63.—Ptolemy X. at Edfu.

power and wealth, which makes an alliance with them
imply the command of large resources in men and money;
mutual hatred; disregard of all ties of family and affec-
tion; the dearest object fratricide—such pictures of de-
pravity as make any reasonable man pause and ask
whether human nature had deserted these women, and
the Hyrcanian tiger of the poet taken its place.

But happily for us in this history, these adventures
and murders took place in Syria, and did not directly
affect Egypt, where Cleopatra and her sons held sway
with only two times of ταραχη, the expulsion of Soter II.
in 108 B.C., and the passage of arms and diplomacy
(about 101 B.C.) wherein Alexander outwitted and
murdered his unnatural mother. So far as the evidence goes, which I am about to quote, even these
dynastic troubles did not affect the native population.
There is, indeed, among Mr. Grenfell's recent acquisitions one papyrus dating from this period (I. xlii.), a
petition from mercenary horse stationed at Diospolis
Parva (Thebaid), complaining that other stations are
better supplied with pay and provisions. Not only do
they speak of cavalry stations at Ptolemais, Cheno-
boskion, and horse and foot in other stations,[1] but plead
that they have behaved bravely in the war and great
dangers during a desperate crisis. If this document
stood alone, historians would have inferred a very
unsettled condition of the country. But scores of
other documents which Mr. Grenfell has published in
the same collection show nothing but peaceable contracts, loans of corn, sales of property, wills—all the
occupations of a quiet society. In vain do we look
in these papers for any allusions to contemporary
history. According as the mass of these documents
increases, their silence regarding any disturbance becomes more and more distinct evidence of peace and
prosperity. They become no longer negative, but

---

[1] These frequent stations of ιππεις μισθοφοροι seem to tell us that
the ιππεις κατοικοι of the middle of the second century were either
reduced in number or not in actual service. At all events, they
are not the ordinary garrison.

positive evidence. We have from Crocodilopolis in the Pathyrite nome, and from the surroundings of Thebes, a host of texts mentioning crowds of people, almost all with Egyptian names. The Persians of the Epigone in particular are remarkable in almost always bearing purely Egyptian names. One called Apollonios has his Egyptian name added, and perhaps Tisres, in the same document, may be Persian. But if a regiment of Persians did settle in the Thebaid, they did not, like the veterans in the Arsinoite nome, import Greek wives; consequently they must have merged rapidly into the native population, merely retaining their title and its consequent privileges. The great list of names (Casati Pap., Louvre) of people buried in the Memnonia, the care of whose sepulture was a matter of revenue bought and sold among the Choachytæ, shows us among some 380 heads of families only 22 Greek names, and of these several residing at Diospolis Magna, and none in the villages with native names whence the majority of the rest comes. Pap. viii. of the Turin Collection shows us a company not of Choachytæ, but of Paraschistæ, the openers and embalmers of the dead, and therefore the most utterly Egyptian of trades, making a contract in L 51 (to which they appeal in L 2 of this reign) concerning the division of profits arising from this horrible occupation. Each party is to confine itself to a certain group of villages or towns, chiefly on one side of the Nile. But this contract is made δια του εν τηι Διοσπολει ξενικου αγορανομου, in other words, before a Greek official, though this office is distinctly qualified as foreign by the contractors. A breach of the agreement leads to the complaint recorded in the papyrus. The boundaries of every property described in any sale of this period are in possession of people with purely Egyptian names. It is, in fact, only when we find mention of high officials that for the most part they have Greek (not Macedonian) names. Yet even here such men as Phommous, epistrategus of the Thebaid, prove to us that the natives were making their mark in the administration.

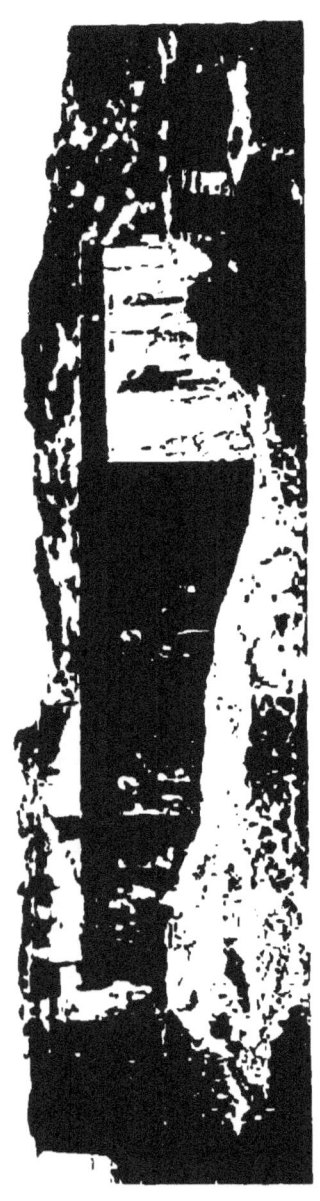

FIG. 69.—Dendera from S.-W.

Turning to the extant inscriptions of Soter II.'s reign, we find hardly any in Egypt beyond the Aswan stele already mentioned ; but a good many, as we might expect, from Delos and from Cyprus. They are mere votive inscriptions, with no information but that the αρχιδεατρος (Strack, 133) or chief butler was now a grandee, and that, at Delos at least, the recent Euergetes and the living Soter were each recognised as second (του δευτερου) of the name. From the later period of his long interrupted reign (88–81 B.C.) we have none.

But if there is but scanty Greek record of this king, and that mostly foreign, there is ample evidence of his activity in the building of Egyptian temples,—this too, I conjecture, from his first period, as it is not likely that the last seven years, occupied by a great war against the revolt of Thebes, could have been fruitful in these works of peace. Perhaps the most interesting of all the remains he has left us is the underground work (foundations and crypt) of the great temple of Dendera (Tentyra), which was indeed built upon an ancient site and according to an old plan, but which is, as we see it, wholly due to late Ptolemaic and Roman munificence. The fact that here, as elsewhere, Ptolemy Alexander continued his brother's unfinished work, points to the permanent and undisturbed influence of Cleopatra III., the queen-mother, during the first twenty years of the disturbed reigns. To build afresh this great temple from the ground was not a moderate undertaking, like the adding of a pylon or a gateway, but points both to wealth and leisure on the part of the government. At the same time Soter added (like his father) to the Pharaonic temple of Medamût, some miles north of Karnak, and rebuilt the pylon of Taharka at the small temple of Medinet Habu on the opposite bank. These favours to the Theban district are very interesting, when we remember that the king was ultimately the destroyer of Diospolis Magna, the royal Thebes. At El-Kab, the rock temple commenced by Physkon was completed by this king ; and, like all his predecessors back to Ptolemy III., he worked at Edfu. But now it was only the surroundings which remained to be completed. Of these Soter II. is specially credited with the great forecourt (F on the plan, p. 125), with its surrounding thirty-two pillars, and the high circuit wall (which was completed by Ptolemy Alexander). "He has built the court of the appearance of the protecting Horus, the lord of the gods, as a copy of the building of the sun mountain with the god of the sun mountain, completed in his excellent work in good sandstone ; offerings are made to his divine image in it" (Eisenlohr in Baedeker, p. 250). This court is minutely described in the inscription. Its measurements are 155 feet by 138 feet, the surrounding wall is $34\frac{1}{2}$ feet high by $8\frac{1}{2}$ feet thick,—truly a splendid piece of work for one of the degenerate and degraded Ptolemies ! He added inscriptions and decorations to the great temple of Philæ, and even in far Talmis (Kalabsheh in Nubia)

and in the great oasis of Kargeh we find traces of
his activity.   The tenor of the Edfu inscription implies that the work was taken up in succession to

Fig. 70.—Temple of Edfu, west side.
(Showing outer wall of Temple on the left, and the great boundary
wall on the right.)

that of his father, and it is mentioned before that of
Alexander.   This confirms what I have said, that the
temple work of Soter II. dates from the first ten years

of his reign. It is remarkable that the priests of Edfu do not mention the reigning queens. The innovation of Cleopatra II., maintained by succeeding queens down to the close of the dynasty, may have seemed to them a violation of tradition. Still it is difficult not to suspect, in the continued building at the same temples of Philometor and Euergetes II., of Soter II. and of Alexander, the influence of the great ladies who lived through the change of kings without stay or intermittence of their royalty.

When Soter was turned out, and Alexander came back from Cyprus to the throne of Egypt, he was a grown man, and not so likely to be subject to his imperious mother; yet in the wars around Cyprus and Palestine that ensued it is the queen-mother who is mentioned by Josephus and Justin as the main figure in fighting against her elder son, and for years she occupied the first place in the protocols, and even a distinct year of rule was assigned to her: ὑπερ βασιλισσης Κλεοπατρας Θεας Ευεργετιδος και βασιλεως Πτολεμαιου του και Αλεξανδρου Θεου Φιλομητορος, Lιγ του και ι is the usual formula.[1] But this protocol, pompous and respectful to the queen as it seems, was the prelude to her being excluded from such honours. For when Alexander married his niece Berenike, our poor evidence points to strained relations between the king and his mother, and the assumption on his part of independent sway. In the four interesting inscriptions of his eighteenth to twentieth years recovered from the Fayyum, we find the king alone named (Strack, 142–5). They all point to a peaceful state of affairs in that province, as well as to a continuance, perhaps in an exceptional extent, of the Greek influences in that province. Two of them give the limits of a sacred enclosure dedicated to the great God Sobk (Souchos) by the *ephebi* of two several schools

---

[1] This I copy from the text I had the good fortune to put together from two far-parted fragments, one of them only a squeeze of the lost stone (cf. Strack, 141). We also have in Grenfell Pap. (II. xxiii. a) βασ. Κλεοπατρας και Πτολεμαιου επικαλ- ουμενου Αλεξανδρου του υιον θεων φιλομητορων.

(called *heresies*).   The Greek notion of prolonged education, ending in a philosophical training, which they
now preferred to call a *heresy* to calling it a school,
seems at home in this isolated corner of Hellenism.

FIG. 71.—Stele of Ptolemy Alexander.
(Now in Trinity College, Dublin.)

The god worshipped is Egyptian, the people concerned
have Greek names and habits.   The other two com-
memorate the endowment of the temple of the great

god Soknopaios (at Dimêh) by the officials of the œconomus of the μερις of Heracleides (the northern and principal of the three divisions of the province) with 182½ artabæ of corn yearly (½ artaba per day). Here again the chief officer of the nome is Lysanias, the œconomos Aniketos, the secretary Apollonios, son of Ischurion,—all Greek names. The officials not only make the donation themselves, but bind their successors also. The facts are too few to enable us to draw any inference. If we had other evidence of a Hellenistic reaction in this reign, we might cite these inscriptions to show that, in contrast to the high native officials we know in the Thebaid at the opening of Soter II.'s reign, we have nothing but Greeks here. But then this province was clearly more Greek in population than the rest.

The palace history of the close of this reign is neither intelligible nor edifying. Alexander is said to have gone into exile (no one knows whither), and to have been recalled by his mother (no one knows on what terms). As she disappears from official mention in 101 B.C., and the new queen, Berenike III., takes her place, though not her pre-eminence, in the official datings, we may suppose her to have died at that time.[1] Justin, of course, says she was murdered by her son whom she was planning to murder. He goes on to say that no sooner was this murder found out than a military revolt expelled Alexander, who fled

---

[1] The date is not quite certain, and it seems to me possible that a curious feature in the papyri G-K of Leyden implies her being yet alive in 99 B.C. For the complaint of the Archientaphiastes of Osorapis and Osormnevis (the chief officer having the charge of the pompous burial of these sacred animals Apis and Mnevis), of which several copies remain, says in every case *that he is being annoyed by certain persons* (σκυλλεσθαι υπ ενιων), whose names he evidently does not choose to tell. In all other such complaints known to me the defendants' names are explicitly given. The king at once grants his request to have a notice-board set up before his house that he is not to be molested. I believe this reticence of names to be somehow connected with the court quarrels and the faction of the old queen. The formula of the receipt is simply, βασιλευς Πτολεμαιος ο επικαλουμενος Αλεξανδρος και βασιλισσα Βερενικη η αδελφη L ιγ Διου κθ Θωυθ κθ, which is our 99 B.C.

with his wife and daughter to Lycia, then to Cyprus, was
pursued by an army from Alexandria, and slain by the
General Chæreas.   With this the fragments of Porphyry
also agree ; but the far more trustworthy, though
vaguer inscription of Edfu says that he fled into Arabia
(Punt), and so his elder brother came back to the
throne.   The suggestion of Krall (*Studien*, ii. 56), that
the priests used Punt *mythologically for Cyprus* shows
how insoluble is the difficulty.

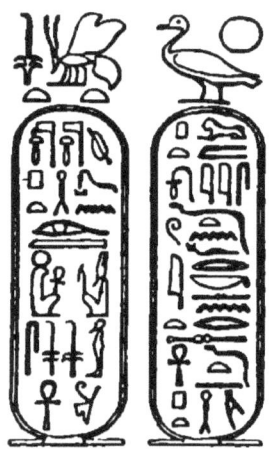

FIG. 72.—Cartouches of Ptol. Alexander.

At all events the change of sovereigns must have
seemed of little moment to the country.   Whether
Soter II., returning after eighteen years of exile, was
a gentle old man, as one tradition (the Jewish?) represents him, or whether he was a cruel tyrant, as
Porphyry's authorities represented him,[1] his home policy
was not likely to produce any novelty.   And yet it
was in these seven and a half closing years of his reign
that a very great calamity befell the centre of national-
ism in Egypt.   This cannot have happened at the
moment of his restoration, for in 87 B.C. Lucullus came

[1] Cf. the instructive note of Gutschmid (Sharpe, ii. 4), who
decides for the latter.

as the lieutenant of Sylla to persuade the king to lend some ships of war to the Romans, in order to prosecute the war with Mithridates. This invader had not only taken possession of the Ægean with his fleet, but had found at Kos the Egyptian regalia and the son of Alexander, whom he treated with great distinction,[1] and who might any day be set up as the legitimate heir to his father and to the crown of Egypt. So Lathyros was civil, temporised, offered presents to Lucullus, but would give no ships.[2] Presently "he made war with the Thebans who revolted, and, subduing them in the third year of the revolt, so ruined them, that not even suggestion was left to the Thebans of their former prosperity."[3] Death overtook Ptolemy shortly after these events (which we may put at L 3–6 of his restoration). "But the Athenians, having received from him many benefits not worth specifying, set up bronze statues of him and of Berenike, who alone was legitimate among his children." Such is our solitary record of these events. The lady would seem to be the wife of Alexander ; but if she was, how is she associated in these gifts with Lathyros, or how was she allowed to marry her usurping uncle? The only solution is to consider these gifts to Athens as sent from Egypt by Lathyros after his return, and so possibly living in peace with his widowed daughter.

The next reign only served to add another empty name to the catalogue of Ptolemies. Alexander II., son of Ptolemy Alexander, was advised by Sylla to marry his stepmother Berenike III., now left in pos-

---

[1] Appian, *Mith.* 23.

[2] Plutarch, *Lucullus*, 2, 3.

[3] Paus. i. 9. It is to be noted that, though the city Diospolis was razed and the people scattered into surrounding villages, the care and adornment of the great temples was not abandoned. The names of the next ruler, Neos Dionysus (Auletes) and of Roman emperors appear still upon the walls of some of the lesser buildings. Moreover, the curious complimentary decree to Callimachus, in Cleopatra VI.'s reign, shows that a whole organised society lived at Diospolis Magna down to 40 B.C.

session of the throne by the death of her father.   But
this adventurer no sooner was established in Alexandria
than he murdered the lady, and was himself murdered
by the soldiery for his pains, after a reign of nineteen
days.   These horrors have none but a dynastic importance.

What was of more moment to Egypt was the
allegation that the late king, the nominee of the
Romans, had bequeathed his kingdom to the republic.
The statements on this subject are confused, and there
is even a doubt whether the testator was not Alexander I., or another obscure person, Alexander or
Alexas, who has even been called Alexander III.   The
probabilities are in favour of Alexander II., who
may have offered this bribe to the men in power at
Rome.   Of his private fortune deposited for safety
at Rome, the emissaries of the senate did take possession, while there was evidently the greatest hesitation
about carrying out the larger provisions of the will, if
such there were.   It seems to me to follow, from these
considerations, that while the bequest of the money
was valid, that of the kingdom, if indeed made, was
not so, Alexander II. being at the time not actually
monarch, nor being indisputably the last direct heir,
who alone could even pretend to make such a will.[1]

At all events, the probability that the Romans would
enforce their supposed rights was the cloud that hung
over the Egyptian court, for the crown was now
assumed, apparently without opposition at home, by a
man who is called an illegitimate son of Soter II., while
his brother likewise assumed the throne of Cyprus.   We
have no clue to the real parentage of this person, nor
to the name and status of his mother, but though the
people and court of Alexandria accepted him, Cicero

[1] I have shown elsewhere (*Hermathena*, xxii.), how in the somewhat similar case of the last Attalid the will seems to have bequeathed to the Roman people only the king's personal estate,
while the Roman demagogues, who were so ready to shout for
the liberty of Greek cities, deliberately ignored the constitutional
rights of Pergamum, and interpreted the king's will as including
all the public revenues of the Pergamene state.

speaks of him as *nec regio genere ortus*, which must at least imply that at his birth his mother was not a reigning queen.[1]   The fear that the Romans would certainly seize the kingdom, if derelict, may have helped the pretender.   But he spent twenty years and most of his wealth in trying to obtain from Rome a recognition of his sovereignty, and all the while constant threats of the enforcing of the supposed will were hanging over his uneasy head. In Egypt he settled himself according to tradition.   He

FIG. 73.—Cartouches of Ptolemy XIII.

is said indeed to have been married before his formal coronation, for a funeral stele (hieroglyphic), translated by H. Brugsch, states that the high priest Pasirenptah, in his own fourteenth year, "placed the uræus crown on the head of the new king of Egypt on the day that he took possession of the crown of Upper and Lower Egypt. . . . He landed at Memphis ; he came into the temple of Qe, with his nobles, his wives, and his children."[2]   This is computed by the same authority

[1] Can she have been the Cleopatra divorced by Soter II. at his accession (above, p. 211), and Auletes, therefore, his son ?

[2] I think this expression rather excludes the existence of a royal or legitimate wife, and that he probably did not marry Tryphæna till the coronation was accomplished.

IV—15

to be the year 76 B.C., so that the king delayed the important ceremony almost four years—an extremely improbable statement. But no doubt seems expressed by the critics (cf. Strack, p. 209, note *b*). He and his wife, named Cleopatra (V.) Tryphæna, whom he of course calls his sister, assumed the title of Gods Philopatores Philadelphi, and besides he called himself the God Neos Dionysos. His nickname is in strong contrast to this pomp; the Alexandrians called him the *piper* (Auletes), because of his dis-royal proficiency upon the instrument. We know not of his devotions to Dionysus; the Isis of Philæ he certainly endowed with additional temple buildings, and the dedications of officials and soldiers (all foreigners) still extant at Philæ show that this sanctuary was now in high favour and under the king's control (Strack, 150–153). One of these, in his nineteenth year, set up by Callimachus, his "cousin," and epistrategos and strategos of the Indian and Red Sea, who comes to worship Isis, shows how far the king's claims reached. Whether this officer really controlled such far country we cannot say. The crypts of the great temple of Dendera, which Lathyros and Alexander had not finished, were completed by Auletes; he set up an altar at Koptos to Khem, Isis, and Heh; put his name more than once on the temples at Karnak (Thebes); set up bronze-bound gates at the great pylon of Edfu; enlarged Philometor's temple at Kom Ombo; and set his name on older work both at Philæ and Biggeh; indeed, the greater part of his activity at these temples was confined to surface work, adorning older structures. It would seem that he desired the credit of being a temple-builder without incurring any considerable expense. It is to be observed that at the date of the setting up of the gates at Edfu (57 B.C.) he was in exile, and not the acknowledged sovereign.

The long game of counter-diplomacy between the Roman magnates or demagogues who desired the spoil of Egypt, and the king's party who were bought by enormous bribes and supported by the mutual jealousy of would-be plunderers, occupied Rome at every breathing time of her civil disputes. The kingdom of Bithynia was bequeathed to them in 75 B.C., and the formal occupation of this kingdom, as well as of the still vacant Cyrene, in 74 B.C., brought on the second

FIG. 74.—Colonnade adorned by Ptolemy XIII. at Philæ.

Mithridatic war. In the troublous time that followed, two Syrian sons of Selene (not her sons by Lathyros) went to Rome (72 B.C.) to claim that they were better heirs to the thrones of Egypt and Cyprus than the actual holders, but they only succeeded in being plundered by Verres. Then came the Pirate and the third Mithridatic wars,[1] and men at Rome, in need of finances, began to press for the annexation of Egypt. Crassus, Cæsar, the tribune Rullus, all endeavoured to secure the huge prize, but were baulked by counter-jealousies; and so the king, with the aid of a bribe of 6000 talents (about a year's revenue), extracted from Cæsar when consul (59 B.C.) the long-sought recognition. It was not a moment too soon, for in the very next year Clodius proposed and carried the annexation of Cyprus, which its king could have saved had he not been a miser and kept his talents in his useless treasury. Yet he showed the spirit of the royal race in committing suicide in preference to tolerating deposition.

FIG. 75.—Ptolemy XIII. and Goddesses. (Kom Ombo.)

But before the catastrophe we are told that the people of Alexandria rose against Auletes and drove him into exile. The debasement of his coinage, which

[1] So powerful did Mithridates appear in the East, that the two Ptolemies ventured to betroth themselves to two of his daughters in 63 B.C.

we can still appreciate, points to financial straits in paying his enormous bribes, and therefore to probable exactions or confiscations which set popular discontent aflame.   He left behind him, perhaps, his wife Cleopatra Tryphæna,[1] though her omission from protocols points to her death some years earlier (viz. 69 B.C.); at all events, an eldest daughter, Berenike IV., born, I imagine, shortly after his coronation, as well as a younger family by another wife, of whom the eldest, born 69–8 B.C., became afterwards the famous Queen of Egypt.   Berenike became the practical heiress, and upon the disappearance of the other princess, whether mother, sister, or stepmother, seized the reins with the true spirit of that dominant race of women.   The Alexandrians were determined to keep Auletes from his throne, and even sent an embassy to Rome to state their griefs against him.   But he, with private influences and bribes, and even, we are told, with assassinations of their ambassadors, foiled their attempts, though he could not induce the senate to restore him. Meanwhile they sought a suitable husband at Alexandria for Berenike IV.   The first, a Seleucus from Syria, turned out so worthless and mean that he was choked off in a few days.   It is to this intruder, nicknamed *Kybiosaktes*, or pedlar in pickled fish (τάριχος), that I would attribute the scandal of stealing the golden coffin of Alexander the Great and replacing it by a glass one.[2]   Her second choice, Archelaus, then high priest at Komana (these Asiatic high priesthoods were positions of almost royal dignity), was of a different sort.   He ruled formally with her, counting his years separately (*L 1, which is also 3*, as a Grenfell papyrus has it), till at the end of six months Gabinius, governor of Syria, for a bribe of 6000 talents from Auletes, and with the consent of Pompey, invaded Egypt, slew Archelaus in battle, and restored Auletes

---

[1] Cf. the difficulties discussed in Strack, pp. 66–68, who decides in favour of an elder sister to Berenike being meant.

[2] As ταριχεύω is used for embalming, so I suppose τάριχος may have been a vulgar word for a mummy.

with much bloodshed,[1] including the murder of Berenike IV.

We are not concerned with the storm which this high-
handed and illegal proceeding excited at Rome, except
that a great deal of Gabinius' bribe was borrowed by
the king from Rabirius Postumus, a former creditor ;
and when this speculator could not recover his money,
Auletes consented to make him his Chancellor of the
Exchequer (διοικητής), so that the taxes of the country
might pass through his hands. I do not think that
the real significance of this curious concession has been
appreciated by historians. It was then without precedent, but has in recent times its parallel in the cession of
Turkish taxes made by the Sultan to secure the interest of
their loans to his foreign creditors. The real creditor was
not the obscure Rabirius, but the powerful Julius Cæsar.
For, when he came to occupy Egypt after Pompey's
death, he claimed that the supplies for his small army
were only the repayment of a fraction of the 17,000,000
sesterces due to him from the late king. And hence
perhaps the zeal of a political party to prosecute the
obscure Roman knight.

According to Cicero, who defended him when Gabinius
was convicted of peculation, and Rabirius was im-
plicated in the case, he was first obliged to take his
dangerous post at Alexandria, because it was otherwise
impossible to recover his foolish loan ; he was obliged
to abandon all appearance of being a Roman, and dress
as a Greek ; he was obliged to submit to the humours
of a despotic king, and see his friends imprisoned, and
his own life in danger. But the fact that he had at
last to escape naked for his life points to the other side
of the story. With the aid of the Roman garrison left
him by Gabinius, he was guilty of such ferocious extor-

---

[1] It is usually assumed that this was merely a victory of the
Roman army over the Alexandrian troops of Berenike and
Archelaus. This is not so. Cæsar (*De Bell. Civ.* iii. 109) expressly tells us that it was the disorderly and mutinous household
soldiery of Alexandria which restored Auletes. They probably
deserted to Gabinius before the battle, in order to gain credit for
the result, and in any case to be found on the victorious side.

tion, that the people of Alexandria rose against him, and would have murdered him, no doubt justly, if they had caught him.

Auletes, restored in 55 B.C., only reigned till 51 B.C., when death removed the most idle and worthless of the Ptolemies. There is nothing more left to record about him.

We need only sum up in a word what impression he has left upon the world. Idle, worthless, devoted to the orgies of Dionysus (whence his title), and disgracing himself by public competitions on the flute (whence his nick-name), he has not a good word from any one. He poses at Rome as king of Alexandria. Probably the ruin of Thebes by his father had crushed the national aspirations, for we hear of no revolt of the natives during his oppressive reign. With the priesthood and native religion he seems to have stood on friendly terms.

But we are indeed fortunate in having, from Auletes' later years, not only the impressions of Cicero concerning the country, but the personal record of Diodorus Siculus, who visited Alexandria and some of the upper country about 60 B.C., and reports with faithfulness what he saw and what he heard from the Greek expounders of the old Egyptian civilisation in the great religious centres of the country. Diodorus' impressions, or rather the impressions we receive from his account, correspond very well with what we learn from the monuments and our other authorities.

First as to Alexandria.—He unfortunately gives us only one personal anecdote of what he saw in that city.

He is telling us that if any one kills an ibis or a cat, whether deliberately or by accident, he must inevitably die, for the crowd comes together and hounds him to death, without legal inquiry. This in itself proves that the mob of Alexandria was no longer Greek as it professed to be, but deeply saturated with native blood, for no Hellenistic mob ever showed such deep intolerance on a matter of local superstition. This feeling in the crowd of Alexandria is so strong, he adds, " that

at the time when king Ptolemy was not yet acknowledged
as a friend by the Roman people, and the populace was
most anxious to show every respect to people from
Italy who were sojourning there, and to give no pretext
or excuse for a quarrel through their fear of Rome, a
Roman happened to kill a cat, and when the mob
attacked the house where he lived, neither the officers
sent by the king nor the public fear of Rome sufficed
to save his life, though he had done it unintentionally.
This fact we report not from hearsay, but having
ourselves witnessed it during our stay in Egypt."

I cannot but think that, in spite of Diodorus, the fact
of the felicide being a Roman gave him a smaller chance,
for the Romans, always unpopular abroad for their
rude and overbearing manners, were now well known
throughout the East as the most cruel and heartless
extortioners, so that the mob may have naturally
seized a religious pretext for its vengeance.

Diodorus also tells us [1] that at the time of his visit the
population of Alexandria (free citizens) was, according
to the official census, more than 300,000, and the king's
revenue from the rest of Egypt more than 6000 talents.
Strabo,[2] however, quotes Cicero to the effect that
Auletes' revenue was 12,500 talents.[3]

When we come to consider the inner country, how
great is the contrast! "Ut occulte latet! ut tota
recondita est!" exclaims Cicero, feeling that his words
were true, even apart from their connection with his
argument. Diodorus translates us into the far past,
when he repeats from the priests their traditions of the
old royalty and the old religion of Egypt. Hellenism
seems powerless among such people. Diodorus feels
that, in the priests and their ritual, in the manners
and customs of the people, in the legislation which
surrounds the old monarchy, in the strange beast-
worship, he describes a country and a race still foreign

---

[1] XVII. 52.   [2] XXVI. i. 13.
[3] Neither of them specifies what particular talent he means, but
the metrologists have made out that their computations agree, and
that the amount is about three millions sterling.

to the new civilisation of the world, but possessed of an equally advanced though primæval culture. Even in his own day the keepers of sacred animals had been known to spend 100 talents upon their obsequies.[1]

Throughout the reign of Auletes, we find the usual votive inscriptions and devotions to the national gods on the part of the king,[2] who was probably the least attentive of all the series to the sentiments of his people. He completed the great temple of Edfu, at which every Ptolemy since the founder, Euergetes I., had laboured, in 58 B.C., and put his dedication upon it, along with that of his queen, Cleopatra (V.) Tryphæna. On the great pylon we see colossal reliefs of the king smiting his enemies. He enlarged the temple of Kom Ombo, building the still extant hypostyle pronaos. One of the pylons at Philæ was decorated by him, and he even built a small temple on the island of Biggeh, close to Philæ. The crypts at Dendera, an altar of black granite at Koptos, and several temples at Karnak, show his cartouche, and consequently his dedication of labour and money to the national gods; in the last case the destruction of the city by Lathyros had not abolished the sanctity of the temples which it contained. Under his children's reign we shall find the building of great Egyptian temples more active than it had been under many a native dynasty.

But there is one source, which by some accident dries up at this time, though it is abundant enough in the next century. We have hardly any papyri of the reigns of Auletes or of Cleopatra to give us an insight into the internal state of the country. Diodorus could learn from the priests their traditions, and could wonder at their hereditary corporate dignities; he can describe, but from the much older Greek source Agatharchides, the horrors of the Nubian gold mines; he can copy from Hecatæus (of Abdera) the account of the conquests of Osymandyas (Ramses II.), as they appear in relief or in text on the great temples at and over against Thebes. But most of his account is at second hand. Like

---

[1] I. 85. [2] Murray's *Egypt*, II. pp. 427, 429, 431.

Strabo after him,—indeed, like most Greek authors,—
he preferred copying froin books to making personal
observations, and so his painstaking and trustworthy
account is very deficient in such anecdotes as that I
have above cited.   Here and there we surprise him in
something modern, as when he speaks of catching
quails by raising nets along the coast,[1] into which they
fly by night on their passage, as any one may now see
on the southern coasts of Italy in May-time.   We feel
that he has been on the Nile, when he notes that it is a
most tortuous river, departing from its general course

FIG. 76.—Philæ Ptolemy XIII.

northwards in bends to the east and west, or even to
the south, and that in high summer the inundations
make the country look like the Ægean with its
Cyclades.[2]   He also knows the *sakya*, which he tells
us was the invention of Archimedes ; and this is probably true, for the old Egyptians only used the *shadoof*.[3]
We know further that he produces a true general
impression, when he says that the queens received
greater honours than the kings, and that even in the

I. 60.   [2] *Ibid.* 32, 36.   [3] *Ibid.* 34.

ordinary marriage settlements the husband was bound
by contract to respect his wife. He knows too about
the use of kiki oil for lamps, and about sundry industries
like the feeding of geese,[1] which are amply corroborated
by the papyri. His account of the ordinary legal process [2] by written documents, and not by oral pleading,
is correct, as well as the curious statement that the
educators of the people objected on theory both to
music and gymnastics in education, as injurious to mind
and body. Even in these matters it is most difficult to
say how far he has himself observed, and how far he
has copied from books. Thus his account of Thebes
and of the tombs of the kings seems to be borrowed
from Hecatæus; and even as regards the pyramids,
his statements are open to the same suspicion. He
speaks of inscriptions on them, and of other details
which cannot be verified, and so he gives us but one
more example of the very reprehensible habit of Greek
historians, who ordinarily passed off second-hand
information as if it were observation of their own.

[1] I. 74.   [2] *Ibid.* 75.

CHAPTER X

AUTHORITIES. — For this chapter we have fortunately several ancient writers on Roman history and biography—Appian, *Bell. Civ.*; Dio Cassius, *lib.* xlvii. ; above all, Cæsar's unfinished narrative *De Bello Civ.* ; and Plutarch's Lives of Cæsar and Antony. Except the inscriptions of Cleopatra at Dendera (which give us no history), and the stele of Turin (dated in her reign), our knowledge of the internal history is practically *nil.*

HOWEVER idle or wicked may have been the life of Ptolemy XIII., his testament shows a strong feeling for his family, and perhaps even for his country. He was evidently in great fear of Roman greed and grasping ; he took every care that no forged or sham will should be produced after his death. He bequeathed his kingdom to his elder daughter and elder son, and appealed by all the traditional friendship of his house with Rome, that the Roman people should not thwart his legitimate dispositions. He sent an attested and sealed copy to Rome, to be laid up in the public archives : the original was preserved at Alexandria.[1] But Rome was now in so troubled a state, the issues at stake were so tremendous, that even this rich prize—the absorption of the wealth of Egypt—attracted no public attention. The king's will was not even formally deposited in the *aerarium*, but remained in Pompey's keeping.

So Cleopatra VI. (those who assume that there was a second Cleopatra Tryphæna, eldest daughter of Auletes, call her the VIIth), then about seventeen years of age, came to the throne with her eldest brother (a boy of ten), on the usual understanding that she should presently marry him. We hear not a word of any

[1] Cæsar, *De Bell. Civ.* iii. § 108.

FIG. 77.—Egyptian Portrait of Cleopatra VI. (Dendera).

dissentient party in the state. Most unfortunately, now that foreign sources begin to tell us of Alexandrian affairs, the indigenous notices, inscriptions, or papyri fail us altogether. This must be an accident, for contracts must have been made daily all through the country, and the one permanent activity of the dynasty—that of building and beautifying temples—was certainly not arrested. It appears that in her second or third year (49 B.C.), when Pompey was preparing for his struggle with Cæsar, he sent his eldest son Cnæus (afterwards killed at Munda) to obtain ships and other supplies in Egypt. Pompey's name was all-powerful in the East, and his son must have been regarded as a sort of heir-presumptive to the Roman empire. We hear from subsequent allusions that Cleopatra was alive to these considerations of ambition, and that she made herself so agreeable to the young man, that there were not wanting suspicions of a serious intrigue. Had Pompey been victor in the coming conflict, we should probably have heard more of this affair. All we now know is that in the fourth year of the nominally joint reign, that is, when the king attained his majority at fourteen, and was probably proclaimed at Memphis, his advisers, especially the eunuch Pothinos, who was his boy intimate,[1] urged him to assume sole control, and Cleopatra was driven into exile. But, with the spirit and the wonderful resources of Ptolemaic queens, she hastened to gather an army in Syria, and proceeded to reconquer her crown. The king's army was encamped over against Cleopatra's, near Pelusium, when the fugitive Pompey, after his defeat at Pharsalia, came with a band of 2000 followers to claim a refuge in Egypt. The king's advisers thought it best to propitiate the rising sun Cæsar, by receiving Pompey on shore, and then murdering him.

We are not told how the war between brother and

---

[1] It seems to have been the usual custom with this royal house to have a eunuch boy brought up in special intimacy with the princes. These persons often obtained great influence, *e.g.* Eulæos with Philometor.

sister proceeded, but we may safely infer that the king won a victory, and that Cleopatra lost her army (which in those cases generally joined that of the victor), but that she did not renounce her claims, nor did she retire into Syria, for she was near enough to carry on negotiations presently with Cæsar.

When Cæsar arrived at Alexandria, the history of that city and its complicated warfare becomes for a moment Roman history, nay, rather the history of the world, and is to be found not in native sources, but in Cæsar's own account of the great civil war, and in the historians and biographers of the period (Plutarch, Dio Cassius). We need here only cull from their narratives the facts that bear upon the condition of Alexandria, which, though a very mongrel and even foreign city, cannot but be regarded as the capital, and so far the exponent of the country. The first point of interest is the angry reception of the conqueror, because he entered the city as Imperator, with his twelve lictors as consul, or twenty-four as dictator (I cannot find which). It would seem strange that the Alexandrian populace, accustomed to royal state, should take umbrage at this display of power. Possibly recollections of the entry of Gabinius, and the bloody scenes that followed the restoration of Auletes, may have alarmed them.

But from Cæsar's account of the composition of the mob we can give clearer and better reasons for this popular indignation. The forces which were presently arrayed against him under Achillas' command were not to be despised, says he, either as to numbers or fighting qualities. There were under arms some 20,000 men in all, consisting (1) of Gabinian soldiers, who had adopted the habits and licence of Alexandrian life and forgotten Roman discipline. Most of them had married there, and were the fathers of families. We see, in fact, a new settlement of κατοικοι, leading by their intermarriages with the natives to a new επιγονη. (2) There was a mixed multitude of pirates and brigands from Syria, Cilicia, and the surrounding regions.

Though Cæsar does not note it, wrecking and coast piracy was always so rife along the wild and difficult coast of the Delta, with its channels of the Nile, shoals, and swampy lakes, that even on Pharos shipwrecked boats and their cargoes were regarded, under Ptolemaic rule, as the property of the natives. There may, therefore, have been a considerable admixture of Egyptian accomplices with the Cilician pirates, lately driven from the sea by Pompey, in this section. (3) Many criminals and exiles from Italy, and fugitive slaves, to whom Alexandria had for years been a safe refuge, on the understanding that they should be enrolled as soldiers—I presume as μισθοφόροι in contrast to (1). "If any of these was claimed by his master, he was rescued by his comrades. This was the body that would demand the death of an unpopular minister ; that would pillage private property ; that exiled or recalled whom they would, according to the old traditions of the Macedonian garrison at Alexandria. They had 2000 horse. They had seen many wars ; had restored Auletes to his kingdom ; had murdered the two sons of Bibulus (we know not when or why) ; had warred against the natives. This was their history."

This all-too-brief description calls for many more observations. In the first place, however, it is quite obvious that, to such a horde as the last, the appearance of lictors with their fasces and axes was very terrible. For they well understood what natives might not : that it meant the establishment for the time of Roman martial law at Alexandria. They might recognise among Cæsar's staff former masters, or men cognisant of their past history and its crimes. They, therefore, from personal alarm raised an outcry constitutionally correct. Cæsar had no right to invade the capital of a friendly sovereign in the guise of a dictator imposing military law on Egypt.

The growth of this force, and its omnipotence at Alexandria, is, however, of more moment to us in the present connection. It is implied that the victorious soldiers of Gabinius were not the principal armed force. They seem to have desired to sink into the condition of civilians, with the mere name of old soldiers. They thus remind us of the old settlers in the Fayyum, with their house in Alexandria, and the charger which they fed and bequeathed to their sons, but in the main peaceful occupants of land throughout the country. Either they or their fathers had come as a conquering caste to Alexandria, and had originally formed the αγημα or household force of the king. But according as they drifted away into peaceful pursuits and sat by the fleshpots of Egypt, they were gradually replaced by absolute mercenaries, men hired for so many years under a mutual contract of pay and obedience, such as we have it described in the treaty between Eumenes and his mutinous troops (*Inschriften von Pergamum*, No. 13).

But what is remarkable, and what we may accept without question upon Cæsar's authority, is that these hirelings, gathered from the four winds of heaven (as indeed the original army of invaders had been), and living round the palace in direct relation to the court, assumed or drifted into the prerogatives and dignities of the old Macedonian household troops. Symptoms of this change may be found in the course of Ptolemaic history. When an Ætolian freebooter or a Jew was commander-in-chief, the old traditions of the Macedonians could only subsist in name.

It was in the face of this dangerous populace and garrison, that Cæsar, as the representative of the Roman people, proposed to adjudicate the claims of the royal brother and sister. In this he was constitutionally justified. The king, in his will, had implored the Roman people to see his dispositions carried out. But when Cleopatra reappeared at Alexandria under Cæsar's protection, her brother soon saw that the Roman was no umpire, but a hostile partisan, the acknowledged lover of the queen. So the army of the king and Pothinos, under the command of Achillas, came suddenly upon Cæsar in the palace, and very

nearly concluded his victorious career. After full
consideration of the circumstances, it seems to me
most probable that Cæsar, though no novice in adventures of this kind, was really subdued into forgetfulness
of his great mission by the charms of this matchless
siren, and that his dangers and difficulties, including an
enforced delay in Egypt of many months in the midst
of a great world-crisis, were the mere consequence of
that snare which has overthrown, and will overthrow,
the mightiest of men. His advent in Alexandria
was not unlike the arrival of Nelson from the battle
of the Nile at Naples, and the eclipse of his higher
qualities for many months from a similar cause ;
and, like Nelson, Cæsar remained faithful to the idol
of his mature years, in spite of the censure of public
opinion.

In the war which ensued—a matter of life and death
with Cæsar—the army of Alexandria showed, as he
says, fine fighting qualities, and made desperate
attempts to storm the palace, to cut off Cæsar from
the sea and its succours, or from fresh water, to
intercept also such help as came to him slowly and
sporadically. It required all the courage and resource
of that famous leader, and all the steadiness of his
small army of two thousand veterans, to hold his
ground till adequate help reached him with the advance
of his general Mithridates from Syria, by the usual way
of Memphis. To bring an army across the Delta was
of course impossible. Meanwhile Cæsar was obliged
to burn the fleet in the harbour, which he could not
man, or even save from the enemy ; and in this conflagration a great quantity of books (papyrus rolls) in
stores beside the quay was destroyed. This accident
of the siege produced no impression whatever on contemporaries, even such as Cicero, whose correspondence of those years is extant. Strabo, who saw Alexandria in the next generation, and gives us a general
description, says not a word on the subject. By and
by, in Seneca's day, people had come to believe that
the great library had been burned. The general silence

of contemporaries is to my mind conclusive against the occurrence of so terrible a catastrophe to letters.

Cæsar had tried every conciliation at the outset; he had read them the king's will, and undertaken to carry out strictly its provisions; he had even proposed to give back Cyprus, and send the younger pair of children to rule over it. But his relations with Cleopatra seem to have set all the other princes absolutely against him; they probably knew they had nothing to hope, if she obtained the control. So Arsinoe, a girl hardly grown up, escaped from the palace with her eunuch Ganymedes, and sought to organise war against the invader. When the elder Ptolemy was sent out at the people's request, under the transparent excuse of arranging terms with the victor, he too headed the people, and, though a boy without experience, behaved with decision and with bravery. But he lost his life in the battle against Cæsar and Mithridates; Arsinoe was carried off to grace Cæsar's triumph at Rome. The younger boy was only of account in supplying a nominal husband for Cleopatra, who, when all things were settled, and the country restored to her and her brother, followed Cæsar to Rome, and lived there, his acknowledged mistress, till his assassination. She brought with her the younger Ptolemy (XV.), her brother and husband, whom she is said to have poisoned during her sojourn there. Probably also she carried with her the child Cæsarion, whom she asserted, no doubt, quite truly, to be Cæsar's; but though we have a note of Cicero's telling of his visit to her, we hear from him no details, except that she was haughty in manner, and yet promised to procure some books from Alexandria for him. Patriotic Romans disliked her, and feared her influence on the Dictator; they thought she would orientalise him and wean him from Rome. Meanwhile he kept Alexandria, and no doubt the upper country, quiet for her by three legions left at Alexandria under Rufinus, a freedman of his own, but an able and trusty soldier. The old organisation of the provinces seems to have survived all the troubles and disturbances of the capital, and even the absent sovereign was loyally obeyed.

When she returned hastily to Egypt upon Cæsar's murder, she associated in the throne her child Cæsarion as Ptolemy Cæsar, the God Philopator Philometor.[1] The chronologers assign four years to her rule with her elder brother Ptolemy XIV., four with her younger, Ptolemy XV., who must therefore have died in the same year as Cæsar. Then came her association with her son, a child of not more than five or six years of age. Dio Cassius (xlvii. 31) says expressly that she obtained Roman consent for this act, promising alliance and succour to the party of Dolabella in the year 712 A.U.C. = 42 B.C. In the great tumults which came upon the Roman world through Cæsar's death she maintained a practical neutrality, though probably making promises to more than one party, and watching eagerly the chances of victory. All her ability must have been required to steer clear of offending the rival partisans. But it is about this time that we hear from a solitary Greek inscription, found at Thebes, that Egypt had been visited with famine, and that Thebes, which had been nominally destroyed by Lathyros, was still sufficiently alive to vote formal thanks to Kallimachos, a leading official there, for his good offices in protecting the inhabitants from starvation.

This stele of Thebes, now at Turin, is interesting enough to detain us a moment, especially as monuments of the time in Greek are exceedingly rare. The text, as given by A. Peyron in his publication of it (*Turin Acad. Memoirs* of 1829[2]), is indeed mutilated, but the general sense is clear. It is bilingual, demotic and Greek, and the native language (now wholly obliterated) occupied as usual the leading place. I am not aware that it was ever studied with any success.

The Greek runs somewhat as follows: " In the reign

---

[1] Maspero (*Annuaire*, etc., p. 21) quotes a curious deification even of this prince's pedigree from the temple of Erment.

[2] Also in C.I.G. 4707, with some corrections.

of Cleopatra, Goddess Philopator, and of Ptolemy also
called Cæsar, the God Philopator Philometor [year 13?
month Art]emisios *x* Phamenoth *x*.[1] It is decreed by
the priests of the [great god Amon]rasonther from
Diospolis Magna and the elders and all the rest (I
suppose of the inhabitants).   Since Kallimachos the
Cousin and [Epistates and over the] revenues of the
nome Peri-Thebes and gymnasiarch and hipparch has
also formerly, when terrible and manifold troubles
wasted the city, nursed it kindly [so as to keep the
district] in perfect peace, and the temples of the
greatest and national gods [and in such manner did
he manage the affairs of the people, that they were
able to live in happiness, in spite of a time of want and
famine.   This seems to be the general sense of lines
7–10].   And when all were in such despair as to call
upon death to free them, he, imploring the assistance
of Amonrasonther, relieved by his generosity all this
distress, shone out like a star, and like a good genius
consecrated his life to the inhabitants of Peri-Thebes,
and having saved them all with their wives and children
brought them from great tempests into a placid
harbour.   But his greatest and highest praise is that
he took religious care of all that appertained to the
worship of the gods, as his grandfather had done, and
restored the local feasts and panegyries of the gods.
Hence it is decreed with good fortune that he is to be
called Saviour of the city, and this title is to be inscribed on his natal day in conspicuous places in the
temple of Amonrasonther, and his statue to be erected
of hard stone, and this inscription set up in demotic

---

[1] Peyron in his Comm. desires to supply in this gap a double
year, viz. L ιγ του και δ as was usual when a queen and king were
thus associated.   But then, owing to a space of eighteen letters
only being available, he is obliged to omit the word μηνος before
Αρτεμισιον, which is surely essential.   There was therefore more
probably only one year mentioned.   At this period the months
had been assimilated, so that the day was the same in both.
Indeed, whether Cleopatra as yet allowed her son to count his
years separately is more than doubtful.   Cf. the learned note of
Strack, pp. 35, 211, who rather decides against it.

and Greek characters to show the gratitude of the city."

This, in spite of the many lacunæ, can be confidently given as the general sense of the text. It is curiously unlike all the other Ptolemaic inscriptions we find in Egypt. There is not a word about royalty after the mere dating. The whole subject matter is in praise of an official Kallimachos. The style is rhetorical and inflated; the honours assigned to this man are such as earlier sovereigns would hardly have tolerated. He evidently, during the queen's absence in Rome, took affairs at Thebes into his own hands, and acted with perfect independence. The allusion to his grand-father's benefits to Thebes points probably to the crisis when Lathyros stormed the town some forty years before, and seems to imply that by the interference of this grandfather the privileges of the city had been spared more than our other sources admit.

When the great civil war was in progress, Cassius demanded from Cleopatra men and money, which she refused, pleading that famine and pestilence had ravaged her country, and to this the text just cited is supposed to refer. But she would have endured worse than ordinary famine and pestilence from that base and cruel villain, had not the decisive day of Philippi thrown the power into the hands of Octavian and Antony. To the latter the regulation of the East was entrusted, and when he summoned her to meet him and account for her neutrality (or worse) in the recent war, she entered upon that new romance of her life, in which Antony was her slave as well as her lover. Cæsar had kept his head after his first intoxication in Egypt; Antony had far less head, and did not regain it.

I may fairly refer the reader to Plutarch's *Antony*, nay, more, to its splendid transcript in Shakespeare's *Antony and Cleopatra*, for the details of a story, to the picturesqueness of which fiction can give no aid. Antony had indeed, when Alexandria was taken by Gabinius, met the young princess; but at that time she had not thought of subduing him. Presently she got Julius Cæsar within her reach, a higher quarry for her flight. During her residence in Rome under Cæsar's protection she must have had many other opportunities of knowing Antony, the Dictator's favourite officer ; still we hear not a hint that would point to the coming tragedy.

But when Antony, desirous of money and dissatisfied with the doubtful neutrality of Egypt, summons her to Tarsus, she sends him no submissive reply, but appears in splendour on the Cydnus, in the garb and with the attendants of Aphrodite.   We should note that she assumed Hellenistic, not Egyptian grandeur. Antony was allowed to pose as Dionysus beside this Aphrodite, and the acclaim of the people was quite such as met the apostles Paul and Barnabas a century later, when they were called Zeus and Hermes at Lystra.[1] The result of this meeting was that Cleopatra carried him captive to Egypt.

So while his wife Fulvia was maintaining his cause against the ambitions of Octavian at Rome, and the renegade Labienus, at the head of the Parthians, was invading Syria, he went off to enjoy the company of the "Inimitable Livers" in Egypt. Never did a man risk such gigantic interests for the enjoyment of the moment.   But behind all this feasting and jollity there was darkness and blood.   Cleopatra persuaded him to order the murder of her sister Arsinoe, who, after being exhibited in the triumph of Cæsar, had sought refuge from her hated sister in the temple of Artemis at Miletus.[2] After some time Antony was compelled to leave Egypt and enter upon his proper sphere at Rome, where apparently every effort was made to wean him from the Egyptian siren, even so far as to marry him to Octavian's gentle and noble sister Octavia.

---

[1] Acts xiv. 11 : "And when the people saw what Paul had done, they lifted up their voices, saying in the speech of Lycaonia, The gods are come down to us in the likeness of men. And they called Barnabas, Jupiter ; and Paul, Mercurius, because he was the chief speaker."

[2] Appian, *Bell. Civ.* v. 9 ; Dio Cassius, xlviii. 24.

Even now, when Cleopatra was left alone, we know
nothing of her internal government; but we may conjecture, with some probability, that at this time she
gave attention to the building of national temples,
especially that of Dendera, where the royal titles of
herself and her son, Ptolemy Cæsar, still appear upon
the walls.   This is to be noted, as she had borne twins
to Antony after his departure (probably 40 B.C.), neither
of whom she ever attempted to set up in the place of
the Dictator's son.   The portrait of Cleopatra (see
Fig. 77) which appears on the walls of Dendera is a
good specimen of the conventionality which pervades
Ptolemaic Egyptian art.   Like the statues of Philadelphus and of Arsinoe II., this figure has no semblance
whatever of reality.   It is even probable, to judge from
the extant coins (cf. Fig. 79), designed by Greek crafts-
men, that she was a fair woman, and not the swarthy
gipsy that she seemed to Shakespeare; even though
she was fond of appearing in state as the new goddess
Isis, and therefore in Egyptian array.

In 36 B.C., however, it was arranged at Rome, probably with a secret hope in the minds of each of the
rivals of what would happen, that Antony was to
command the army against the Parthians.   Thus his
fate was sealed, for when so near as Syria there was
no chance that he would not again meet his mistress.
He did not even wait for her to approach him, but sent
an officer to bring her to him at Antioch; and when she
arrived he lavished royal gifts upon her,—the dominion
of Phœnicia, Cœle-Syria, Cyprus, Cilicia, and parts of
Judæa and Arabia,—gifts which shocked Roman opinion
far more than his execution of harmless kings and his
promotion of private persons to great governments.
Still worse, he acknowledged his twins, and gave them
the significant names of Alexander Helios and Cleopatra
Selene.

Presently he started for the East, sending Cleopatra
home to await his triumphant return.   But on her way
she came to Jerusalem, where she found the man of all
others who must have hated her with deadly hatred.

Herod the Great, one of the handsomest and most
persuasive adventurers that ever lived, was building
up a kingdom for himself out of the favour of the
Romans, of the Hellenistic cities which he courted,
and his own abilities, when he found that this terrible
queen was likely to oust him of all his hard-gotten
gains.   Nor is it doubtful that, if Antony had been the
ultimate victor, the kingdom of Egypt would have
regained its widest bounds, and the Asmonæan house
been reduced to subjection or extinction.   So these two
Oriental sovereigns must have met with very dramatic
urbanity—while in their hearts each saw in the other a
deadly rival.   Josephus says she tried her wiles upon
Herod, and that he made this campaign against his virtue
a reason for proposing to slay her, but that his council
warned him of Antony's vengeance, which no persuasion would turn aside.   So she was escorted to the
Egyptian frontier with studied ceremony.   When
Antony returned, not a victor, but defeated, and saving
little more than his life and a sorry remnant of his
force, she met him again in Syria with provisions and
succours, and so kept him from his wife Octavia, who
had come to meet him as far as Athens.

His second campaign of vengeance (34 B.C.) against
the Parthians was more successful, at least sufficiently
so to warrant his celebrating a Roman triumph, with
the Armenian Prince Artabazus led in chains, at Alexandria.   This was worse than all to Roman sentiment,
and we may be quite sure Herod, among lesser tale-
bearers, made the most of it to his friends at the
court of Octavian.   But Antony, blinded to all except
Cleopatra's desires, formally, and in public assembly,
proclaimed her and her son Cæsarion lords of Egypt,
Cyprus, Libya (including, I suppose, Cyrene), and
Cœle-Syria.   His son Alexander was to be called *king
of kings*, and to possess Armenia, Media, and Parthia;[1]
his younger boy, Ptolemy, who must have been a mere
infant, was to govern as king Phœnicia, Syria, and
Cilicia.   All this was evidently suggested to Cleopatra

[1] This is confirmed by Livy, *Epit.* cxxxi.

by the traditions of her house ; she only claimed in the
Greek world what had formerly, and had long, belonged
to Egypt.

These things showed plainly what was to come.
But if Antony had attacked Octavian at once, the latter
was not ready and in sore distress for funds, as the
Eastern revenues were in his opponent's control. The
demand for money at Rome caused seditions, and
Octavian was obliged to use all means, fair and foul,
to cast odium on Antony and rouse Roman opinion
against him. For this purpose Antony's will was even
taken from the custody of the Vestal Virgins, and its
provisions criticised—a most outrageous proceeding.
But Cleopatra seems to have shown less tact than we
should expect towards Antony's followers, and to have
so caused some of them to abandon him and carry their
knowledge of his doings to Rome.

It was felt by his remaining officers that Cleopatra's
decision to go with him to Samos, his centre of armament, and then into the campaign to Actium, was a
fatal mistake, from a military point of view. When
she was present he thought of nothing else, and the
only chance of victory lay in leaving him free and un-
shackled. But from her point of view the matter may
have seemed different. How could she trust these
Romans when she was absent? What attractions
might not Octavia still possess to carry him back to
Rome? If his fleet were taken at Actium, she would
be a helpless prisoner, with nothing to offer the victor.
And in any case she was only the mistress of kings and
victors, not of the defeated and disgraced. Which of
her ancestors—Cleopatras, Arsinoes, Berenikes—could
be named that would not have discarded a defeated
husband, that would not have affected to give her
heart with her hand to any royal victor?

As soon as the fall of Antony seemed inevitable (and
she may have expected it beforehand), she fled with her
fleet and carried him with her away from his duty and
his shattered army. She reached Alexandria before
the news of her defeat, and is said to have sought to

get rid of dangerous people there by murder and
confiscation.   But she found that Antony must be
abandoned, and some other bid made for royalty.   Her
attempt to fascinate Octavian, when he came to Alexandria, failed, as it was sure to fail upon that cold and
calculating nature, even had she herself not been past
her prime in beauty.   He made, however, some stupid
attempts to deceive her, in order that he might secure
her treasures and her person for display at his triumph.
But she was not deceived for a moment, and escaped
by poison from the fate which she had imposed upon
her luckless sister.

FIG. 78.—Cleopatra and her Son Cæsarion
(Dendera).

Though the dynasty closes with Cleopatra, we must
not omit to notice the fortunes of her children.   If
there be one redeeming point about her character, it
is her constant love and care for Cæsarion, her eldest
and Cæsar's son, whom she associated with her in the
sovereignty, whose figure she engraved on the national
monuments, whose life and interests she strove to
safeguard in every extremity.   Nor do we hear that
she ever diminished his claims in the interests of
Antony's children, who might well have shown some

jealousy of the young prince.   Cæsarion is one of those
figures about whom we should gladly learn more, but
about whom history preserves an obstinate silence.   It
is a case like that of the son of Alexander the Great and
Roxane, whose life is hidden from us, though his titles
to fame and sympathy are not only his superb origin,
but the gigantic heritage of which he was defrauded,
and the captivity and early death to which his bitterest
foe consigned him.   Yet who had better claims to be
known of all men than the young Alexander?   So it is
with Cæsarion.   He had reached an age when several of
his dynasty had not only sat upon the throne, but led
armies, begotten children, and engaged in councils of
state.   Yet not one word of his appearance, of his habits,
of his betrothal in marriage to any princess, is recorded.
We are only told by Dion that, upon their final return
to Alexandria, Antony and Cleopatra had his eldest son
Antyllus (Antonius), and her eldest Cæsarion, declared
ephebi, that the populace might regard them as men,
fit to rule if any casualty removed their parents.   This,
he adds, was the cause of both their deaths at Octavian's
hands.

When the day of Actium had made Octavian master
of the Mediterranean, Cleopatra's first thought was of
the Red Sea and the far Ethiopian lands, whither many
expeditions had gone from Egypt, and which seemed
to promise a safe refuge from the turmoils of the
Hellenistic and Roman worlds.

She even sought to carry her fleet across the isthmus
of Suez,—Plutarch says a distance of 300 furlongs,—
and so secure herself with her treasure beyond the
limits of the Roman world.   But the first galleys
which were actually carried over were burned by the
Arabians, and then the proximity of Antony and his
despair seem to have paralysed her further action.   For
she was not without suffering herself from the same
weakness on which in others she had based her triumphs.

It seems from this narrative that the canal of Philadelphus was no longer passable for ships, and this
again suggests that the later Ptolemies had found the

desert roads to the Nile (from Berenike and Myos
Hormos to Koptos) more practical than the dangerous
navigation of the Red Sea.[1] Presently she sent away
her son Cæsarion, now a lad of 17 years, to the far
Berenike, to hide him from his enemies under the care
of his tutor.   But this faithless knave, that he might
curry favour with the conqueror, brought the lad back,
when Octavian cruelly put him to death.[2]   The conqueror thus acknowledged the asserted parentage of
the divine Julius, and could not brook in the world a
nearer heir to the great Dictator.

As we hear that he only put to death one son of
Antony, Antyllus (who had been declared a hereditary
prince), the rest remain to be accounted for.   But
history tells us nothing of their fate, save that the
young princess, called Cleopatra after her mother, was
married to Juba, the literary king of Mauretania, a
friend and companion in arms of Octavian, who came
with him to Egypt, and was probably struck with her
beauty, and impressed with the great traditions of her
race.   Dion adds that Octavian allowed Juba and his
wife to carry off her two brothers, Alexander and
Ptolemy, with them to their African home.

With these events the Ptolemaic epoch of the history
of Egypt comes to a close, and we pass to the Roman
period, when the land became a province of the Empire
managed by Roman officials.   Most fortunately, the
change did not take place during the Republic.   The
reader has learned from the foregoing pages how this
long designed catastrophe was delayed by rivalries and
jealousies at Rome.   Consequently that much-enduring
country was saved the oppressions and exactions of
such men as Verres and his crew, with the exception of
the momentary tyrannies of Rabirius.   The Empire at

[1] Dion speaks of the fleet which the Arabs burned being built
on the Red Sea coast, not transported from the Mediterranean.

[2] Plutarch (*Antony*, 81) charges the tutor of Antyllus, Theodoros,
with the murder of this boy, whom he betrayed to the soldiers
(what soldiers?).   He adds that it was the epigram of Areios, οὐκ
ἀγαθὸν πολυκαισαρίη, which cost Cæsarion his life.

least brought with it a great reform in the provincial management, and Egypt, kept jealously under the immediate control of the Emperor's deputy, and never under the Senate, may have at last attained a stable and sober management. Fortunately, too, recent discoveries have added enormously to the business documents which date from the Roman period, so that the materials for the succeeding volume are far more ample than those of the Ptolemaic era. When these later evidences have been sifted, we shall no doubt be able from them to throw new light upon the later Ptolemaic history, which is now so wofully deficient in anything but dynastic quarrels. For there is ample reason to assert that the Romans changed as little as possible in the inner management—the *Verwaltung*—of the country. When the masses of Ostraka are published by Wilcken —most of them from the centuries after Christ; when the huge mass of papers from Oxyrynchus has been sifted and printed by Messrs. Grenfell & Hunt, then we may hope to revise the preceding chapters, and fill in with some social and economic details the mere framework left us by the stray notices of foreign historians. Who knows whether we may not also recover some mine of late Ptolemaic papyri, which will tell us of the internal state of Egypt in the days of Cleopatra VI., what the extant groups tell us of the reigns of Philometor and of Physkon ?

With the earnest hope that these anticipations may be verified in our own day, we close our very difficult and unsatisfactory task.

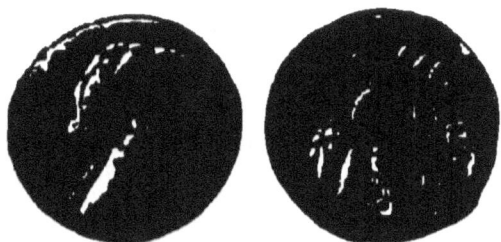

FIG. 79.—Coin of Cleopatra.

APPENDIX

THE THRONE-NAMES OF THE PTOLEMIES

(Transliterated by F. Ll. Griffith)

Soter, Alexander III., and Philip Arridaeus have the same prenomen: *Stp n R', mr n Ymn*, "chosen of Ra, beloved of Amen."

Alexander IV. is distinguished as: *H"yb Ymn, stp n R'*, "joy of the heart of Amen, chosen of Ra."

Ptolemy II. *Wsr k' Ymn, mr R'*, "strength of the *Ka* of Amen, beloved of Ra."

Ptolemy III. *Yw' n ntrwi snwi, stp n R', shm 'nh n Ymn*, "heir of the (two) fraternal gods, chosen of Ra, living image of Amen."

Ptolemy IV. *Yw' ntrwi mnhwi, stp n Pth, wsr k' R', shm 'nh Ymn*, "heir of the (two) beneficent gods, chosen of Ptah, strength of the *Ka* of Ra, living image of Amen."

Ptolemy V. *Yw' ntrwi mrwi ytw, stp n Pth, wsr k' R', shm 'nh Ymn*, "heir of the (two) father-loving gods, chosen of Ptah, strength of the *Ka* of Ra, living image of Amen."

Ptolemy VII. *Yw' n ntrwi prwi, hpr Pth, stp n Ymn, yr m' 't R'*, "heir of the (two) manifest gods, form

255

of Ptah, chosen of Amen, doing the rule of Ra"
(distinguished at a glance by the presence of the
scarab *ḫpr*).

PTOLEMY IX.   *Yw' n ntrwi prwi, stp n Pth, yr m"t
Ymn, šhm 'nḫ R*, "heir of the (two) manifest gods,
chosen of Ptah, doing the rule of Amen, living image
of Ra."

PTOLEMY X.   *Yw' n ntr mnḥ, ntr·t mnḥ·t, stp n Pth, yr·
m"t R, šhm 'nḫ n Ymn*, "heir of the beneficent god
and of the beneficent goddess, chosen of Ptah, doing
the rule of Ra, living image of Amen."

PTOLEMY XI.   *Yw' ntrwi mnḥwi, stp n Pth, yr m"t
Ymn, snn 'nḫ n R*, "heir of the (two) beneficent
gods, chosen of Ptah, doing the rule of Amen, living
image of Ra."   The second cartouche reads : Ptolemy
—*sd·tw·n·f Yrksntrs, 'nḫ st, mr Pth*—"called Alexander, living for ever, beloved of Ptah."

PTOLEMY XIII.   *Yw' n p ntr nti nḥm, stp n Pth, yr m"t
Ymn, šhm 'nḫ R*, "heir of the god that saves, chosen
of Ptah, doing the rule of Amen, living image of Ra."

[Cartouches of Ptolemy I. (cf. above, p. 52) are not
familiarly known ; those of Ptolemies XIV. and XV.
have not yet been found.]

z.

l:

l'

l'

l'

fa
h.

INDEX

IV—17

PRINTED BY
MORRISON AND GIBB LIMITED, EDINBURGH

www.ingramcontent.com/pod-product-compliance
Lightning Source LLC
Chambersburg PA
CBHW021059030726

47496CB00006B/1911